COACHES' GUIDE TO TEAM POLICIES

American Sport Education Program

with

Laurel T. Mackinnon, PhD, FACSM

HUMAN KINETICS

Library of Congress Cataloging-in-Publication Data

Coaches' guide to team policies / American Sport Education Program.
    p. cm.
  Includes bibliographical references and index.
  ISBN-13: 978-0-7360-6447-7 (soft cover)
  ISBN-10: 0-7360-6447-8 (soft cover)
 1. Coaching (Athletics)   2. Coaching (Athletics)--Moral and ethical aspects.
I. American Sport Education Program.
  GV711.C583 2007
  796.07'7--dc22

2007008513

ISBN-10: 0-7360-6447-8
ISBN-13: 978-0-7360-6447-7

Copyright © 2007 by Human Kinetics, Inc.

The Web addresses cited in this text were current as of December 2006, unless otherwise noted.

Acquisitions Editor: Emma Sandberg; **Developmental Editor:** Anne Hall; **Assistant Editor:** Cory Weber; **Special Projects Editor:** Anne Cole; **Copyeditor:** John Wentworth; **Proofreader:** Anne Meyer Byler; **Indexer:** Dan Connolly; **Permission Manager:** Carly Breeding; **Graphic Designer:** Robert Reuther; **Graphic Artist:** Sandra Meier; **Cover Designer:** Keith Blomberg; **Photographer (cover):** Human Kinetics/Tom Roberts; **Photographer (interior):** Neil Bernstein, unless otherwise noted; photos 3, 4, and 5 on page iii © Human Kinetics; **Photo Asset Manager:** Laura Fitch; **Visual Production Assistant:** Joyce Brumfield; **Photo Office Assistant:** Jason Allen; **Art Manager:** Kelly Hendren; **Illustrator:** Al Wilborn; **Printer:** Versa Press

Copies of this book are available at special discounts for bulk purchase for sales promotions, premiums, fund-raising, or educational use. Special editions or book excerpts can also be created to specifications. For details, contact the Special Sales Manager at Human Kinetics.

Printed in the United States of America

10 9 8 7 6 5 4 3 2 1

Human Kinetics
Web site: www.HumanKinetics.com

United States: Human Kinetics
P.O. Box 5076, Champaign, IL 61825-5076
800-747-4457
e-mail: humank@hkusa.com

Canada: Human Kinetics
475 Devonshire Road Unit 100, Windsor, ON N8Y 2L5
800-465-7301 (in Canada only)
e-mail: orders@hkcanada.com

Europe: Human Kinetics
107 Bradford Road, Stanningley, Leeds LS28 6AT, United Kingdom
+44 (0) 113 255 5665
e-mail: hk@hkeurope.com

Australia: Human Kinetics
57A Price Avenue, Lower Mitcham, South Australia 5062
08 8372 0999
e-mail: liaw@hkaustralia.com

New Zealand: Human Kinetics
Division of Sports Distributors NZ Ltd.
P.O. Box 300 226 Albany, North Shore City, Auckland
0064 9 448 1207
e-mail: info@humankinetics.co.nz

WITHDRAWN
UTSA Libraries

CONTENTS

PREFACE

Whether you are a sport administrator or a coach, this book provides you with the tools to improve the sport experience for your athletes. All too often, coaches receive little direction on implementing effective team policies. Most coaches implicitly follow league and school rules without giving them much thought.

Coaches' Guide to Team Policies offers sound rationale for establishing team policies. Chapters 1 and 2 examine team policies from a philosophical perspective. You will consider your own coaching philosophy and how it relates to six moral values:

1. Respectfulness
2. Responsibility
3. Caring
4. Honesty
5. Fairness
6. Good citizenship

After developing a team philosophy that is based on these moral values, you will learn how to create, communicate, enforce, and revise effective team policies. As you read the final three chapters, you will be guided through specific examples that are organized according to the six moral values. For each subject, two suggested rule wordings are provided. One is general, and the other is more explicit.

Throughout *Coaches' Guide to Team Policies*, fictitious "coach A" and "coach B" guide you as you determine your own style on team policy. Coach A offers general wording, whereas coach B prefers to be very detail oriented. Both approaches are valid, but you will find that one style or the other better suits your goals and your team.

After reading this text, you can visit the ancillary Web site for *Coaches' Guide to Team Policies* at www.HumanKinetics.com/Coaches GuideToTeamPolicies. On this site, you have access to tools that will help you create a customized set of team policies without having to reinvent the wheel. Easy-to-access documents that include all of the suggested policies are provided.

This text complements the ASEP Professional Coaches Education Program, which also includes *Coaching Principles, Sport First Aid*, and many sport-specific books and courses. For more information about ASEP, be sure to visit www.ASEP.com.

ACKNOWLEDGMENTS

I wish to acknowledge the following people for their invaluable help with this book:

Rainer Martens for the original idea and conceptualization of the book's content and approach; Amy Tocco, Emma Sandberg, and Anne Hall at Human Kinetics for editing and helping to develop the book conceptually and structurally; and the coaches who contributed their thoughts about coaching young people—these thoughts give life to the policies and rules described in the book.

Why Have
Team Policies?

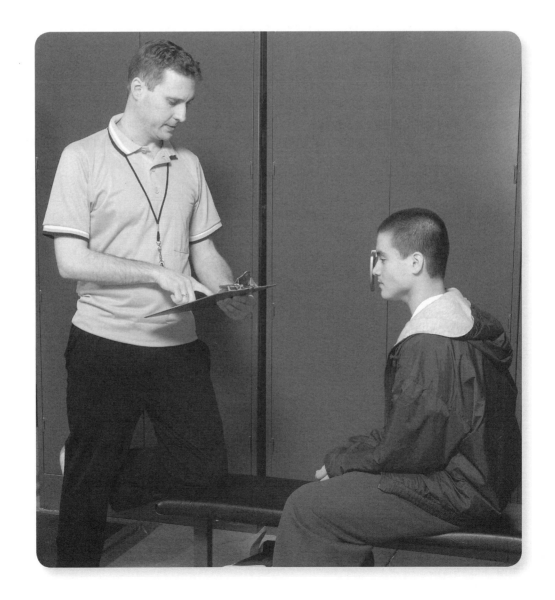

*Y*ou are coaching a club basketball team for 16-year-olds. It's time for you to select a representative team to participate in a major tournament in another city. Your club has a rule that to be selected for the representative team you must have taken part in a weekend team camp held a month earlier. Your second-best scorer and one of the team leaders missed the camp because of his grandfather's unexpected death. He knew at the time that he would forfeit his chance to play in the tournament by missing the camp to attend the funeral and remain with his family. The other players seem to want him on the representative team.

What would you do in this situation? Does your team policy require you to strictly enforce rules, or do you have some flexibility and discretion? Does your team policy allow athletes to appeal decisions?

As a coach, you probably recognize the challenges of this situation and might recall similar difficult decisions you've had to make about your team, your athletes, and others involved in your sport.

Having clear and complete team policies will help you make complex decisions such as this one more easily, consistently, and fairly; policies will also help you to communicate the reasons behind your decisions to all involved. This book is designed to help you create practical policies and rules to help you guide your team. In this first chapter, we'll begin by defining team policies and rules and discussing their importance. Tips are offered for transferring your philosophy into workable policies. Chapter 2 proposes methods for structuring your policies and rules within the framework of the six moral values (respectfulness, responsibility, caring, honesty, fairness, and good citizenship) as stated in the Arizona Sport Summit Accord of 1999. Chapter 2 also shows you how to construct a code of conduct and presents ideas for enforcing rules and resolving conflicts. The final three chapters apply these concepts to help you develop policies and rules for athletes (chapter 3), coaches (chapter 4), and others involved in organized sport, such as parents, support staff, spectators, and the media (chapter 5). This book has been designed to help you construct and develop your team policies, but it is understood that you will not want, or have the time, to start from scratch and write a complete set of policies and rules. Instead, the book contains a range of policies and rules for you to select from; choose the ones that best fit your philosophy and approach and that are otherwise most appropriate for your team. In some cases, you might be able to use the suggested policies and rules as they are written; in other cases, you will likely want to modify them to suit your situation.

UNDERSTANDING TEAM POLICIES

A policy can be defined as a method or course of action or a set of organizational guidelines that guide decision making. Team policies, then, are a set of principles, guidelines, and procedures to direct decision making about the team and the people involved with the team.

Team policies provide a general set of guidelines, which should be flexible and interpretable, to help you make decisions. When correctly written and applied, team policies help a team function effectively to fulfill its objectives; they help everyone involved (athletes, coaches, parents, supporters, the media) understand the reasons behind decisions.

All sports teams—whether you have an informal community team for young children or a highly structured professional team—need team policies. Regardless of a club's size or competition level, it is important to be able to clearly articulate how your team is run and how decisions are made.

HOW TEAM POLICIES HELP YOU AS A COACH

Team policies provide a structural framework for making decisions, communicating responsibilities and expectations, and enforcing rules. Team policies allow you to make coherent, consistent, timely, and transparent decisions. They let athletes and others know how they are expected to behave on and off the playing field. Team policies let others see how you make decisions. They also provide consistency and continuity over time and in different situations, for example, across seasons, at different levels of competition, or if one coach leaves and is replaced by another.

You can think of team policies as a collection of road maps to a destination. The collection of road maps allows you to plan your journey, visualize your destination, and travel there efficiently. Without a road map, you might eventually reach your destination (a successful sport program), but your journey will likely take much longer and include many detours along the way (see figure 1.1).

Effective team policies help free up your time to focus on your coaching responsibilities, such as training your athletes, teaching sport skills, promoting team cohesiveness, and formulating strategies. Policies ease the burden of administrative tasks by giving you a clear direction when you must make a decision.

A lack of team policies will not always spell disaster. However, without team policies, your decisions might appear to be ad hoc (apart from others or out of context), inconsistent, or arbitrary. Ad hoc decision making can be confusing because people might not be able to see and understand the reasoning behind your decisions.

Properly written team policies make rights, responsibilities, and expectations clear to everyone involved. For example, a team policy that clearly specifies the grades required for eligibility leaves little doubt in your athletes' minds about the expectations placed on them academically.

Clear team policies help provide direction for how people should act in new or different situations. For example, if your

COACHING TIP

"Players need and want guidelines. They need to know the expectations of your team and program."

—Jill Prudden, girls' basketball coach, Oak Ridge High School, Oak Ridge, Tennessee

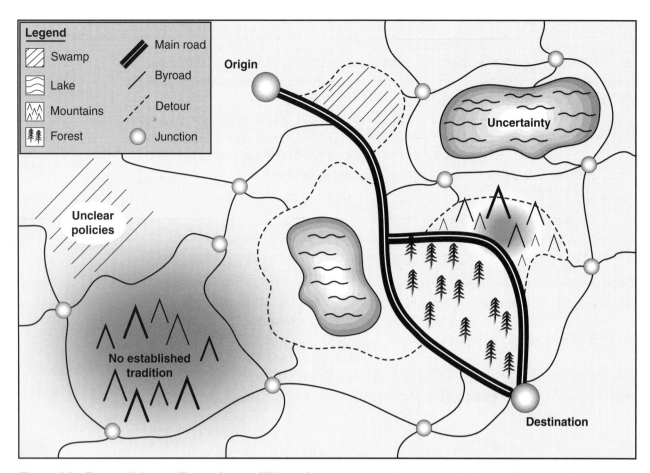

Figure 1.1 Team policies are like road maps. Without them, you may arrive at your destination (a successful sport program), but your journey will take longer and include many detours along the way.

team has a well-detailed policy on fighting, a new athlete challenged by an opponent to fight during a heated game will know that he or she is expected to walk away and avoid a skirmish.

Team policies make it more likely that athletes and coaches are treated fairly by everyone involved, including coaches, teammates, competitors, officials, parents, sponsors, the media, and supporters. Good policies prevent harassment by educating everyone on what constitutes harassment and how to avoid it.

Personal growth and skill acquisition are two important functions of sport for young people. Team policies that reflect concepts such as fair play and sportsmanship help teach these important life skills during a critical time of development.

Effective team policies reduce the chance of conflicts arising, and when conflicts do arise, a policy can help settle the dispute. Many times, conflicts arise because no clear policy is in place or because a policy is misunderstood or inconsistently applied. Policies promote due process and fair treatment. For example, an athlete suspended because of rough play or absence should have a right to appeal the decision.

TEAM POLICIES CANNOT DO EVERYTHING

While good team polices can help you make decisions fairly and consistently, they cannot coach your athletes or make decisions for you. You must still provide the leadership to teach, guide, and discipline your athletes to achieve your team's philosophies and goals.

Team policies do not absolve you of the responsibility for enforcing rules and making decisions. In the end, it is the person responsible, not the policy, who makes the decision and accepts responsibility for that decision. When faced with a difficult situation, you must weigh the various factors involved and make a decision. The team policy guides you by providing a firm basis on which decisions can be made. You might find with strong policies in place that the process of making a difficult decision becomes simpler and the path to that decision clearer, but *you* must still make the decision. For instance, cutting a star player from the team because of poor grades or discipline problems will always be difficult. Your team policy provides you with a basis and a process, but a decision on each situation must still be made. (Keep in mind here that a policy is different from a rule. A discussion on how policies differ from rules comes later in the chapter.)

Written team policies should not take the place of or discourage regular, clear, and open communication. You should discuss team policies with everyone early in the season and continually refer back to them in regular meetings. Athletes, coaches, and others involved should feel free to voice their opinions and discuss important issues. When making a decision, you should highlight how the decision fits within the team policies. If you are constantly under siege for your decisions about issues such as athlete discipline or eligibility, you need to look closely at whether your policies are effective, whether the athletes understand them, or whether you are applying your policies consistently.

Team policies should not be inflexible rules with little room for discretion and interpretation; they should never replace due process. It is difficult to always strictly interpret and enforce rigid rules; there are gray areas and different viewpoints. Athletes and coaches are human, and we should maintain some level of humanity in our decisions. The scenario at the start of this chapter (the basketball player who missed a team camp because of a death in the family) is one example in which discretion might be appropriate, and in which an athlete might have the right to appeal a decision.

Finally, team policies are not written in stone. A policy can and should be modified if necessary. Situations and rules, scientific knowledge about sport, and a community's expectations all can change; what is considered acceptable might change over time.

Team policies are a set of principles to guide the many decisions you make about your team. Effective team policies are understandable, flexible, and adjustable; they help

COACHING TIP

"There needs to be some flexibility whenever one works with human beings, especially teenagers! No two people are exactly alike, just as no two situations are exactly alike."

—Laura Sundheim, girls' volleyball and track and field coach, Hardin High School, Hardin, Montana

your organization and team fulfill their objectives. Clear and effective policies set a level of expectation for behavior on and off the field by athletes, coaches, parents, and others involved in sport. Team policies let others see how you make decisions. All teams, regardless of the age of participants or level of competition, need team policies to help the team run smoothly and achieve its goals. Team policies free up your time to focus on coaching responsibilities and ease the burden of administrative tasks by giving you clear direction when you must make a decision. Team policies should be solidly based on your team and organization's philosophy.

Let's now consider how you develop your team philosophy, if you don't already have one, and the relation between the team philosophy and policies and rules.

DEVELOPING YOUR TEAM PHILOSOPHY

What do you value, or think is important, for your team members? Performing their best? Winning a championship? Learning important lessons in life, such as fair play? Developing sport skills and physical fitness? Learning to work together as a team? Having fun?

A philosophy is a basic theory or set of beliefs, ideas, and principles held by an individual or group. This set of beliefs and principles represent what you, your team, or your organization value. Everyone has philosophies—be they simple or complex—about various things, and a person's philosophies might change over time. Your philosophy reflects what you value in life and the type of person you are.

Philosophies guide our everyday decisions as well as our short- and long-term planning. When developing team policies, you must first examine your own philosophies about your sport and team. A policy is often developed by first stating the philosophy behind the policy. For example, a policy on harassment might begin with a statement such as this: "Our team believes that all individuals have a right to play sport in an environment free from harassment because of sex, race, religion, ethnic background, sexual orientation, or disability." A policy on athlete discipline might start by stating: "All team members have a responsibility to behave in a manner that reflects positively on the team at all times." Your team's policies should flow naturally from and be consistent with your philosophies.

If you don't have a clear team philosophy, you might start with these three steps:

- Identify your organization's, team's, and personal objectives; consider what you and your team hope to achieve.
- Determine the principles that guide you and your team; consider what things in life and in sport you value the most.
- Use these basic principles to guide your policies and rules; think about how you might translate these principles into action.

If your organization, such as a high school, already has a well-defined philosophy or a clear set of general principles meant to apply school wide, it is relatively easy for you to apply this philosophy or these principles to your team. For example, if your school has a strict zero-tolerance philosophy regarding alcohol and substance abuse, you have little flexibility when developing your team's philosophy on this issue.

Depending on the situation, you might find that your own personal coaching philosophy differs slightly from your team philosophy. Organizational and team philosophies are rarely the work of one individual but tend to reflect the collective thinking and values of a group or community. Thus, the process of developing program and team philosophies might involve a variety of stakeholders (people affected by the policy), such as you, your athletes, your athletes' parents, your school or organization, the sport association or conference, people with particular expertise (e.g., sports physicians, physical therapists, or trainers), and the local community. Of course, not all of these people need be involved at any given time or must be involved in every step.

When involving others in developing your team philosophy and then expressing the philosophy through your team's policies and rules, you can take one of three approaches.

> *Approach 1*: Create a draft document yourself, circulate it to stakeholders (e.g., coaches, athletes, parents, the school or organization), and ask for their comments. Then meet with stakeholders to discuss your proposal or ask people to communicate their thoughts directly to you by phone, letter, e-mail message, or Web site. Revise your document based on their comments and circulate it again to achieve consensus.
>
> *Approach 2*: Call an open meeting of stakeholders to discuss their ideas about developing a philosophy, and then use these ideas to draft a document. Circulate the draft document to stakeholders, using their suggestions to refine your final document.
>
> *Approach 3*: Form a small subcommittee of people representing various stakeholders to draft a document for all stakeholders to consider.

Part I of *Successful Coaching* by Rainer Martens presents detailed information about developing your team philosophy.

POLICIES VERSUS RULES

Policies and rules are not the same. Policies are broader than rules; they state the underlying philosophy and guidelines that direct decision making. Policies are more general, flexible, and open to interpretation than rules are.

Rules are more specific and restricted and are directly applicable to particular situations. The difference between a policy and a rule is subtle but important. When selecting team policies, it is important for you to differentiate policies from rules. Rules will form part of your policy and are the basis for enforcing your

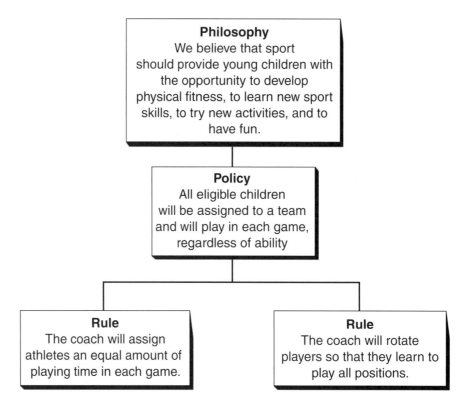

Figure 1.2 Team leadership follows a logical flow. In order to assemble your policies and then implement rules, you need a background philosophy that reflects your team's core ideals.

policy, but your team policies should not be simply a collection of rules (see figure 1.2).

Your team policy on any issue, such as substance abuse, violence, or harassment, should include the rules outlining how you expect your athletes (and others whom the policy covers) to behave in specific situations. Your policies should always be consistent with your team and individual philosophies, objectives, and attitudes. As a living, working document, an effective team policy should readily integrate into and guide everyday procedures and decisions. For example, if you are coaching a developmental team of ninth graders and your policy is that all members play an equal amount of time each game, then you will naturally rotate your players, even if this means your best players spend time on the bench or your team does not score as much.

Above all, team policies should be consistent with and reflected by the attitudes and behavior of all involved with the team. For example, in your team policy on athlete discipline, you would outline why discipline is important for athletes and the team, how athletes are expected to behave, the reasons they should behave this way, definitions of infractions of the policy, consequences of infractions, and the process to deal with infractions. Your discipline policy might include a rule that foul language is unacceptable. To be consistent, no one involved with the team (coaches, athletes, support staff, parents, and volunteers) should be permitted to use such language during any of the team's activities.

To be taken seriously and to be effective, your team philosophies, policies, and rules should be consistent with each other. Remember that philosophies

Figure 1.3 Another way to visualize team guidelines is with an organic image: A tree represents growth and change to accommodate an expanding sport program.

dictate policies, and policies dictate rules (see figure 1.3). If your philosophy is that sport performance should reflect achievement, effort, and talent through legitimate means, then your policy will encourage fair play without resorting to performance-enhancing drugs. Your policy would state this philosophy and instruct how it should be reflected in attitude and behavior. The consequences of infractions would also be stated. The rules within your policy would identify and define banned substances and outline the procedures for enforcing the rules. Policies not reinforced through rules become empty and ineffectual.

In this chapter we have defined team philosophy and policies, discussed how policies can help your team achieve its goals, and differentiated between policies and rules. Let's now move to the next chapter to discuss how to select, develop, structure, and communicate your team policies.

Coach's Exercise

- In writing, state your current team philosophy. (If you don't have a team philosophy, develop a draft of your team philosophy using the process presented in this chapter.) List four principles based on this philosophy that inform your team policies. Closely examine each of the four principles to make sure they are consistent with your team philosophy. If a principle is inconsistent, propose a new wording of that principle to make it consistent with your team philosophy.

- Recall a difficult decision you have made regarding your sports team (either your current team or a past team). Did you have a team policy to guide you when making the decision?

  —If yes, did the team policy help you make the difficult decision? How so?

  —If no, would you have benefited from having a team policy when making that decision? How so?

- What common issues with your team do you run into year after year?

  —Have you developed either formal or informal team policies to deal with these issues?

  —What is the benefit of having formal team policies to deal with these issues?

- Consider one of your team's current policies. How effective is this policy?

  —If you think the policy is effective, consider why.

  —If you think the policy is not effective, consider how you could improve it.

Selecting Effective Team Policies

*Y*ou are coaching a gymnastics team. One of your athletes has been accused of taking a banned substance contained in a new type of appetite suppressant. The gymnast admits that she took the substance for a few days early in the season to try to lose weight, but she pleads ignorance because she did not know the suppressant contained an ingredient on the list of banned substances.

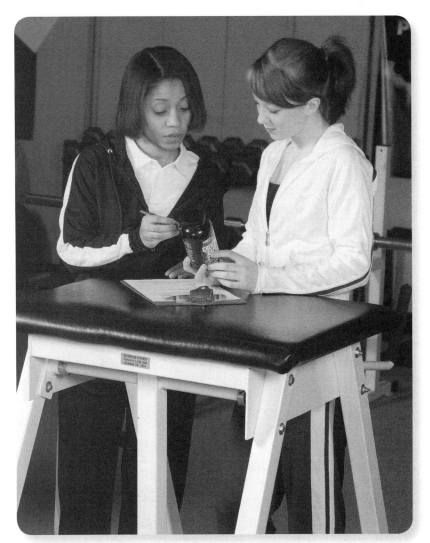

How would you handle this situation? Does your current team policy on drug abuse and supplements cover the possibility of newly developed substances? How would you address your athlete's belief that it was acceptable for her to take the appetite suppressant because she didn't know it contained a banned substance?

After reading chapter 1, you understand that your team needs to develop policies (or, if you already have set policies, you might need to update or expand them). You should also have a better understanding of the purposes of team policies and what can happen without them.

This chapter discusses how to develop your team policies, including how you might select and structure your policies, how they can reflect your team philosophy, what areas your policies should cover, and how you can put your policies into action.

DEVELOPING EFFECTIVE POLICIES

By now, you might be convinced that you need team policies and wondering how to go about developing them. As mentioned in chapter 1, this book offers options for you to select and modify the policies and rules that best fit your philosophy and situation. Let's start by discussing the overall format and structure of policies.

Policy Format

Policies can have different formats, depending on their purpose and complexity. Your own management style and preferences may also influence the format and extent of your policies. A more relaxed coach might believe that his or her team needs only a few general rules, whereas another coach might like to have everything spelled out clearly and precisely. We will return to this idea of different approaches later and throughout the book.

Despite different formats and complexity, effective policies have several common characteristics based on recommendations by the Centre for Sport and Law Inc. (www.sportlaw.ca/policyw.htm).

A good policy should be

- clearly and concisely written,
- reader centered (i.e., in language and format readers can understand and apply),
- consistent in terms and language,
- thorough in coverage but not overly complex or long,
- relevant and appropriate to those involved, and
- based on the most recent information.

Your policies will be more effective if they clearly communicate your team's philosophy and specify how this philosophy is to be reflected in attitude and

Examples of the Differences Between Policies and Rules

Examples of a policy statement	Examples of rules relating to the policies
Athletes will represent the team with honor and display good sportsmanship.	• Athletes will accept officials' decisions without argument. • Athletes will shake hands with opposing team members after the game. • Athletes will applaud outstanding play by players on both sides.
Each athlete is responsible for all uniforms and equipment assigned during the season.	• The athlete will wear a clean and neat uniform for each practice and game. • The athlete or his or her parents will pay for equipment damaged or lost during the season.
Coaches will act respectfully to everyone involved in sport.	• The coach will refrain from publicly criticizing an official. • The coach will refrain from using offensive or aggressive language or gestures during a game. • The coach will shake hands with the opposing coach after the game, regardless of outcome.
Parents will respect the professional abilities of coaches.	• Parents will not criticize a coach in front of their children, other athletes, or other parents. • A parent wishing to speak with a coach will make an appointment to meet with the coach. • A parent may not question the coach's decisions about team lineup or playing time.
The media will respect the privacy of athletes and their families.	• The media will seek permission from the coach before trying to interview an athlete or his or her family. • Before publication of a story about our team, the media will seek confirmation of facts from the coach.

behavior. You might find it a challenge to balance your policy's length and detail to cover all areas while keeping it understandable to your athletes and their parents.

To assemble a reader-centered policy, you should take the reader's viewpoint. Consider how your athletes will read and understand your policy. Use a format, style, and language appropriate to your readers so they will be able to understand and apply the policy. For example, a 10-page, single-spaced document using a formal style and legal terms will probably confuse your athletes and their parents. Use direct, unambiguous language, subheadings, bulleted points, and bold type to enhance the readability of the document. Also use consistent terms and language throughout your policies. Using different words to mean the same thing in different parts of the document can confuse readers, especially young people or those whose first language is not English.

It is a good idea to ensure that each part of the document is consistent with the others. For example, if you choose a zero-tolerance policy on use of illicit drugs or alcohol, then the consequence (e.g., suspension) must match the seriousness; giving warnings for repeated drug abuse would undermine your policy's intended message on the seriousness of drug abuse.

You will want to allow time to revise, edit, and proofread the document before releasing it for others to see. If possible, ask others outside the team to read and comment on the document to ensure that it is consistent and understandable.

Consider whether your policies are broad enough to cover every conceivable possibility. This might seem a difficult task, but it works best if you can consider, in advance, what could happen and how you would handle every situation. You should not discount something happening simply because it has not happened before. For example, you might assume that everyone on your ninth-grade team shares your philosophy that fair play, learning new skills, and having fun are the most important things at this age. However, your policies would be more effective if they covered the possibility that a player might occasionally take the game too seriously and behave inappropriately (e.g., argue with the referee, intentionally foul opponents, fight with teammates). You are much better equipped to deal with this possibility if you have anticipated and planned how to handle such a player.

Team policies that are relevant and appropriate to the athletes and others involved are more effective than generic policies that might apply to everyone. For example, coaching a team of female athletes might require you to have a policy on playing when pregnant.

Finally, we suggest that you periodically update your team policies to include the most recent scientific and medical information and social trends. Policies based on out-of-date information or personal bias will be constantly challenged, possibly in the courts. Continuing the previous example of a female athlete competing while pregnant, the most recent medical and scientific evidence considers competing during pregnancy to be safe up to a certain point in certain sports, and that the decision to compete is best made by the woman and her doctor. A coach cannot ban a pregnant athlete from competing simply out of personal concern or belief that sport is inappropriate during pregnancy.

How to Structure Team Policies

There is no one best way to structure a team's policies. Your policies must reflect your particular team's athletes, situation, needs, and interests. However, good policies answer the following questions:

- What is the purpose of the policy?
- What is the team's philosophy on the issue?
- Who does the policy cover?
- What situations and behaviors does the policy cover?
- How will infractions be handled?

Common Features of Comprehensive Team Policies

1. Introduction
   1. Purpose of the policy
   2. Statement of the team's philosophy
   3. General description of what the policy covers
2. Application of the policy
   1. Who does the policy cover?
   2. What situations does the policy cover?
3. Definitions
   1. Special terms used in the policy
   2. Descriptions and examples of behavior covered by the policy
4. Expectations and responsibilities of people covered by the policy
   1. Specific situations
   2. Specific expectations, roles, and responsibilities
5. Enforcement of the policy and process to deal with infractions
   1. Definitions of infractions (minor and major)
   2. Disciplinary action
   3. Consequences of infractions (minor and major)
   4. Reporting infractions
   5. Process of investigating infractions
   6. Confidentiality
6. Appeals process, dispute resolution
   1. Time frame
   2. Procedures for appeal and hearing

When selecting your policies, consider the importance of each of these factors relative to your situation. For example, if you coach a team that travels often, you will need a detailed section on behavior on the road. If you coach a varsity team of 18- and 19-year-olds, you might need more detail on policies outlining the consequences of infractions than you would need if you coached a developmental team of 15-year-olds. Regardless of how many topics your policies cover, the most essential thing is to clearly spell out how your athletes (or others) are expected to conduct themselves and the consequences of failing to meet those expectations.

When an athlete or other person violates a rule, it is often because he or she is not fully aware of that rule, how the rule fits within the context of the policy, or the consequences of breaking the rule. Returning to the example at the beginning of this chapter—the gymnast who pleads ignorance after taking a banned substance contained in a weight control supplement—unless specifically told by the coach, trainer, or health professional, a young athlete might not be aware that she must check supplements for banned substances or even that common supplements can contain banned substances.

Having organized, well-written, and clearly explained policies is one way to prevent or reduce the chance that your athletes will break the rules. You might not be able to prevent all infractions, but you will be better equipped to deal with the consequences of infractions if your policies are clearly written and explained.

AREAS TO COVER IN TEAM POLICIES

When selecting your team policies, it's reasonable for you to ask what these should and should not cover. Again, the extent of your policies and rules will depend on your team philosophy, the age of your athletes, the level of competition, and how many people the policy covers. Keep in mind that team policies and rules specify the standards of acceptable and unacceptable behaviors and the responsibilities each member is expected to accept. Policies and rules prescribe the expectations and outcomes from team members and others involved, including coaches, athletes, support staff, volunteers, parents, spectators, and the media. So, it is essential to carefully plan and develop your team policies and rules.

We encourage you to develop team policies and rules that cover important aspects of behavior and organizational issues that might affect how your team functions. You cannot legislate every aspect of your athletes' behavior, nor would you want to be responsible for enforcing such restrictions!

Consider the purpose of your team policies: to communicate to your athletes (and others involved) your team's philosophy and how this philosophy should be reflected in attitude and behavior. Such consideration should lead you to identify the areas to cover in your team policies.

The Six Moral Values

To help you focus the scope of what your team policies should include, this book has been structured to reflect the six moral values developed by the Arizona Sport Summit Accord in 1999. The six moral values are as follows:

- Respectfulness
- Responsibility
- Caring
- Honesty
- Fairness
- Good citizenship

These moral values encourage character development through sport and have been endorsed by many sport organizations.

Character can be described as the type of person you are, what you stand for, and your tendency to do the right thing. Character is revealed by how you behave when no one is watching or when you do not expect to be rewarded; it includes the types of judgments you make, how you interact with others, and how you put into action your personal philosophy.

We generally associate good character with behavior that is kind, trustworthy, honest, faithful, and responsible. Sportsmanship is said to represent good character for those involved in sport.

Most sport policies and codes of conduct (or behavior), whether for athletes, coaches, support staff, parents, or others involved in sport, incorporate these aspects of character. These six moral values are considered universal principles that allow us all to live and work productively in a civilized society. Let's take a closer look at each of them.

Respectfulness

Respect is enshrined in the golden rule: treating others as you wish to be treated by them. Respect applies to oneself as well as to others. Respectful athletes and coaches accept decisions by officials or superiors without arguing, avoid violence in and out of sport, act considerately toward all people, and seek to resolve differences without anger and insults.

Examples of respectful behavior in sport include using considerate language and nonverbal body language even when you are angry or disappointed, walking away from confrontation during a game, speaking respectfully (e.g., without sarcasm or profanity) even when you are provoked, accepting victory and defeat without disparaging your opponents, and accepting officials' decisions without argument.

Responsibility

Responsibility involves perseverance and doing the right thing. Responsible athletes and coaches are reliable, self-disciplined, and considerate; they do not act impulsively without first considering the consequences of their actions.

Examples of responsible behavior in sport include always trying your hardest, even against a much better opponent or when the outcome doesn't matter; showing up regularly for practice, even when you are preoccupied or don't feel like training; letting the coach and team know if an emergency prevents you from attending practice; and accepting responsibility for actions that lead to unexpected consequences.

Caring

Being caring involves compassion, gratitude, and empathy (the ability to experience the feelings of others). It might sometimes seem incongruous that you are supposed to be caring while also trying your hardest to win. But you can be both highly competitive and caring at the same time. Athletes and coaches who are caring are gracious in both victory and defeat; they readily acknowledge the contributions of others to their success. Caring athletes play for their team rather than just for themselves. Caring also involves promoting the health and safety of everyone involved in sport, particularly athletes.

Examples of caring behavior in sport involve complimenting your opponent's efforts, win or lose; thanking your teammates, coaches, and supporters after a game; encouraging an injured teammate; and helping an opponent up after a fall or tackle. For example, the coaches of the 2003 Rugby Union World Cup finalists, Australia and England, openly praised each other's accomplishments in the week before the final match. Such behavior is not uncommon among effective and successful coaches.

Honesty

Honesty involves being truthful and forthright (i.e., not hiding important information) and acting with integrity and loyalty. Athletes and coaches show their honesty by speaking and acting consistently and by always doing the right thing. The motives and actions of honest coaches and athletes are rarely questioned because their actions are backed up by a personal sense of integrity.

Examples of honest behavior in sport include being a team player (loyalty), dealing honestly and openly with other athletes and coaches (honesty, loyalty), and playing fairly within the spirit and rules of the game (honesty).

Fairness

Fairness—playing by the rules and the spirit of the game whether you are winning or losing—is one of the key elements of sportsmanship. Athletes and coaches are often under enormous pressure to be successful, sometimes with huge financial rewards and incentives. Such pressure often seems inconsistent with fairness; sometimes playing fairly means losing the point or even the game.

Athletes and coaches who play fairly will always play by the rules, regardless of how doing so affects the outcome of the game. Athletes and coaches display a sense of fairness by not taking unfair advantage by bending or circumventing the rules. Occasionally, you see tennis players correct a line judge's call for a ball that hits the baseline, although it means he or she loses the point. Fairness can also be applied to criteria for determining awards or playing time.

Good Citizenship

Perhaps the hardest to define because it encompasses attitudes and behavior outside of sport, good citizenship involves contributing positively to your community, whether local, regional, or national. Athletes and coaches who are good citizens proudly represent their country in an international competition, volunteer their time and effort to worthwhile causes, follow the law, and act as positive role models. The media readily report behavior—both good and bad—of high-profile athletes and coaches, who must recognize how their actions influence young people. Many high school athletes are active in community and charity events and are well known in their communities.

COACHING TIP

"We participate in a fund-raiser for cancer. Our athletes run a relay—each runs a half-mile at a time and each has the name of someone he or she knows who has died from or survived cancer. We've raised over $2,000 each of the past three years."

—Arnie Miehe, cross country coach, Darlington High School, Darlington, Wisconsin

Conflict Resolution

So far, we have discussed how team policies will help you manage your team and how to develop your policies. Sometimes, though, conflicts can arise even with the best of intentions and clear policies supported by good management. Conflict is part of the complexity of human behavior and cannot be completely avoided. However, having within your policies a means to address conflicts will make it easier to solve them and to minimize distractions when conflicts arise. Let's discuss how you can include a process for conflict resolution within your policies.

As we have said, disagreements and conflict arise even with the best policies and consistent enforcement of rules. If handled well, conflict is not always a bad thing, as it helps clarify boundaries and expectations. To be fair and effective, your policies should include some mechanism for athletes to question a decision, and for them to be heard in a fair and objective process. This is especially important if you are coaching teenagers; a common complaint among this age group is that adults do not listen to them or consult them when making important decisions.

Policies on conflict resolution clarify the process through which an athlete or others can question a decision or express a grievance. This process usually involves a hearing before a discipline or grievance committee. The committee should be objective and represent the entire team or organization; a player representative can be a member of the grievance or discipline committee.

Above all, it is important to ensure due process—the legal procedure that guarantees an individual's rights are protected—at every step. Not adhering to due process can cause several undesirable effects, such as giving the impression that your decision making is unfair or arbitrary, confusing your athletes because they cannot see how you make certain decisions, alienating your athletes or making them feel powerless, and leaving you and your school open to legal action by the aggrieved player.

Let's now discuss areas that you probably won't need to cover in your policies.

AREAS NOT TO COVER IN TEAM POLICIES

You might be relieved to know that your team policies do not have to cover every aspect of your athletes' and staff's behavior. In fact, team policies should cover only those aspects of behavior that directly affect the athletes' and others' participation on your team. Areas outside of sport or not directly relevant to participation on the team are difficult, and often inappropriate, to include in team policies. Here are some areas that we suggest you leave out when developing your team policies:

- Personal relationships. Policies should not restrict whom your athletes or staff associate with, provided there is no conflict of interest or illegal activity. You might think an athlete is associating with the wrong crowd, but you can create many problems by making rules or exerting pressure to force him or her to abandon a friendship. As long as the behavior is legal and does not directly influence participation on your team, you need not try to police it.

- Interests outside of sport and during the off-season. Policies should restrict outside interests only if they directly affect the athlete's participation on the team. For example, it would be fair to ban your athletes from high-risk sports during the season for fear of injury or because they might affect their ability to train. However, it might prove impossible to enforce such a ban during the off-season.

- Personal beliefs and choices. Policies restricting athletes from pursuing a particular hobby, lifestyle, personal philosophy, or religious belief violate their rights and are likely to alienate your athletes. Moreover, in some situations, making decisions about an athlete or treating him or her differently because of a personal belief or lifestyle choice can be construed as harassment or discrimination.

THE CODE OF CONDUCT

A code of conduct, sometimes called a code of ethics or code of behavior, is a document that clarifies how people associated with your team are expected to behave and their duties and responsibilities. A code of conduct will be an integral part of your team policies. This document gives life to your policies in that it translates those policies into the practical terms of everyday behavior. The code of conduct should be a list of the most important rules that indicate the attitudes and behavior expected of your athletes or others involved in sport.

A general code of conduct can be contained in a single document to cover all people involved with the team (athletes, coaches, support staff, parents, and so on.) You can list the expectations for each group in separate sections for each role. Another approach, taken by many teams these days, is to develop separate codes of conduct for each role, in particular for athletes, coaches, parents, and support staff.

A code of conduct can be viewed as a contract or agreement between the team and the person whom it applies to. Many teams now require their athletes, staff, parents, and others involved to sign a statement indicating that they have read and understood the relevant code of behavior or conduct. A signed statement serves as a record that the policy was explained, that they understand the code of conduct, and that they agree to act as required. Having them sign the code of behavior also emphasizes how important you and the team view the code.

Regardless of age, sport, and level of competition, all codes of conduct have some common features:

* Statement of purpose and philosophy behind the code
* Duties and responsibilities expected of the person covered by the code
* Situations covered by the code

Your athletes and others involved will find it easier to understand a code written in plain and concise language (no legal terms) appropriate to their age and education level. Fairly short codes work best; most codes of conduct are no more than a few pages in length, although some are longer if they include detailed information about infractions and appeals procedures, or if they apply to more than one group.

When developing your code of conduct, consider including both positive and negative wording to describe behavior that should be encouraged or avoided. Here are some examples:

* Coaches should ensure that activities are suitable for the athletes' ages, experience, fitness level, and ability to ensure the safety of athletes (positive wording).
* Coaches should refrain from using alcohol, drugs, or tobacco products when working with athletes or involved in team events (negative wording).

Codes of conduct are mentioned throughout this book. Chapters 3, 4, and 5 provide sample codes of conduct for athletes, coaches, parents, spectators, support staff, and the media. These chapters present specific examples that you can incorporate into your codes of conduct. These have been written from a general perspective to cover a wide range of situations. They might be useful to you as they are, or they might provide a starting point for you to develop your own codes of conduct for various people involved with your team.

Up to now, we have focused on what your policy should and should not cover and how to develop a code of conduct that is consistent with and gives life to your policies. Let's now discuss how to communicate with your athletes, their parents, and others so that everyone understands your team's policies and how they fit with your philosophy.

COMMUNICATING TEAM POLICIES

Once you develop your policies, we encourage you to openly discuss them with those involved so they are aware of and understand your team's policies. It is self-defeating to have written policies that are kept in a file drawer and brought out only in times of crisis. Even worse is to have vague, unwritten policies that rely on someone's memory or team precedent, or to take a crisis mentality and develop policies only when needed.

The best way to communicate your team policies is to provide brief and concise documents that are both thorough and written in a way that everyone can understand. It is a good idea to spend time in a meeting early in the season to discuss the policies with your athletes, their parents, coaching staff, volunteers, and others involved. You might need to have separate meetings for different groups. You are encouraged to discuss the reasons for and the benefits of your policies. Clarify each policy and its underlying rationale, expected behavior, consequences of infractions, and the appeals process. Be sure to define any new terms and give illustrative examples so that everyone fully understands concepts such as code of behavior, harassment, conflict of interest, and dispute resolution. It is always a good idea to allow time for questions and discussion about the policies and code of conduct. Let your athletes, coaches, and support staff know that they are welcome to discuss these issues with you throughout the season. Then be sure to follow through when someone comes to discuss a policy.

The example at the start of this chapter, the gymnast who took an appetite suppressant not knowing it was banned, can be considered as a failure in two parts. First, the drug policy should have been fully communicated to her, and she should have been educated on which substances were banned and which were not. Second, it was her responsibility to check before using any supplement.

It is especially important to ensure your policies are evident in every aspect of how you coach your team; that is, put your policies into practice. Consider a few examples:

- You are coaching a team of ninth grade basketball players. Your team philosophy and policy emphasize team commitment, learning new skills, enjoyment, and social and personal growth. As a result, you do not think twice about having each player play an equal amount of time in each game, even if it means your best players are on the bench during some of the game.

- You are coaching a high school varsity football team. All your players have signed a code of conduct that clearly states that any athlete who gets into a fight with an opposing player during or after a game is automatically suspended for the next game. Your star running back picks a fight with an opponent after a loss. You do not hesitate to enforce the code, even though it means your running back will miss the next game, which determines the conference championship.

- You are coaching a swim team. Your personal philosophy and team policy emphasize fair play and treating others with respect and dignity. In the final event of an important meet, your relay team is disqualified for an illegal changeover. From your position in the stands, you thought the changeover looked legal and are preparing to protest, when two of the relay swimmers quietly admit to you that their teammate did leave the blocks early. You immediately praise your swimmers for their sense of fair play and do not lodge the protest.

ENFORCING TEAM POLICIES

Enforcing your team policies and codes of conduct, especially when it involves infractions and disciplining your athletes, is one of the most difficult aspects of coaching. But the job of enforcing your policies is made easier if your policies clearly state what is and is not acceptable behavior and the consequences of infractions.

The consequences will depend on several factors, including the seriousness of the infraction, whether it caused personal injury or loss of property, whether it was an isolated incident or repeated behavior, and whether a prior warning had been given.

The methods you use to define consequences and to discipline athletes who violate rules will depend on your personal and team philosophies, your management style, and community expectations. Discipline does not always have to be negative—a punishment—but can be turned to advantage, as a way of instructing, changing behavior, and teaching important life lessons to your young athletes. In *Successful Coaching*, Rainer Martens defines "positive discipline" as "training that develops self-control" (page 143). With positive discipline, you proactively teach and model correct behavior in the hope that you can prevent poor discipline or inappropriate behavior. You focus on discipline and self-control that encourages athletes to do the right thing as opposed to simply trying to avoid punishment. The interested reader should consult chapter 8 of *Successful Coaching* for more ideas about positive discipline.

DISCRETION AND FLEXIBILITY

Your team policies will be more effective if you build in some discretion and flexibility. Theoretically, your decisions will be simpler and more straightforward if you enforce your policies and rules strictly without exception. However, human behavior and events can be complex, and the situations that are common to sport are not always simple and straightforward. There might be different viewpoints or "truths" about the same event.

Because of this complexity, including some degree of discretion and flexibility allows you to better express your team's philosophies and goals, rather than locking you into the simplest and most expedient decision.

COACHING TIP

"I ask team members for their input because sometimes peer pressure can be a positive motivator. It also gives players a sense of ownership and accountability for decisions, which builds cohesion."

—Jim Caputo, boys' soccer coach, Blue Ridge High School, Farmer City, Illinois

Consider the example of the teenage basketball player presented at the start of chapter 1. He had missed the training camp because of his grandfather's death. The rule on team selection for the upcoming tournament states that athletes must have attended the camp to be considered for selection. The easiest decision is to strictly follow the rule and not select the player because he missed the camp. Consider the consequences, however: Your team will play without one of its stars, his teammates want him to be there (so their morale might suffer if he does not play), and the player might feel torn between loyalty to the team and to his family. Consider also the reasons behind the rule about attending the team camp—to create team spirit, to work on plays and fitness, to keep players motivated and committed. Does a decision to leave him off the team truly serve the reasons behind the rule? Probably not. Consider also your team philosophy and goals—to teach your athletes about life and sport skills, to perform to their ability, to work together as a team. Thus, naming him to the team despite his missing the camp is more consistent with your team philosophy and goals than strictly following the rule and leaving him off the team.

Consider another situation. During a high school basketball game you see one of your players push an opponent for no obvious reason, which starts a fight between the two players. Your player is charged with a foul. Your team policy states that an athlete who starts a fight during a game is suspended for the next two games. If your policy has no flexibility or appeals process, you would automatically suspend the player. In doing so, however, you might miss hearing your player's side of the story—that she had already mentioned to the referee and your assistant coach that her opponent was constantly standing on her foot to prevent her from rebounding, and that her opponent grossly overplayed her nudge to move her off her foot. Hearing this directly from the player provides an opportunity to reinforce the ideas of fair play and respect for one's opponents, and to teach your player other ways to handle such a situation. It is doubtful that an automatic suspension would be beneficial for this young player.

REVISING POLICIES

As we mentioned in chapter 1, you should not consider your policies and rules as written in stone. Rather, you might find the need to change your policies and rules as your team's situation or community expectations change, or as advances in technology or training methods occur. For example, 10 years ago, your small high school might have had an "everyone plays" policy. However, if your community and school have grown, and parents and children now want a program that also offers the opportunity for gifted athletes to train and compete at a high level, you might need to change your policies and rules to accommodate this change in your community's objectives.

You might consider regularly reviewing your policies and rules to see how they suit your team's current situation. This could be done through informal (e.g., casual interactions) or formal (e.g., meetings, committees) consultation with stakeholders. At the start or end of each season, you could circulate the current policies and rules and invite comment. In chapter 1, we suggested some processes to use to develop your philosophies and policies. These same methods can be used to evaluate and, if needed, update your current policies. What's important is that you see your policies and rules as dynamic and responsive to your team's needs rather than as absolutes.

Coach's Exercise

1. Do you currently have a process in place to review and evaluate your team policies? If so, do you believe the process is working as effectively as it could be? Why or why not? If you don't currently have a process to review and evaluate policies, identify the steps you would take to develop one over the next six months.

2. If you currently have a code (or codes) of conduct, examine these in the context of the six moral values. Is any moral value not covered in your code(s) of conduct? Do you think you should add this to your code(s) of conduct?

3. Which of the six moral values is the easiest to model for your athletes? Which is the most difficult? Why do you think this is?

4. Can you recall an incident or conflict that was not resolved to your satisfaction? What caused or contributed to your feelings of dissatisfaction with the outcome? Have you changed or would you change your rules or policies as a result to prevent this problem from happening again?

5. What problems have you encountered in trying to communicate your team policies and rules to your athletes? To their parents? How have you dealt with these problems? Can you think of ways to improve communication with your team's stakeholders?

THE COACH'S LEGAL RESPONSIBILITIES

As a coach, you have legal responsibilities, or a "duty of care," to your school and your athletes. It is beyond the scope of this book to discuss these responsibilities in detail. *Successful Coaching* lists the nine legal duties of coaches:

- Properly plan the activity.
- Provide proper instruction.
- Warn of inherent risks.
- Provide a safe physical environment.
- Provide adequate and proper equipment.
- Match your athletes appropriately.

- Evaluate athletes for injury or incapacity.
- Supervise the activity closely.
- Provide appropriate emergency assistance.

Adapted, by permission, from R. Martens, 2004, *Successful Coaching*, 3rd ed. (Champaign, IL: Human Kinetics), 470.

Essentially, as a coach you must ensure that your knowledge and coaching skills are up to date, that you use "best practice" methods of coaching, and that you provide a safe and supervised environment for your athletes. The legal expectation is that your actions will be reasonable, prudent, and up to date. At the end of this book you'll find a glossary of basic legal terms relevant to coaches.

Putting Team Policies in Context

These questions are provided as examples to illustrate the overall structure of team policies, using the framework discussed in this chapter.

What is the purpose of the policy?

This policy outlines the team's policy and rules on use and abuse of alcohol and illicit substances (e.g., illegal drugs, performance-enhancing substances) for members of the team.

What is the team's philosophy on the issue?

There is overwhelming evidence that alcohol and substance abuse has many adverse effects on mental and physical health, especially in young people. As a community, our highest priority is the health, safety, and well-being of our student athletes. We believe that use of alcohol and illicit substances is incompatible with the ideals of sport. Participation in extracurricular activities, such as sport, is a privilege that carries a responsibility for athletes to themselves, their team, their school, and their local community. Our athletes have a responsibility to ensure that they are healthy and fit and able to perform to their potential. Thus, this policy prohibits the use of alcohol and illicit substances by all athletes during the competitive season.

Whom does the policy cover?

This policy applies to any athlete who is a member of the team, even while that athlete is on academic probation, recovering from an injury, or not practicing or competing with the team for any other reason.

What situations and behaviors does the policy cover?

This policy covers all team members while they are participating in any activity, both inside and outside of school and sport, whether involved with sport or other activities, and whether during school hours or outside of school hours. This policy applies from the beginning of training at the start of the season through the last game, practice, or tournament at the end of the season.

Student athletes are responsible for knowing and understanding this policy and the situations in which it applies. They are also responsible for knowing which substances are on the conference list of banned substances and for checking the status of any substance they take or are given (e.g., an over-the-counter medication or one prescribed by a doctor). Athletes are expected to abide by the following guidelines:

- Athletes shall not knowingly possess, use, consume, transmit, or be under the influence of alcohol, controlled substance(s), or banned performance-enhancing substances at any time. (Note: Athletes of legal drinking age in this state are still subject to this policy.)
- Athletes should avoid situations in which alcohol or illicit substances might be used.
- Athletes who unwittingly find themselves in settings where other people are illegally possessing or using alcohol or controlled substances should leave that situation as soon as possible.

How will infractions be handled?

First offense: The athlete found to have broken the rules on alcohol and substance abuse will be referred to the school counselor or another specialist counselor and will complete an approved educational program aimed at preventing substance abuse. The athlete may continue to practice and compete with the team while completing the educational program. No further action will be taken if the counselor considers that the athlete has satisfactorily completed the educational program.

Second offense: The athlete found to have broken the rules on alcohol and substance abuse for a second time, even if for a different substance, will be suspended from the team for four weeks (28 days). He or she may train with the team but may not sit on the bench during games, compete, or otherwise represent the team during the time of suspension. The athlete will complete a second educational program and may be reinstated only on recommendation of the counselor that the athlete has successfully finished the program.

Third offense: The athlete found to have broken the rules on alcohol and substance abuse for a third time, even if for a different substance than the previous two times, shall be suspended from all school sport for the remainder of the season or for one full term, whichever is longer. This suspension may carry over from one school year to the next. The athlete will complete another drug education program and perform community service as decided by the school counselor. The athlete may be reinstated after serving the suspension only on recommendation of the counselor that the athlete has successfully completed the drug education program and community service.

All information about athletes investigated for an alleged breach of this policy will be considered strictly confidential and will be discussed only with those directly involved in enforcing the policy (i.e., coach, athlete and his or her parents, disciplinary committee). This information will be discussed only in disciplinary committee hearings on the incident. For a first offense, no mention will be made on the student's school record.

Any student athlete found to have broken the rules on alcohol and substance abuse may submit a written appeal to the school's disciplinary committee within

(continued)

(continued)

10 days. The committee shall be required to consider the appeal and make a decision within 30 days. For a second or third offense, the athlete may practice with the team but may not compete while the appeal is being considered. The decision by the disciplinary committee will be considered a final decision, and no further appeals will be permitted.

HOW TO USE THIS BOOK

We hope you were convinced in chapter 1 that your team will run more effectively with well-defined team policies. In this chapter, we have discussed how to choose, structure, and develop your team policies as an extension of your personal and team philosophy. If you do not already have team policies, we are not suggesting you start from scratch and write a complete set of new policies. Instead, the next three chapters provide you with a range of suggestions and options for compiling your team policies. Chapter 3 addresses policies and rules for athletes, chapter 4 for coaches, and chapter 5 for others involved in sport, such as parents, spectators, support staff and volunteers, and the media.

The next three chapters are structured on the six moral values framework introduced earlier in this chapter. Each section begins with a brief description of that moral value, followed by a general policy statement that might serve as an introduction to your policy on that area, and then options for each rule within each moral value. For example, the area of "being responsible" for athletes presents rules relating to issues such as attendance at school and practice, eligibility, academic progress, self-discipline, and so on. Within each area, we present two policy and rule options—one that reflects a more relaxed management style of a coach who believes that athletes respond better to a limited number of rules, and another that reflects the style of a coach who thinks young people need more rules that are explicitly worded. We'll call these coaches "coach A" (more relaxed style) and "coach B" (more explicit rules).

This book is organized so that you may assemble a complete set of policies and rules from these suggestions, selecting those that reflect your style and are relevant to your situation, and modifying them as needed. You will be able to identify the suggested policies and rules by the check box that precedes each one. Select your preferred policies and rules as you go, or make your choices by visiting the book's Web site at www.humankinetics.com/CoachesGuideToTeamPolicies.

Coach A vs. Coach B

"A few rules are good. They help athletes and others involved know what is expected, but we should also let people use their common sense and judgment. Young people have enough rules in their lives without needing lots more to govern something fun like sport."

"Young athletes need rules. They need to know where they stand, what they should do and what they should not do, and the consequences of not following the rules. It is up to adults to provide that guidance."

Selecting Team Policies and Rules for Athletes

*I*t is late in a hotly contested soccer match between your school and a rival, the two top teams in the conference. Your team is down 3 to 1. Your opponents have a well-deserved reputation for physical—bordering on dirty—play, which they have demonstrated throughout the game, eliciting loud cheers from their supporters. To make matters worse, because of a shortage of officials available for the match, the referee is a coach at the other school. Your players think he has not been entirely objective and fair. Your best midfielder and an opponent are fiercely chasing the ball when they appear to collide, and the opponent falls to the ground. It looks to you, your coaches, and players that the opposing player tripped himself trying to illegally tackle your player. The referee calls a foul on your player, giving a free kick to the opposing player, who taunts your player with both words and gestures. Your player begins to run toward him, retaliation in mind. Then loud voices from the sideline call out, "Don't do it, Sam! Don't stoop to his level!" The yells come from Sam's parents. Sam stops, shrugs, smiles, and turns away. The parents of your other players cheer wildly.

© Human Kinetics

How many different layers of rules, attitudes, and behavior related to sport can you find in this example? Would your current team policies cover them all? For the moment, let's just look at the issue of respect. How many examples of respect (or lack thereof) can you find in this example? Let's list them: self-respect of the players involved, both teams' players' respect for opponents, coaches' and players' respect for officials, parents' respect for their children and the officials, respect by everyone for the game of soccer, and respect for the concept of fair play.

You can see by this example that we have many expectations of attitude and behavior for our athletes, coaches, officials, and parents. These sometimes get lost in the heat of an important contest. Think of a team, maybe even your own, that you remember as well disciplined and well coached. What characteristics did these athletes display that made you think that? Think of another team about which you remember thinking, *How undisciplined, how unruly!* How were those athletes different from the ones on the well-disciplined team?

When you think about your ideal players, you don't think only in terms of athletic ability; you also consider qualities such as leadership, self-respect, and self-discipline, the way they react in difficult situations, an ability to inspire their teammates, a sense of fair play, and love of the game.

You probably already recognize the many benefits of sports participation by young people. Sport contributes to good health; teaches many important life skills, including fair play, sportsmanship, leadership, and teamwork; and helps develop other social and physical skills. You can probably recall that some of your most satisfying moments as a coach did not center on winning but on helping your athletes develop character and achieve personal growth.

Although sport is not the only means through which young people can develop skills and character, parents, school, communities, and government actively encourage and support participation in sport because of the many benefits.

Although all young people should be presented with opportunities to participate in sport if they choose, accepting the challenge to participate carries some responsibility. Participation in sport is a privilege that carries a certain level of accountability. Consider what you expect of your athletes once they join your team: that they attend practice regularly, show respect for themselves and others, abide by school and team rules, try their hardest in all contests, and accept both victory and defeat graciously. How do you communicate those expectations clearly to your athletes and their parents? Establishing clear policies on how you expect your athletes to behave, on and off the field, is a good start.

In this chapter we will discuss the many issues involved in selecting team policies and rules to guide athletes' behavior, attitudes, and effort. We will use the six moral values introduced in chapter 2 as a framework to discuss these issues. To refresh your memory, the six moral values are respectfulness, responsibility, caring, honesty, fairness, and good citizenship. In the rest of this chapter, the policies and suggested rule options will be presented within the context of this framework. For example, you will learn about sports policies on these topics:

- Respectfulness: interacting respectfully with others; respect for oneself, the environment, and property
- Responsibility: eligibility, attendance, effort, reliability, self-discipline
- Caring: being compassionate, generous, and forgiving; ensuring athlete safety; avoiding injury and illness
- Honesty: being truthful, trustworthy, and loyal; acting with integrity; being courageous enough to do the right thing; being a team player
- Fairness: playing fairly and within the spirit of the rule, sharing and being tolerant of others, demonstrating good sportsmanship
- Good citizenship: being a good role model, being educated and informed about lawful and ethical behavior, obeying laws and rules, cooperating and contributing to the community, and avoiding and discouraging substance abuse

Along with these policies, we will discuss accepting consequences and dispute resolution (enforcing rules, appeals procedures) and review two examples of an athlete code of conduct (one for more relaxed coach A and one for stricter coach B) that you can use as a template as you create a code of conduct for your team.

POLICIES ABOUT RESPECT

Respect is an integral part of sport. Consider all the facets of sport that feature respect: We sing the national anthem before a game, introduce players at the start of a match, cheer outstanding play, expect players to shake hands at the end of a match, applaud athletes when they receive their medals or trophies—all of these are signs of respect that have become part of the ritual of sport.

Respect has several levels:

- Self-respect
- Respect for others on the team (e.g., teammates, coaches, support staff)
- Respect for opponents
- Respect for others involved in sport (e.g., officials, volunteers, media, spectators)
- Respect for the game, its rules and traditions, and the spirit of competition
- Respect for property and the environment

You expect that everyone involved in sport should be treated with respect. Policies on respect cover how your athletes interact with teammates, opponents, coaching and support staff, officials, spectators, the media, police, fans, and members of the local community. These policies might also cover how your athletes treat property (e.g., sports equipment) and the environment (e.g., sports facilities and those in the local community). A clearly worded policy on respect is a powerful tool in educating your athletes and others involved with your team about the expected standard of behavior and attitude; such a policy will guide them to achieve a high standard of respectful behavior in all their activities.

☐ *Coach A's policy introduction*: All team members should show self-respect and respect for others and for the game.

☐ *Coach B's policy introduction*: Our team believes that respect is an integral part of sport. All athletes are expected to act with respect and dignity and have the right to expect others to treat them similarly. The athlete is expected to demonstrate self-respect and to act respectfully at all times toward everyone involved in sport, including teammates, coaches, parents, support staff, officials, opponents, spectators, volunteers, the media, and members of the public.

Here are some examples of respectful actions by athletes:

- Using positive words, even when discussing an opponent or an unfavorable situation or event
- Walking away from a confrontation
- Shaking the opposing team members' hands before and after the game, regardless of outcome
- Standing and participating sincerely in pregame rituals
- Following the coach's instructions, even if they disagree

- Refraining from disagreeing with or reacting emotionally to an official's decision
- Signing autographs for fans
- Answering questions from the media with sincerity

Here are some examples of disrespectful actions by athletes:

- Vulgar or offensive talk about opponents
- Offensive or obscene gestures aimed at opponents or spectators
- Physical aggression or violence directed at teammates, coaches, opponents, officials, spectators, or others involved in sport
- Overly emotional displays of anger or sarcasm (verbal or nonverbal) directed at officials, opponents, teammates, coaches, or spectators
- Refusing to participate, or doing so reluctantly, in established rituals, such as shaking an opponent's hand after a game or match or standing respectfully during player introductions or during the national anthem
- Refusing direction from the coach or team captain or intentionally changing a play called by the coach or team captain
- Intentionally damaging property

The following sections discuss rules on various aspects of respect, including language, respect for property, and harassment.

Respect for Other People

We often view acting with respect toward others as an extension of respect for oneself. Teaching young people to act respectfully can be difficult, especially if they have had few positive role models. We often focus on telling young people how not to behave, but it is more effective (and more challenging) to define, model, and encourage acceptable behavior.

Appropriate Language

What do you think of a young person who uses offensive or profane language? Most people are put off by offensive language; we tend to think the person using such language is inarticulate, undisciplined, or lazy and simply does not care what others think. Offensive language is usually perceived as a sign of disrespect, although such language has become accepted in popular culture (e.g., some forms of popular music). In sport, offensive language tends to reflect poorly on the speaker and, by extension, on the team and school he or she represents.

Offensive language extends beyond profanity or swearing; it also includes derogatory, insulting, demeaning, or disrespectful language and gestures.

Here are some examples of disrespectful language:

- Profanity, vulgar words or sayings
- Disrespectful or lewd chants, songs, cheers, or gestures aimed at opponents, officials, teammates, or spectators

- Booing or heckling of opponents or officials
- Taunting or name calling of a teammate, opponent, official, or spectator

Continuing from our previous statement about modeling acceptable behavior, it is important to clearly define and explain why these examples are disrespectful. It might be helpful to have your athletes self-reflect on how they feel when they witness or (better yet) are subjected to such behavior.

When selecting your rule on respectful language, consider the age, maturity, and experience of your athletes and whether they already understand the importance of speaking respectfully. Of the two following rules suggested, option 1 is more general and less prescriptive, the type of rule favored by coach A. This option might suit athletes who already understand what is and is not respectful language. Coach A's option might also be your choice if you use another means to educate your athletes about what speaking respectfully means (e.g., if this topic is covered in the classroom or another program). Option 2 is more detailed and prescriptive, the type of rule that coach B prefers. This option gives examples of what is and is not acceptable language. You might choose this option for a large program or with athletes from diverse backgrounds, when you might not be certain of their understanding of the issue, or if language has been a problem in the past.

☐ *Coach A's rule*: The athlete should speak respectfully at all times.

☐ *Coach B's rule*: The athlete should speak clearly, directly, and politely. The athlete should use positive words and phrases whenever possible. When representing the team, the athlete should not use offensive, profane, vulgar, or lewd language, cheers, comments, or gestures. The athlete should not participate in booing, heckling, taunting, or name calling of anyone involved in sport, including teammates, coaches, opponents, officials, and spectators. An athlete who speaks disrespectfully or who uses offensive language will be disciplined, which may include suspension from the team.

We have presented some ideas about the importance of respect in sport and given examples of both respectful and disrespectful behavior. Language is one of the more obvious ways to show respect or disrespect in sport. Let's now consider other aspects of respectful behavior and some options for rules regarding respect.

Respect for Opponents

Sport is often likened to battle, and sometimes it is difficult for young people to understand that they can compete hard and strive to win without feeling negative emotions toward their opponents. Learning to respect one's opponents while being competitive is an important life lesson for young people, who probably learn this best by observing how adults act toward opponents.

Of the following suggested rules, option 1 is more general and might work with athletes who understand the issues relating to respect toward others or when you do not expect disrespectful behavior to be a problem (e.g., with younger children). You might consider option 2 when you need to more clearly define and give examples of how athletes should act toward others in the context of sport.

☐ *Coach A's rule*: The athlete should act respectfully toward opposing players and coaches.

☐ *Coach B's rule*: The athlete should show respect for opposing players and coaches before, during, and after the game by shaking hands and observing other pre- or postgame rituals.

Respect for Officials

In the heat of competition, many young athletes tend to react emotionally to an official's decision, especially one that affects the athlete's performance (e.g., the last permissible foul in a basketball game). However, an overly emotional reaction by the athlete shows disrespect on the athlete's part, which in addition to being disrespectful can sometimes backfire (e.g., the official calls a technical foul or sends the player off the court) and further disadvantage the team. Most would agree that respect for officials is vital if they are to maintain control over the game.

Option 1 requires simply that athletes not argue with officials. This option could be construed as permitting or even encouraging the athlete to use other means to express disagreement with the official's decision. Like coach A, you might choose this option when you are confident that your athletes will not overreact to a decision. Option 2 is more restrictive and gives examples of behavior to avoid when athletes disagree with an official's decision.

☐ *Coach A's rule*: The athlete should not argue with an official's decision.

☐ *Coach B's rule*: The athlete should accept all officials' decisions without arguing and without displaying excessive emotion or sarcastic or offensive language or body language.

Respect for Property

Sport can be an expensive activity, both for athletes and for sponsoring organizations, such as a school or club.

Respect for Uniforms and Equipment

Given the importance of proper equipment to performance and safety, you should expect your athletes to show respect by taking care of their uniforms and equipment.

The first rule states an expectation that athletes should respect and treat accordingly (with proper care) any equipment and uniform they are issued. This minimal view can be open to interpretation; for example, what does "proper care" mean? This option does not clarify who is responsible for any loss or damage. You might choose this option when athletes provide their own uniforms or equipment (e.g., swimming, tennis, golf) or for experienced athletes who understand what proper care implies. The second option might be most appropriate for larger programs or those that provide athletes with much of their uniforms and equipment (e.g., football, baseball, hockey). If you choose this option, consider the implications of making athletes themselves responsible (e.g., that this rule extends to the parents as well because most young athletes are financially dependent on their parents) and how to make parents aware of this commitment.

☐ *Coach A's rule*: Athletes should take proper care of their equipment and uniforms.

☐ *Coach B's rule*: Athletes are responsible for all equipment and uniforms assigned to them during the season. They are responsible for taking care of the equipment and uniforms, ensuring the equipment is cleaned and remains in good working order, and returning the equipment and uniforms in good condition at the end of the season. The athlete is responsible for paying for uniforms or equipment that is lost or damaged beyond normal expected wear and tear.

Respect for Personal Belongings

You might expect your athletes to be responsible for securing their own personal property, such as sport shoes, equipment they have purchased themselves, books, cell phones, computers, and other personal belongings. Owning an assortment of high-tech gadgets has become almost a prerequisite for many young people. But if items go "missing" and athletes become suspicious of other team members, team cohesiveness can be damaged. One might argue that respect for oneself extends to respect for one's property.

Option 1 expects athletes to take responsibility for any personal property brought to practice or games. The concept of "taking care" to secure personal property could be interpreted in different ways. You might choose this option for athletes who are less likely to own expensive possessions or to bring them to practice and games. The second option gives more direction for securing personal property and suggests the obvious preventative of simply not bringing such items to practice or games.

☐ *Coach A's rule*: Athletes should take care to secure their own personal property when attending practice and competition.

☐ *Coach B's rule*: Athletes are responsible for their own personal property, including apparel and equipment, when participating in sport. They should secure personal belongings in their locker during practice and competition and should avoid bringing expensive or personal items not required by the sport.

Respect for Personal Property of Others

Respect for property extends beyond the equipment and uniform assigned to athletes. You also expect your athletes to respect the property of others, the sport facilities at your school, other facilities at which they practice or compete, and any nonsport property at the school or in the community. Vandalism or accidental damage to property resulting from carelessness or unrestrained horseplay can reflect badly on your team and school, even when caused by only one or two team members. Being forced to spend precious resources on replacing or repairing mistreated facilities can burden the team or organization and limit the funds available for items such as equipment, uniforms, or travel.

The first option informs the athlete of the expectation of respect for others' property. Option 2 is more informative and educational and has a broader scope, extending beyond school and sporting events. You might choose this option if you want your athletes to gain a broader view of their responsibility or if your team practices or competes at various venues, travels frequently, or has a history of problems. Anyone who has lived with teenagers might agree that including the last sentence (keeping the locker room neat) could require some incentives.

☐ *Coach A's rule*: The athlete should respect the personal property of others and community property.

☐ *Coach B's rule*: Athletes are expected to respect the personal property of others (e.g., teammates, coaches, opponents), the sports facilities used in practice and games (home and away), and other public and private property not directly associated with sport (e.g., the school or community). Athletes should keep locker rooms neat and clean.

So far in this section we have talked about respect for others involved in sport and respect for property. Now let's move on to discuss a more subtle concept, especially for young people or those relatively new to sport, that of respect for the game itself.

Respect for the Game

Respect for the game is a more abstract concept for young people to grasp than respect for property or not using offensive language. Respect for the game, and for sport in general, involves understanding the broader principles of sport participation. According to Clifford and Feezell (authors of *Coaching for Character*), respect for the game is one of the underlying principles of sportsmanship that gives meaning to sport participation.

> "... just as a team effort is more than the sum of the individual efforts of the players and coach, the game is more than a particular game played on a particular day, more than a set of rules that determine how you go about trying to win.... '[T]he game' refers to a historical entity.... There wouldn't be a game without the efforts and achievements of all the participants.... [T]he game is something greater than each of us." (page 62)

Respect for the game goes well beyond performing well and winning. It is at the very heart of why sport exists and why we view sport as important to young people's development. We want young people to take away more from their participation in sport than just the feelings associated with winning and losing. Some might argue that concepts such as accepting outcomes and contributing to and feeling part of a larger experience beyond one small team are equally as or even more important than other aspects of participation, such as winning or developing fitness and skill.

Policies and rules on fair play and playing within the spirit of the game are covered later in this chapter. How athletes accept the outcome of a match can be viewed as an extension of respect for oneself, others, and the traditions of the game. Let's consider a rule to cover how you'd like your athletes to act at the end of a game.

All serious athletes invest a great deal of emotion in their participation, and it is only natural that they feel and express emotions, both positive and negative, at the end of a game. You probably do not want your athletes to be emotionless automatons who respond the same regardless of outcome. However, it is fair to expect your athletes to react with respect and dignity in both victory and defeat.

Here are two options for rules regarding respectful behavior after a game. Option 1 is in keeping with coach A's minimalist approach and permits the athlete to display emotion providing his or her behavior is respectful. Without specificities, the term "respectful" could be interpreted in different ways. Option 2 limits how much emotion an athlete can show and, as coach B likes to do, provides specific direction on ways the athlete should and should not act. This option might suit larger programs at a higher level of competition, when athletes might be more emotionally involved in sport.

☐ *Coach A's rule*: The athlete should act respectfully in both victory and defeat.

☐ *Coach B's rule*: The athlete should show respect to teammates, opponents, officials, and spectators in all situations, regardless of the outcome of a game or match. The athlete should avoid excessive displays of emotion in both victory and defeat.

Let's take a moment to summarize and reflect on this section so far. Respect has many levels and involves respect for oneself and for others involved in sport, such as teammates, coaches, opponents, and officials; respect for the game and its integrity and tradition; and respect for property and the environment. When selecting rules about how athletes show respect, consider addressing issues such as language and gestures, accepting decisions and victory or defeat with honor, respecting personal and community property, and observing the rituals associated with competition with sincerity. Your choice of rules might depend on your own personal and team philosophy about the importance of each issue and what role you think sport should play in helping young people develop and show respect.

Let's now move on to discuss harassment. Some view harassment as an issue that is contentious, subjective, or difficult to define and enforce. We have included harassment in this section on respect because in a broad sense harassment is a failure to respect others.

Harassment

Harassment is difficult to define precisely because it includes a subjective element and sometimes more than one viewpoint, but most agree that any conduct or behavior that is cruel or intimidates, humiliates, embarrasses, harms, or is offensive to a person or group constitutes harassment. Harassment can take physical, sexual, emotional, and verbal forms. Examples of such behavior include (but are not limited to) the following:

- Hostile verbal or nonverbal forms of communication (comments or gestures)
- Threatening, patronizing, or demeaning talk, actions, or gestures intended to intimidate or demean another
- Unwelcome jokes, teasing, ridicule, innuendo, or comments about another person's appearance, lifestyle, age, race, sex, religion, ethnic origin, nationality, disability, or sexual orientation
- Physical or sexual assault
- Unwelcome comments, jokes, or advances about sex or requesting sexual favors or unwelcome physical contact of a sexual nature
- Hazing or initiation in any form, whether with or without consent of the victim
- Other types of behavior that might create a negative or hostile environment, retaliation, or threatened retaliation

Sexual harassment includes unwelcome remarks, advances, or actions of a sexual nature when such remarks or actions affect decisions or performance or when they create an intimidating, awkward, or offensive environment.

Some schools and organizations view harassment as a serious enough issue to warrant a separate policy; others treat harassment as a form of unacceptable behavior that can be covered by wider policies on respect and codes of behavior.

You may or may not choose to have a separate policy on harassment, depending on whether your school or organization already has an antiharassment policy and preventive program, whether harassment has been an issue in the past, the size of your school or organization, and the age of your athletes. Whichever option you choose, We suggest that you clearly define harassment and give plenty of examples both within the policy and in face-to-face meetings with athletes and others involved to clearly indicate how you define harassment, what is unacceptable, and the consequences of infractions against the harassment policy.

You are encouraged to deal with complaints of harassment quickly, sensitively, fairly, and confidentially. Victims of harassment can be reluctant to come forward because of embarrassment (especially if hazing or sexual harassment is involved) or for fear of retribution or that a complaint might sour relationships with teammates or coaches. In addition, many aspects of what we now consider harassment (e.g., practical jokes or initiation rituals) were in the past considered a part of the traditions in some sports or teams, the school culture, or simply "growing up." Because harassment can be a serious accusation that can lead to disciplinary or even legal action, it is important to fully investigate the facts before making any decisions.

Here are two options for rules on harassment. The first option is brief and flexible and leaves open to interpretation precisely what could be considered harassment. Because of the subjective element of the definition of harassment, this option might work if your athletes are either well informed about harassment (e.g., if your school covers harassment in other policies and programs) or if there is little likelihood of harassment occurring because of constant supervision.

Option 2 is more detailed and states a team's position in both positive (e.g., "the right to be treated with respect") and negative (e.g., "harassment will not be tolerated") terms. You might select this option if you wish to use your policy to educate your athletes on the various aspects of harassment and to stress how seriously you view this issue. If your team has a history of problems relating to harassment, consider supplementing this rule, for example, with other educational materials or with a presentation by a counselor to ensure that your athletes understand this complex issue and your expectations.

☐ *Coach A's rule*: The athlete will not initiate or participate in any activity that could be considered harassment.

☐ *Coach B's rule*: Our team is committed to creating a positive environment for our athletes that is free of harassment in any form. Each athlete has a right to be treated with respect and to participate without fear of harassment on the basis of sex, race, nationality, religion, ethnic origin, sexual orientation, family status, or disability. Harassment in any form will not be tolerated, and an athlete who engages in harassment may be disciplined. Members of our team will not engage in harassment of teammates, opponents, officials, coaches, spectators, other students, members of the public, or any others involved in sport.

The following section discusses procedures for reporting, investigating, and responding to complaints of harassment.

Dealing With Harassment

Anyone who experiences or who witnesses harassment or who believes that harassment has occurred should report this behavior to the coach as soon as possible.

The coach will encourage the person reporting the harassment to complete a written report describing the incident(s).

Depending on the seriousness of the reported harassment and whether it is ongoing behavior or a single incident, the coach may elect to

- investigate further by talking directly with witnesses or the person(s) who experienced the harassment (complainant),
- confront the person(s) accused of harassment, or
- report the incident(s) to school or organizational authorities.

The complaint shall be investigated and acted on promptly.

Some harassment can be handled informally, for example, by confronting the person accused of harassment and explaining the unacceptability and consequences of the behavior. Sometimes young people might not realize that their behavior is offensive; in such cases, it is often more effective and less disruptive to deal with the issue informally through education rather than through punishment. If the person accused of harassment accepts responsibility for the behavior, the coach may require him or her to apologize to the offended party, and the matter can end there without further action.

If the harassment is ongoing or serious, or if the person accused of harassment refuses to accept responsibility, the coach or school may

- suspend the athlete accused of harassment from participating in team events pending resolution of the complaint, or
- convene a committee or panel to formally deal with the complaint.

If a committee is required, it should be comprised of objective members who are not involved with the team. The committee will gather facts about the alleged incident(s) through interviews and written statements. The person accused of harassment will be permitted to submit a written statement about the incident(s). The committee will convene a hearing to allow the complainant(s), person(s) accused, and witness(es) to present evidence and to question each other. The committee will submit a written report of its findings and decision along with any recommended disciplinary action. The committee's decision will be final, subject to appeal under the team's appeals procedures.

Consequences and Disciplinary Actions

Informal resolution may be concluded through a verbal or written apology (or both) from the person accused of harassment to the offended party. Informal resolution may also involve mandatory counseling for the person accused of harassment.

Depending on the seriousness or ongoing nature of the offense, formal resolution of the incident(s) may involve

- verbal or written apology or both;
- counseling of the accused to prevent further harassment;
- letter of reprimand to the accused;
- suspension from participation for a specified period;
- exclusion from participation in all sport;
- other disciplinary or legal action.

Repeated offense: An athlete found guilty of a second incident of harassment shall be excluded from school sport for one calendar year. An athlete found guilty of a third incident of harassment shall be excluded from school sport for the duration of his or her enrollment.

So far, we have presented some ideas to consider and have suggested policies and rules about respect. Respect has several facets, including respect for oneself, others, property, the environment, and the traditions of the sport. Respect makes sport possible because without respect sport loses its sense of fairness and fun, without which an activity is not sport.

Let's now move on to discuss a very broad and important topic that could be considered a natural extension of respect: responsibility. Because respect reflects a sense of valuing oneself, others, and the environment, people who respect themselves and others are more likely to feel responsible for their actions and to act responsibly.

POLICIES ABOUT RESPONSIBILITY

Most team policies begin from the premise that being part of a team carries both rights and responsibilities. You can require athletes to be responsible for their own behavior both in and outside of sport, for example, by maintaining eligibility, by attending class and achieving the required grades, by showing up on time for training and competition, by dressing appropriately for all team functions, and by exhibiting self-discipline. Athletes should understand that they must face and accept the consequences of breaches of policy.

In this section we will discuss policies and rules on

- self-discipline;
- eligibility;
- attendance, punctuality, and effort at practice and competition;
- appropriate dress;
- travel and curfew;
- accepting consequences of actions.

Your experience probably tells you that these are vast topics that attract a range of opinions. It can be a challenge to get young people to recognize the need for and to accept an appropriate level of responsibility. Can you recall a time when an athlete did not act responsibly and if this had an effect on your team? Think about how you handled the situation and whether the athlete learned anything about responsibility from your reaction and the consequences of his or her actions. You can help your young athletes learn to develop their own sense of responsibility by clearly (and patiently) articulating your policies and rules and the reasons behind them and by consistently applying and reinforcing these policies and rules.

In this section we will discuss each of the major topics regarding responsibility, starting with a general policy statement. This first statement is quite simple in its expectation that athletes will act responsibly. This option might be suitable for older teenagers or young adults who are experienced athletes and who understand your expectations, when you have another means to define and give examples of responsible behavior, or in recreational sport. Option 2 is far more expansive in defining the various facets of responsibility relevant to your team. This option also puts the obligation squarely on the athlete to know and follow team policies and rules and to accept the consequences of not doing so.

☐ *Coach A's policy introduction*: All athletes should act responsibly in all aspects of their sports participation.

☐ *Coach B's policy introduction*: It is an honor and a privilege to participate as a member of our team. Team members are expected to commit to the team's goals and to act responsibly, exercise good judgment, and encourage others to act responsibly at all times. Athletes are responsible for knowing and following all team policies and rules, for ensuring that they maintain academic eligibility, for attending practice, for giving full effort in practice and competition, and for following team rules at all times, including when traveling with the team. Athletes are also expected to accept the consequences of lapses in any of these areas.

As discussed earlier in the section on respect, the best place to start discussing responsibility is with the athlete's responsibility to him- or herself and self-discipline.

Rules About Self-Discipline

Consider the self-discipline required to excel at sport. The athlete must practice often, push his or her body past the point of fatigue and even pain, keep motivated against a sometimes superior opponent, play by the rules, avoid overt aggression even in a contact sport, and accept losing with dignity. Without self-discipline, sport could become chaotic.

COACHING TIP

"We vote for a best practice player each day, and the student athlete [who receives the most votes during the season] receives a plaque at the end of the year. We also read the same book as a team for each season, usually one about respect and sportsmanship; we discuss the book's themes as a team several times during the season."

—John Staab, baseball coach, Champaign Central High School, Champaign, Illinois

You expect a certain level of self-discipline from your athletes. How much you expect probably depends on their age, commitment, and level of competition. Obviously, the higher the level of competition and more complex the sport, the more self-discipline you require from your athletes. Although some undisciplined athletes might achieve a certain level, natural talent in the absence of self-control can only take them so far.

Rules about fighting and other forms of physical or emotional aggression can be considered in your rules about self-control; after all, an athlete who fights clearly demonstrates a failure in self-discipline.

The following discussion presents two suggested rules on self-discipline and aggression. Option 1 is probably the bare minimum acceptable for youth sport and requires the athlete simply to exercise self-control and avoid fighting or excessive aggression. The terms "self control" and "excessive aggression" are somewhat open to interpretation. For example, a certain level of physical aggression is inherent in sports such as ice hockey and football. You might consider this option for young athletes or in sports that rarely involve physical aggression, such as swimming or gymnastics. This option might also work if you can clarify what constitutes an acceptable level of aggression. However, this rule might be interpreted as condoning a certain level of violence or aggression. Option 2 is clearer on what is expected of the athlete. This option requires the athlete to avoid fighting and also requires a higher level of responsibility: to discourage fighting and aggression by teammates. This rule is less likely to be misinterpreted as condoning violence and aggression, especially if athletes are expected to discourage their teammates from fighting.

☐ *Coach A's rule*: The athlete should exercise self-control during practice and games. The athlete will not fight or display excessive aggression.

☐ *Coach B's rule*: The athlete should exercise self-control during practice and games or matches and in other sport-related activities. The athlete should not show excessive emotion, anger, frustration, or physical or verbal aggression and will not start a fight or become involved in a fight in any situation. The athlete will help his or her teammates avoid fights or other displays of aggression.

Athlete responsibility extends beyond behavior during sport and the more obvious issues of discipline and attitude. A range of more subtle aspects of responsibility exists, such as athlete eligibility, attendance, appearance, and effort. It can be easy to overlook or downplay these issues when focusing on the more obvious aspects of responsibility in sport. But clear policies and rules on these issues make it easier to clarify your expectations to your athletes. For example, if you had no clear policy about attendance and effort at practice, it might be difficult to deal with the gifted athlete who often misses practice or attends but just goes through the motions. How would you justify his or her inclusion in the starting lineup to other team members who regularly attend practice? How would you explain benching this athlete because of poor attendance? In either case, clear policies are necessary.

Rules About Eligibility

Eligibility refers to whether an athlete has met the requirements to participate in competitive sport. The United States courts have ruled that participation in extracurricular activities is not a constitutionally guaranteed right. That is, although access to public education is considered a fundamental right, the courts view extracurricular activities as optional and are thus not basic rights. This being the case, schools can legally dictate eligibility requirements to participate in extracurricular activities.

Policies and rules about eligibility generally aim to ensure that athletes receive a sound education and that competition is fair and safe.

As a coach, you have probably had to make tough decisions about an athlete's eligibility. You might have had a star athlete who could not compete for several games, or even a season, because of poor grades or after transferring from another school.

Eligibility covers a wide range of issues, including

- age and duration of enrollment;
- academic standards;
- attendance at school;
- residency;
- amateur status and outside-of-school participation;
- recruitment.

Whether your eligibility policy covers all of these issues will depend on the age of your athletes and the level of competition. For example, if you coach a highly successful football team at a large private high school, you might need policies about recruitment and outside-of-school participation, but these are less important issues for a public high school team. Some of your policies might be dictated by the sport association or school district that your team is part of.

You have probably found that some eligibility issues are fairly straightforward and that others can be more complex. Some issues occur far more often than others. For example, rules about maximum age of student athletes and minimum grade point average to maintain eligibility are clear-cut and easier to enforce than more complex issues such as whether a student has accepted financial gain or inducement to transfer to your school and play on your team. You have likely spent more time on the issues of academic eligibility and student attendance than on the others.

Option 1 is a more general and less prescriptive rule, as coach A prefers. The second option is more explicit and puts the obligation clearly on the athlete to know and meet eligibility criteria.

☐ *Coach A's rule*: All athletes must meet the minimum eligibility standards to participate in sport.

☐ *Coach B's rule*: The athlete is responsible for understanding and making every effort to meet eligibility criteria. An athlete placed on academic probation for poor grades must fulfill the terms of that probation before resuming participation. No student with a disability shall be denied the opportunity to try out for a sport because of his or her disability.

Maximum Age in School Sport

Most high schools have policies that restrict the age of their athletes to either 19 or 20 years by a certain cut-off date early in the school year or start of the sport season (e.g., March 1 for spring sports). The maximum age will vary according to the minimum age at enrollment in first grade, which varies among states. Having a maximum age ensures that athletes compete against others of roughly similar age and helps ensure that students make progress toward graduation.

Here are two options for rules about maximum age. The first option permits any student enrolled in school to participate in sport, regardless of age. You might choose this option if your school has athletes older than the average student population and you think it is important for them to participate fully in school activities. The second option is more restrictive because it adjusts maximum age according to the season's starting date. For example, an athlete reaching the maximum age on October 1 would be permitted to participate only in fall sports under option 2. You might use this option if you feel it is important to restrict eligibility based on age (e.g., if older athletes have an unfair advantage over athletes of normal school age) or as an added motivation for athletes to make steady progress toward graduation

☐ *Coach A's rule*: Any student enrolled in school is eligible to participate in sport regardless of his or her age.

☐ *Coach B's rule*: An athlete is ineligible to participate in school sport if he or she has reached the age of 19 (or 20, depending on your state) before September 1 for fall sports, December 1 for winter sports, and March 1 for spring sports.

Total Duration of Enrollment

Many high schools have policies that restrict the duration a student athlete can be enrolled and still participate in sport; this duration is usually 8 semesters or 16 quarters, equivalent to 4 years of full-time enrollment in grades 9 through 12.

This policy ensures that athletes make steady progress toward graduation, which is consistent with other rules regarding academic eligibility.

Of the two options for rules provided, the first is more general in that it allows any enrolled student to participate. This rule allows flexibility for a student who withdraws from school and later returns to compete without losing one season or year of eligibility. This option also allows a student who progresses through the system at a slower than average rate to continue to participate. Option 2 limits eligibility to students who progress through the system at the expected rate. You might choose this option if you have a large pool of athletes to choose from or to encourage student athletes to achieve at the level necesssary to graduate on time.

☐ *Coach A's rule*: Any enrolled student may participate in sport for the duration of his or her enrollment regardless of the length of enrollment.

☐ *Coach B's rule*: A student is eligible to participate in sports for a total of 8 semesters (or 16 quarters) from the time he or she first enrolls in ninth grade.

Academic Eligibility

Ideally, school sport is considered a vital part of the total educational process and not just an isolated activity. Many schools and communities take the view that athletes are first and foremost students. Ensuring that your athletes achieve and maintain their academic eligibility is vital to their development and future educational and vocational goals.

Much debate has taken place regarding the minimum standards athletes should achieve to maintain eligibility (Bukowski 2001). A nationwide trend toward more stringent guidelines and enforcement of high school academic eligibility requirements started in 1983 and was met with mixed responses. Some maintain that high school athletes tend to achieve higher grades than nonathletes and that academic eligibility standards have minimal impact. Others believe that school sport is sometimes the only motivator for low-achieving students to stay in school and that enforcing a minimum grade point average would cause these students to drop out. Schools with high academic standards (e.g., minimum grade point average of 2.5 to 3.0) report that student athletes generally adjust to the standards, provided they are publicized and that struggling students receive support.

It is important to stress to students that they are ultimately responsible for their own grades and progress toward graduation. Although your policies should reflect this, we also encourage you, your support staff, and the school to actively support your students in achieving to the best of their abilities. Some ways your school might provide this support include

- weekly grade checks by coaching, teaching, or counseling staff;
- extra study sessions or tutoring run by teachers or high-achieving students;
- a program to identify students at risk of failing and to intervene before they fail;
- a program of academic probation to ensure that students who perform poorly can quickly achieve the needed standards.

Most state school athletic associations and local school districts have rules about academic eligibility for extracurricular activities, including sport. Your policies must be consistent with these organizations' policies. You might have more stringent requirements than the larger organization (e.g., a higher minimum grade point average), but your policies must at least meet the larger organization's minimum standards.

Minimum Grades   School sport policies vary widely in the minimum grade point average and number of courses that students can fail and still remain eligible. These range from the strictest (athletes must pass all courses with a 2.5 grade point average) to the most lenient (must pass at least half your courses, with no consideration of grade point average). For sports starting at the beginning of the school year, the most recent grades from the end of the previous school year are counted.

Of the two rules described, option 1 is less prescriptive, allowing any enrolled student to participate in sport, regardless of grades. You might choose this option if your athletes generally achieve at a high level without the need for a minimum standard or, at the opposite end of the spectrum, when the school and community believe that sport plays an important role in helping to keep poorly performing student athletes in the school environment (i.e., without sport, some young people are likely to withdraw from school). Option 2 demonstrates a commitment to the academic achievement of athletes. Modify our suggested minimum grade (D) and grade point average (2.5) to suit the expectations of your school, parents, and community.

☐ *Coach A's rule*: Any student enrolled in school may participate in sport as long he or she attends classes regularly.

☐ *Coach B's rule*: To remain eligible, athletes must pass all courses (grade of D or higher), have a 2.5 (C) grade point average in the preceding semester (or quarter), and be passing all courses in the current grading period. For sports starting at the beginning of the school year, the final grades from the end of the previous school year apply.

To this point we have discussed rules about eligibility, both general and stricter options, and the arguments for these. Let's now turn to what you can and should do to ensure that your athletes achieve the grades they need to participate in sport and what to do about those who do not.

Consequences of Failing to Maintain Academic Eligibility Rules about the consequences of failing to maintain academic eligibility vary widely, depending on the minimum standard required and how closely the school monitors grades. The period of ineligibility because of poor grades ranges from one week to one full semester, depending on how often the school or coach can check grades and student progress. Some schools offer or even require ineligible students to develop an action plan with their academic counselor or coach to ensure that they can achieve the necessary grades to regain eligibility. Some schools require failing student athletes to attend extra study periods or to submit regular progress reports.

Consider how remaining ineligible can affect the student athlete's attitude toward school and academic progress. One view is that the more the school can do to encourage student athletes to improve, the less they will see ineligibility as a punishment and the less disruptive it will be to the athlete and to your team. On the other hand, more progressive policies require your school to commit adequate resources, such as staff, to monitor student compliance. You will need to consider these factors when choosing your policy on academic eligibility.

Two rules are provided regarding how to handle athletes who fail to maintain academic eligibility. Option 1 is more flexible and allows each student athlete to be treated as an individual and the school to provide a tailored program for the student. This option also provides flexibility for students experiencing personal, health, or family problems that might interfere temporarily with academic progress. However, this option requires adequate resources for the student to be given individual attention and to be monitored by an academic counselor, which may not be practical in every school. Option 2 is more prescriptive and less flexible, clarifying that all athletes must achieve at a certain level to maintain eligibility. You might choose this option if your school emphasizes academic achievement above other activities or if your school does not have adequate resources to provide an individualized approach.

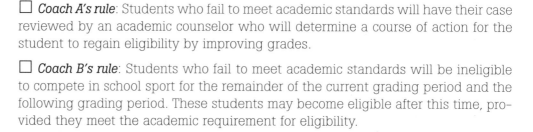

☐ *Coach A's rule*: Students who fail to meet academic standards will have their case reviewed by an academic counselor who will determine a course of action for the student to regain eligibility by improving grades.

☐ *Coach B's rule*: Students who fail to meet academic standards will be ineligible to compete in school sport for the remainder of the current grading period and the following grading period. These students may become eligible after this time, provided they meet the academic requirement for eligibility.

Once you have decided on rules regarding eligibility and when to allow ineligible students to return to sport, you need to consider what to do with ineligible students during the period of their ineligibility.

Can Ineligible Athletes Practice With the Team? Should academically ineligible athletes be permitted to practice with the team? Opinions vary. Allowing athletes to practice (option 1) encourages them to feel a part of the team and that academic ineligibility is only temporary, which might motivate them to achieve the necessary grades. You might adopt this option to motivate marginal students to improve their grades or if your school does not have a structured and well-resourced system for failing students. This option also works well for sports with long seasons, when maintaining fitness is important and you anticipate that students will improve their grades enough to compete before the end of the season.

Another view is that failing students need to devote full attention to their studies to regain eligibility. Option 2 is stricter and might work best in schools that emphasize academic achievement above all else or when a failing athlete needs extra time to concentrate on studies.

☐ *Coach A's rule*: Academically ineligible athletes are encouraged to continue practicing with the team, even if they are not permitted to compete, while working toward regaining academic eligibility.

☐ *Coach B's rule*: Academically ineligible athletes may resume training with the team only after regaining eligibility. While ineligible, students may not attend practice, wear the team uniform on competition day, join the team (sit on the bench) during competition, or be introduced as a member of the team.

We have looked at several viewpoints and rule options on academic eligibility and the consequences of student athletes failing to achieve eligibility. Let's now consider some methods to help your athletes achieve and maintain academic eligibility.

Academic Probation and Monitoring Progress   One option for students failing to achieve the grades necessary to maintain academic eligibility is to place them on academic probation, allowing a specified period of time for students to raise their grades and regain eligibility. Many schools have started using contracts between the students and teachers involved; these documents explain what students must do to raise their grades to the acceptable level and clarifies the role of the teacher, parents, and student. Whether you allow your athletes to practice but not compete while on academic probation will depend on the policy you decided on in the previous section.

The two options for rules both use academic probation and regular (weekly) monitoring to keep athletes working toward regaining academic eligibility while on probation. In option 1, the school is responsible for checking the athlete's progress against the probation contract. This option allows the athletes to continue to practice (but not compete) while on probation. You might consider this option if your school has adequate resources, such as a counselor and a system to check progress in each class. The second option also uses probation as a means to help athletes regain eligibility but is stricter in placing the responsibility on the students to report on their progress each week and does not allow them to practice or compete until they have regained academic eligibility. You might choose this option for athletes who are failing several classes or if your team numbers are restricted and you have to remove an ineligible player from your team list to make way for a replacement.

☐ *Coach A's rule*: A student who becomes academically ineligible during the school year will be placed on academic probation. The student's progress will be checked by the school counselor each week in accordance with the probation contract. The student may practice with the team but may not compete while on academic probation.

☐ *Coach B's rule*: Students who become academically ineligible during the school year will be placed on academic probation until they achieve the grades they need to regain eligibility. While on academic probation, the student must submit a progress report every week in accordance with the probation contract. While on academic probation, students may not practice with the team or compete or sit with the team during games.

Sometimes a failing student does not have enough time to improve his or her grades and regain eligibility before the end of the school year; this problem affects athletes in spring sports in particular. Consider how to handle athletes who end the academic year having lost their academic eligibility and whether summer school should be an option.

COACH'S HIGHLIGHTS

1. Qualifying for the state volleyball tournament 20 out of 21 years
2. Placing in the top four 14 out of 20 years
3. Playing my brother's team for the state title in 1994
4. Hiring former players as assistant coaches

—Laura Sundheim, girls' volleyball and track and field coach, Hardin High School, Hardin, Montana

Summer School   Some schools allow academically ineligible students to enroll in summer school to repeat classes they failed or that caused them to become ineligible. This policy encourages students to remedy their academic problems sooner rather than waiting until the next academic year and allows them to progress toward graduation with their classmates. Students are required to attend a suitable summer school program that meets the school's standards.

Option 1 is more flexible and allows the student athlete to regain eligibility by successfully completing the necessary classes over the summer. Option 2 is more restrictive and permits students to count classes passed only during the normal school year. This option might be considered harsh but might motivate athletes to concentrate on their studies during the school year, without the "fall-back" option of repeating classes during the summer. Your decision on which rule to adopt might depend on your other choices of rules about eligibility, if your athletes have access to summer school programs, and whether your school limits age or duration of enrollment of its athletes.

☐ *Coach A's rule*: Academically ineligible students may enroll in summer school to repeat the class or classes that caused ineligibility. The summer school grade(s) will count toward determining academic eligibility for the coming school year.

☐ *Coach B's rule*: Academically ineligible students may not count summer school grades toward their eligibility in the following school year.

Academic Ineligibility From the Previous Year   You might sometimes encounter students who enter a new school year academically ineligible because of poor grades in the previous year but who did not repeat or pass the needed classes during summer school. This kind of case presents a problem if you have chosen the more flexible rules about academic eligibility just described.

Here are two options to deal with student athletes who have lost eligibility because of poor grades in the preceding year. Option 1 has no carry-over from the previous year and allows students to start each new academic year fresh. This option might serve your team well by allowing failing students to continue to participate, but it might not encourage your athletes to achieve academically year after year, so you might be perceived as condoning poor academic performance.

Option 2 is stricter in that it considers the previous year's grades in determining whether the student can participate in the new academic year. By refusing eligibility at the start of the new school year, this rule might help motivate athletes to progress through each grade. On the other hand, an athlete in a fall sport might lose most of or even a complete season if a few months are needed until progress can be assessed.

☐ *Coach A's rule*: A student who is academically ineligible at the start of the school year because of grades from the previous year shall regain eligibility at the start of the new school year. The student must meet eligibility standards to maintain eligibility for the new school year.

☐ *Coach B's rule*: A student who is academically ineligible at the start of the school year because of grades from the previous year shall remain ineligible until the end of the first semester of the new school year. The student may regain eligibility at this point if his or her grades meet the minimum academic standards required for eligibility.

In this section we have discussed academic eligibility and how you can encourage your athletes to achieve it in the classroom; we have also looked at some options for ways to deal with poorly performing student athletes. Let's now discuss rules regarding ways to ensure regular attendance at school, which is vital if athletes are to achieve academically and maintain their academic eligibility.

Daily Attendance

Regular attendance and self-discipline among students are important to progress toward graduation. They are also important life skills relevant to future study and work. In most states, school attendance is compulsory until a certain age, and parents are legally responsible for ensuring their children's attendance.

Most schools have a policy regarding student attendance during the school day to maintain eligibility. (This is different from attending team practice, which is discussed elsewhere). Rules cover attendance both over the short term (e.g., student must attend class to practice or play on any given day) and long term (e.g., student must attend a minimum number of school days throughout the year). Rules on attendance also cover issues such as punctuality and legitimate reasons for late arrival, early departure, and absences.

You might consider incorporating some flexibility about attendance to identify unavoidable events that can cause a student to miss class or an entire school day (e.g., car trouble, family emergency, medical appointment).

One way to encourage your athletes to attend class is to create a rule requiring that they can practice and compete only on days on which they attend all their classes. For weekend competition, this can be extended to the day (usually Friday) preceding the game. We present two options for rules about daily attendance. The first allows athletes to practice or compete on any day if they have attended only one-half day of school. This rule also gives the coach the option of allowing an athlete who has missed school to participate after considering the reason for the absence. This option might be a good choice if your school believes that sport helps keep young people involved in school and if you have chosen most of the more flexible options on academic eligibility. The second option is stricter, requiring athletes to have attended a full day of school on the day of competition (or preceding day for a weekend game or match).

☐ *Coach A's rule*: The athlete must attend at least one-half the school day to participate in practice or competition. The coach may make an exception if the athlete has a legitimate reason for absence (e.g., family emergency, doctor's appointment) that has been accepted by the school principal.

☐ *Coach B's rule*: An athlete must attend all scheduled classes to participate in practice or competition on that day. For weekend contests, the student must attend all classes on the school day immediately preceding the weekend.

Attendance and Enrollment Over the School Year

Along with considering attendance at school on the day of practice or competition, you might also consider attendance over the semester or entire school year. Some schools now have a minimum number of school days that students must attend if they are to participate in extracurricular activities. This policy is consistent with the idea that your athletes need to attend class regularly if they are to maintain academic eligibility and progress toward graduation.

The first option is general and simply requires the athlete to meet the minimum attendance standard set by the school, conference, or state. You might choose this option if you are trying to keep marginal or unmotivated students in the system or if your school has flexible rules on attendance. The second option is stricter and permits only excused absences (which you would have to define) such as illness, serious injury, or family emergencies.

☐ *Coach A's rule*: To maintain eligibility, athletes must attend the minimum number of scheduled school days as required by the school district (or sport association) for progression to the next grade.

☐ *Coach B's rule*: To maintain eligibility, an athlete may not have any unexcused absences during the term (semester or quarter) in which he or she competes.

Appeals Regarding Academic Eligibility

Student grades can be affected by personal and outside events such as family breakdown, the death of a loved one, or a failed relationship. Your school may have a policy that applies to all athletes regarding whether they have a right to explain if outside events caused poor academic performance. Option 1 permits the student to participate in sport while a decision is pending, whereas option 2 bans the athlete from practice and competing until the problem is resolved.

☐ *Coach A's rule*: Students shall have the right to appeal a decision about their academic eligibility if they believe there are extenuating circumstances. The student may continue to participate in sport while the appeal is being considered.

☐ *Coach B's rule*: Students shall have the right to appeal a decision about academic eligibility if they believe there are extenuating circumstances. The student may not practice or compete in sport while the appeal is being considered.

You will need to have an appeals mechanism to deal with appeals quickly, consistently, and fairly. General rules for appeals are discussed later in this chapter.

Most student athletes follow the rules. After all, every sport is underpinned by a set of rules. Research shows that student athletes tend to have lower than average rates of truancy and discipline problems and overall higher grades. However, young people are not perfect and can get into trouble because, for many, part of youth involves testing the boundaries and learning through trial and error. Let's now move on to discuss handling athletes disciplined for unacceptable behavior.

Suspended or Expelled Students

As mentioned earlier, the United States courts have ruled that participation in school sport is not a constitutionally protected right, which means that schools can prohibit suspended or expelled students from participating in sport. For suspended students, this may mean for the duration of the suspension; for expelled students, this may mean that they may not participate ever again. Suspension and expulsion may include all or some organized school activities. Consider how you would handle student athletes who have been suspended or expelled for disciplinary reasons outside of sport.

Here are two choices on dealing with suspended student athletes. The first choice permits the athlete to continue to practice and compete during his or her suspension. Similar to the considerations of academic eligibility discussed previously, you might have good reasons to allow the athlete to remain active on the team during suspension. Consider, for example, an athlete disciplined for a first minor offense who has acknowledged and apologized for his or her lapse. Or a student whom you do not expect to become a regular discipline problem and who might be motivated to avoid future problems by remaining involved with the team. The second option is stricter and might be needed for athletes who commit more serious or repeated offenses. Disallowing the athlete from participating in all school activities, including sport, sends a strong message to both the offending athlete and the community that you are serious about the expected level of your athletes' behavior.

Unacceptable behavior may not always lead to suspension, and the school may use some other form of discipline. Rules on good citizenship are discussed later in the chapter.

☐ *Coach A's rule*: A student athlete suspended (whether in an in-school or out-of-school suspension) for disciplinary or other reasons may participate in sport during the period of suspension.

☐ *Coach B's rule*: Students who are suspended (whether in an in-school or out-of-school suspension) from school for disciplinary or other reasons are ineligible to participate in sport during the period of their suspension. They may not practice or compete with the team while on suspension. They may regain eligibility once the suspension has been completed provided that the coach and principal are satisfied that the behavior causing the suspension will not recur. A student expelled from the school may not practice or compete with the team once the expulsion takes effect.

Residency

Residency is important to eligibility in public schools, where students generally attend the school closest to their residence, which is supported by taxes paid by their parents or guardians. Considering the highly competitive nature of high-profile school sports, it can be tempting to try to lure an outstanding athlete from one district to another or from the public to private sector. However, most school districts and sport associations have strict rules about residency. Residency rules aim to ensure the stability and the best interests of student athletes (i.e., they attend their local school for the educational programs) and fair competition (i.e., to avoid one school recruiting all the top athletes).

Of the two rules presented, the first option is more general and allows any enrolled student to join your team, regardless of residency. You might select this rule if you coach in a small school and have a limited pool of students, if your school district has flexible rules about residency, or if your students come from families that move frequently. The second option is stricter and requires you or your school to check where your athletes live.

☐ *Coach A's rule*: All students enrolled in school may participate in school sport regardless of their place of residence.

☐ *Coach B's rule*: An athlete must reside within the boundaries of the school district and designated attendance area. Residence is based on the residence of the parent or legal guardian with whom the athlete lives.

Transfers Between Schools   Many schools and associations specify a time period for legal residence and might limit the number of times student athletes are allowed to transfer schools and retain eligibility during their high school careers. These rules clearly distinguish between a student athlete who transfers because of family situations and one who transfers simply to compete for a particular school. For example, it is generally considered a legitimate cause for transfer if an athlete's family moves or there is a change in legal guardianship, requiring the athlete to change schools. On the other hand, an outstanding athlete who transfers to a new school outside his or her home district for no apparent reason raises questions about the legitimacy of the transfer. In most instances, school administrators are more likely to be involved in developing and enforcing residency policy than are coaches.

Option 1 is flexible and allows any student transferring to the school to participate without concern for the reason for the transfer. This option might suit smaller programs. However, to adopt this rule, you might have to first check that it is consistent with your conference rules on transferring athletes. Option 2 is somewhat more restrictive and requires you or your school to check the reason for the athlete's transfer. This option would permit most, but not all, transferring students to participate. It should filter out any students transferring between schools solely to participate in sport.

☐ *Coach A's rule*: Any student who transfers to the school at the start of or during the academic year is considered eligible to participate in sport, regardless of the reason for the transfer, provided he or she meets academic and attendance requirements.

☐ *Coach B's rule*: A student who transfers to the school is considered eligible to participate in school sport only if he or she meets one of the following residency conditions:

→ The student resides within the designated school district.

→ The student transfers from another school district during the same academic school year or between academic school years because of a change in residency by the student's parents or legal guardians or because of a child protection order, placement in foster care, adoption, or juvenile court order.

→ The student transfers from another school district for reasons other than disciplinary action or because his or her previous school does not offer the next grade level.

A student who does not meet one of the above conditions is deemed ineligible to participate in school sport for one year after the date of enrollment in the new school.

The rules about academic eligibility, residency, and attendance discussed so far apply to typical situations for student athletes who live and attend school in their home district. But how would your team handle an inquiry about participating from an athlete who lives in your district but does not attend school because he or she is home schooled?

Home Schooling In recent years, a movement toward home schooling has evolved in the United States and Canada. The United States courts have ruled that participation in school sport is not a fundamental right that must be extended to home-schooled students. On the other hand, many schools permit home-schooled students living in their district to participate in school sports, provided they meet eligibility requirements such as age and academic standards. This is not an issue that comes up very often, but you might want to think about whether your team should permit participation by home-schooled students.

One benefit of permitting home-schooled students to participate is that you might find a talented athlete who would not otherwise participate in your sport. Although some sports are well organized at the community level (e.g., swimming, gymnastics, tennis, golf), high-level competition in other sports (e.g., football, wrestling) might be available only through the school system. Option 1 states that your team and athletes could benefit by allowing anyone living in your vicinity to participate, even if he or she does not attend your school. Option 2 does not permit nonenrolled athletes to participate. You might choose this option if you coach in a large school with many talented athletes from which to select your team, or if you believe that team cohesion depends on all athletes being students at your school.

☐ *Coach A's rule*: Students exempted from public school education and who are home schooled may be eligible to participate in school sport provided they meet the age, academic, and residency criteria for participating in school sport.

☐ *Coach B's rule*: Only students enrolled in the school may participate in the school's sport programs. Home-schooled students living in the district may not participate in school sport.

Another atypical athlete is the international student who attends your school for a short period, usually up to one year at most. Depending on how often your school hosts international students, you might consider whether you need a rule about the eligibility of these students in your sport program.

International Students Many schools participate in exchange programs to host international or foreign-exchange students, some of whom might wish to participate in school sport as part of their learning experience. Some schools have policies restricting participation by such students, but many do not. Whether you allow all foreign students to participate with the same rights as domestic students will depend on any restrictions imposed by your school district or sport association or conference, your personal philosophy, and the size of the pool of eligible athletes in your school's district. You might approach this issue similarly to whether you permit home-schooled students living in your district to participate in sport.

The first rule option treats the international student much the same as any local student and does not restrict participation in sport. You might choose this option if you coach in a small school that is always in need of talented athletes or if international students bring with them a different level of experience or skill that would benefit your team. The second option is somewhat stricter in giving the international student only one year of eligibility and only if he or she has not previously graduated from high school. You might find this option works better in a larger school or when fierce competition exists for team selection from local students. Some schools also restrict international students to junior varsity or lower level teams; you might consider adding this aspect to your rule if an athlete's progression through the developmental teams is important to his or her selection to the varsity team.

☐ *Coach A's rule*: An international student who enrolls in school under an approved foreign-exchange program is eligible to participate at any level in any sport provided he or she meets all other eligibility requirements (academic, age, residency, etc.) for the duration of his or her enrollment.

☐ *Coach B's rule*: An international student who enrolls in school is eligible to participate at any level in any sport for one year only, beginning on the date of first enrollment. The student must also meet all other eligibility requirements (academic, age, residency, etc.) and must not have previously graduated from high school in his or her home country.

Young people are full of energy, and some are not satisfied to compete on only one team or in one sport. You have probably encountered talented and keen young athletes who "live and breathe" sport.

Playing for More Than One Team

Schools can sometimes restrict athletes from competing in the same sport for more than one team during the same season. This policy helps avoid conflicts in attendance and scheduling and prevents athletes from training excessively, which is likely to lead to overtraining, illness, or injury. Some schools permit athletes to compete for more than one team if no conflict in scheduling of practice and competition arises.

Option 1 leaves it to the athlete and his or her family to determine how many teams he or she can join. The only limitation is a conflict of scheduling that might prevent the athlete from attending practice or games for both teams. This option would work in sports with short seasons or when there is little overlap between the different teams' schedules. You might wish to monitor your athletes for signs of overtraining, fatigue, and injury. Option 2 is more restrictive and ensures that your athletes are available and fully committed to your team's requirements. You might choose this option for teams with full schedules, in sports with long seasons, or if you believe that participating in other sports or teams might jeopardize your athletes' health.

☐ *Coach A's rule*: An athlete may play on as many teams as he or she wishes, provided no conflicts in game and practice schedules arise.

☐ *Coach B's rule*: While a member of the team, an athlete may not compete as a member of another team in the same sport, or in a different sport, for the duration of the team's competitive season, including end-of-season tournaments if the team is competing in the tournament. The school's athletic director or club director may grant exceptions to this rule on an individual basis.

Amateur Status

Student athletes at the high school level are usually expected to participate as amateurs and not to receive financial reward for their participation. However, this can be a difficult policy decision, given the potential for athletes in some sports to capitalize on their success. Requiring young athletes to remain amateurs removes the added pressure to perform that can burden young athletes or limit their enjoyment. On the other hand, you might not have the power to limit the earning capacity of a young athlete. Your sport or conference might have rules about amateur status that your team rules must accommodate.

The first rule option is flexible and allows athletes to become professional and still remain a member of the team. Before adopting this rule, you would need to check whether your conference permits athletes to accept payment, the possible effects on team spirit and cohesion, and whether accepting payment as a professional would jeopardize the athlete's future prospects (e.g., in college sport). The second option restricts participation to true amateurs only. The last part of this option permits the athlete to accept small gifts. We've suggested up to $100, but you might vary this amount depending on the sport and your athletes' situations. For example, you might permit a long-jumper from a low-income family to accept a pair of specialty jumping shoes worth more than $100 donated by a local sporting goods store.

☐ *Coach A's rule*: An athlete may accept financial remuneration and still participate on the team.

☐ *Coach B's rule*: An athlete must retain amateur status to remain a team member. An amateur athlete may not

→ accept any cash award for sport participation,

→ accept payment for expenses above those actually incurred for competition or travel to competition,

→ sign a contract to play professional sport or play sport as a professional or as a member of a professional team,

→ accept a salary or any other form of financial assistance (e.g., scholarship) from a professional sport team, or

→ accept merchandise, gifts, or services in excess of $100 per calendar year.

Let's pause a moment to summarize this rather large section on athlete eligibility. We've discussed some of the issues relating to student athletes' grades, school attendance, residency, and how these fit within the focus of your program and your schools' philosophy about academic achievement. This section has presented rule options that fit the belief that academic achievement is vital for student athletes as well as the belief that sport is an important means to attract and keep student athletes in "the system" regardless of academic achievement. All of these rules are related mainly to the student athlete's activities outside of sport. Let's now turn to issues of athletes' responsibility more directly related to sport, such as their attendance and effort at practice and competition, attire, travel, and curfew.

Attendance and Effort at Practice and During Competition

You naturally hope that your athletes will be as committed to the team and their sport as you are. It's difficult to run a team—to develop their fitness, plan strategy, prepare for important matches—if your athletes don't attend practice regularly or don't give a full effort at each practice. Regular attendance is also essential to developing team spirit and morale; teammates need to trust each other and know that each is giving his or her all. Thus, you expect your athletes to honor their commitment to the team and their teammates and to show up at practice ready to go all-out.

But young people often experience conflicting demands on their time and attention. They can be easily distracted by events needing their immediate attention or causing them concern at the moment, particularly personal relationships. As a coach, you might find it difficult to balance the need for self-discipline, responsibility, and care (discussed later in this chapter) that you are trying to instill in your athletes.

Attendance at Practice

The preceding sections emphasized that being on a team is an honor that carries with it both kudos and responsibility. If your athletes accept the concepts of self-respect and respect for the game and their team, it will be easier for them to understand the importance of attending practice and giving full effort at practice and during competition.

Option 1 implies that attendance is expected but does not stipulate any consequences for not attending. This option relies on athletes to take the initiative to communicate with the coach. This option might work for developmental teams or in individual sports in which attendance is not so crucial or with highly committed athletes with whom you have a long-standing relationship and whom you trust to inform you when they cannot attend practice. Option 2 is more restrictive and makes playing in the game dependent on attending practice. You might consider this option in team sports in which teamwork and complex strategy are crucial or when regular training is essential, such as before major competition.

© Human Kinetics

☐ *Coach A's rule:* Athletes should attend all practices. Athletes missing practice should inform the coach as soon as they know that they cannot attend and should give their reason for missing.

☐ *Coach B's rule:* An athlete must attend all scheduled practices unless excused for reasons of health, injury, or other unavoidable events. An athlete who misses more than one practice in a given week, regardless of the reason, will be ineligible to play in that week's game or match. An athlete missing practice should inform the coach as soon as he or she knows that he or she cannot attend and should give the reason for the absence.

In designing your rule about attendance at practice, you might consider how best to explain to your athletes what is and is not an acceptable reason to miss practice. For example, a family emergency, a religious holiday, a doctor's appointment, or school field trip might be acceptable reasons to miss practice.

On the other hand, time management is one important lesson for student athletes, and you probably would not accept an athlete missing practice to complete an assignment he or she has had two weeks to complete.

COACH'S HIGHLIGHTS

1. Seven state football championships, two state track championships
2. Induction into national and state halls of fame
3. National coach of the year in football (2005)

—Phil Robbins, football and boys' track coach, Powell Valley High School, Big Stone Gap, Virginia

Effort at Practice and During Competition

You expect your athletes to do more than just show up for practice. You want them to concentrate on their training and to give full effort at every session. Have you ever coached an athlete who showed up for practice but seemed to be just going through the motions? If you coach a team sport such as basketball, soccer, or football, and this behavior happened regularly, that athlete's habits probably affected team cohesion.

☐ *Coach A's rule*: The athlete should give full effort at all practices and games. Any athlete who does not feel physically capable of full effort should inform the coach, who may decide to excuse the athlete or modify the session.

☐ *Coach B's rule*: Athletes are expected to concentrate fully and exert themselves to the expected level at all practices and during all games or matches. Any athlete who does not feel physically capable of full effort should inform the coach, who may decide to excuse the athlete or modify the session. Athletes who do not exert themselves as expected during practice and who do not offer a reason to the coach will not be in the starting lineup for the next game.

So far, our discussion has focused on rules about respect and responsibility in the context of athletes' behavior and rule options to cover the varied aspects of respect and responsibility. Let's now turn to another aspect of responsibility: the way athletes dress.

Appropriate Dress

Schools and communities take great pride in their youth's sporting achievements. Consider how much time, effort, and money go into sport at all levels, from community and school sport to national teams competing in the Olympic Games. Think about the different ways that your athletes demonstrate their pride in their achievements. The way they dress is probably one of these. If we accept that participation in school sport is an honor and privilege, then athletes should be proud to represent their school, and the school community has reason to expect their appearance and actions to reflect this pride.

Although neat attire by itself does not guarantee a well-disciplined team, many consider appropriate dress to be a component of self-discipline and self-respect.

Wearing a team uniform is a given in most organized sports. The uniform identifies team members, is in some cases necessary for performance, health, and safety (e.g., avoiding injury or heat illness), and is a crucial part of developing team identity and cohesion. The previous section on responsibility offered rule options about caring for the team uniform. Your team might have a uniform or other dress code to wear for team activities besides games or matches (e.g., during awards ceremonies or travel to and from competition).

Option 1 requires athletes simply to wear the team uniform for games and to dress neatly for other team activities. You might consider this option when it is not that important that the team maintains a certain image outside of practice and games. The term "neatly" means different things to different people, and you might need to define what is and is not acceptable dress for team events when athletes do not wear their uniforms. The second option is stricter; it covers travel and implies that your team has a prescribed standard of dress for activities when athletes do not wear their uniforms. If you choose this second option and prescribe what athletes may wear when they do not wear their uniform, we suggest you seek the athletes' input and consider regularly updating your dress code. Young people are especially sensitive to current trends in fashion; it may be difficult for your athletes to take pride in their appearance if they find the required attire uncomfortable or unfashionable, or if they are ridiculed by their peers or opponents.

☐ *Coach A's rule*: The athlete must wear the team uniform for all games and should dress neatly for all team events outside of practice and games.

☐ *Coach B's rule*: The athlete must wear the prescribed uniform or attire for all games and noncompetition team activities such as awards ceremonies, publicity events, and travel to and from competition.

Cell Phones

Cell phones are an established and accepted part of youth culture, but despite their many benefits, they can be an unwanted distraction to athletes who should be concentrating on practice or competition. Consider if you want to create rules regarding the presence and use of cell phones when athletes are at practice and competition. The first option is more flexible and relies on athletes being considerate, such as by knowing when to turn off the cell phone so it does not ring during a crucial time in practice or competition. The second option makes it clear that cell phones are to be used only for urgent communication, such as to arrange transportation with a parent.

☐ *Coach A's rule*: If athletes bring cell phones to practice or competition, they should ensure that the phone does not disturb practice or competition.

☐ *Coach B's rule*: Athletes may not bring cell phones to practice. An athlete may bring a cell phone to competition but must turn the phone off and may use it only to communicate with a parent, as needed.

Does your team ever travel for competition? If so, what do you do to ensure that your athletes arrive on time, ready to compete and behave appropriately?

Travel

When your team travels to an away game or tournament, you want the travel to go smoothly and safely, without worry. You do not want to have to be concerned about your athletes traveling safely, following directions, and arriving on time. You or someone in your organization probably organizes your team to travel together efficiently, by bus or van. Traveling together helps develop team spirit and cohesiveness and can help mentally prepare your athletes for the upcoming contest.

Travel to Competition

Here are two rule options regarding how your athletes travel to games. Option 1 is flexible and gives athletes the responsibility of arranging their own transport. You might choose this option when you know transport is not a problem for your athletes. For example, older teenagers can drive themselves, some families arrange car pools, and some parents always attend their children's games. Option 2 is more restrictive in requiring the team to travel together (although it permits alternative arrangements, such as if a parent needs to pick up an athlete after a game). This option requires you to know in advance, and to have some control over, how your athletes travel to games or matches. We will discuss issues relating to the coach's responsibility to ensure safety during travel in the next chapter.

☐ *Coach A's rule*: Athletes may arrange their own travel to and from games or matches and other team activities.

☐ *Coach B's rule*: Except by prior arrangement as approved by the coach, all athletes are expected to travel as a team to and from games or matches and other team activities.

Overnight Travel

Here are two options for rules regarding how athletes should behave when traveling overnight to competition. The first rule assumes that your athletes understand what is and is not respectful and responsible behavior. This option might be useful for a well-disciplined team whose athletes travel frequently. The second option is stricter and more explicitly describes acceptable and unacceptable behavior and the consequences of inappropriate behavior.

☐ *Coach A's rule*: Athletes should act respectfully and responsibly when traveling overnight for competition or other team activities.

☐ *Coach B's rule*: Athletes should act respectfully and responsibly when traveling overnight for competition or other team activities. Athletes will not engage in horseplay or other activities that could disturb others. Athletes will observe the team's curfew and not leave their rooms except as authorized by the coach or other supervising adult on the trip. The use of alcohol, tobacco, or other illicit substances is forbidden. An athlete who acts inappropriately may be disciplined or sent home.

Coach's Exercise

Your team is getting ready to travel to an important annual tournament. Last year, several senior athletes got into trouble for irresponsible and disrespectful behavior, and your team's reputation has suffered as a result. Although all of those athletes graduated last year, you expect your current athletes will be subjected to taunts about last year's mishaps. What do you say to your athletes to prepare them?

Curfew

Adequate rest is important to good health and to both academic and sport performance. You can probably recall terrible performances by tired athletes who had not rested enough the night before a big game. Some teams impose nighttime curfews on their athletes to ensure that they are well rested and able to perform at the level expected. Setting a nighttime curfew may emphasize to your athletes the importance of rest. However, a curfew might be difficult to enforce on a daily basis; they are much easier to enforce during travel, when you have tighter control over your athletes' whereabouts.

Option 1 trusts each athlete (and his or her family) to be responsible for deciding on what is sufficient rest. Option 2 prescribes actual hours that the athlete must be at home. Although this option might go further in ensuring that your athletes do not overdo their socializing, you might find this rule difficult to document and enforce. When considering these options, think about the age and level of your athletes (e.g., parents probably enforce their own curfews for younger athletes), parental expectations regarding how much control you can and should have over their children's lifestyle, and whether your athletes are at risk of not getting enough rest.

☐ *Coach A's rule*: The athlete should take care to get enough rest to perform to his or her ability both academically and in sport. Although the team does not impose a curfew, we expect each athlete to rest and sleep sufficiently during the sport season so that performance in school and sport are not compromised by being overtired.

☐ *Coach B's rule*: During the sport season, the athlete is expected to observe the following curfews:

→ Weeknights and nights before a game or match: 10:30 p.m.
→ Weekends, if no game or match the next day: 1:00 a.m.

Anyone who has worked with young people recognizes that it can be difficult to teach some of them how to accept responsibility for their actions. Consider the young people you have coached or worked with over the years. Can you recall some who seemed to naturally understand and accept responsibility for their actions, whereas others seemed less mature or were unable (or unwilling) to understand the concept of personal responsibility?

Accepting Responsibility for Actions and Consequences

As mentioned earlier, participation in sport is a privilege that carries many benefits and responsibilities. A part of growing up is learning to take responsibility for your actions. If coaches' policies and rules are clearly worded and actively incorporated into all team activities, their athletes should not be surprised at the consequences of not following rules. That said, it is important to clearly convey, in both positive and negative wording, the expectation that your athletes accept responsibility for following the rules and the consequences of breaking rules.

Option 1 is minimal and expects athletes simply to follow the rules, without proposing consequences of not doing so. Option 2 is more prescriptive and informative. This rule sets a standard of responsibility (what athletes are responsible for) and the consequences of shirking that responsibility (accepting the consequences of infractions).

□ *Coach A's rule*: The athlete should understand and follow all team rules.

□ *Coach B's rule*: Each athlete is responsible for his or her own actions and for accepting the consequences of those actions. An athlete is responsible for knowing and following the school and team policies and rules. An athlete who violates a school or team rule is expected to accept the consequences, which may involve suspension from the team. Any athlete disciplined for violating a team rule has the right to appeal the decision in accordance with team policy.

This ends a long section on athlete responsibility. Before progressing to the next moral value (caring), let's recap the major points of this section. Being part of a team carries both rights and responsibilities, and it is fair to expect your athletes to accept responsibility for their own behavior both in and out of sport and to accept the consequences of failing to do so. In this section we discussed issues relating to self-discipline, eligibility, attendance, effort at practice and competition, dress, travel, and curfew. Clearly worded rules supported by both positive and negative models, along with an appropriate measure of patience and consistent application and enforcement, are likely to teach young athletes to accept responsibility. Such rules also minimize the distractions that poor discipline can bring to team sports.

Coach's Exercise

Think of a situation in which some of your athletes acted irresponsibly. At the time, did you have a policy regarding athletes' responsibility that covered the particular indiscretion? If so, why did the athletes act contrary to this policy? If not, do you think a strong policy might have prevented the behavior? Have you changed any part of your policy as a result of the incident?

POLICIES ABOUT CARING

In this section we discuss the different aspects of caring. You will learn how to choose rules to help athletes translate the concept of caring into practice, specifically how to cooperate with and encourage teammates, contribute to team effort, and ensure the health and safety of your athletes.

Caring is related to fairness and respect; people who treat others fairly and with respect generally also care deeply about themselves and others. Policies and rules about caring focus on cooperation, compassion, empathy, generosity, and issues of athlete health and safety.

☐ *Coach A's policy introduction*: All athletes should support their team and teammates.

☐ *Coach B's policy introduction*: Our team is committed to a caring environment in which each team member is a valued part of the team and all team members support each other.

Cooperating With and Supporting Team Members

How important is it to your team's success for your athletes to cooperate with and support each other? Different sports require different types and levels of cooperation and support. For example, a team sport such as football, hockey, or baseball might involve complex plays requiring precise timing and coordination among athletes at the same time. In contrast, individual sports such as track and field, golf, or tennis, require a different level of cooperation among athletes on the same team. This does not mean that cooperation and support apply only to team sports, but that cooperation and support among team members can take different forms and be expressed in different ways. Take the example of swimming or track, in which your athletes might compete against each other in individual events and then, a short time later, work together in a relay. Getting them to focus on their individual competitiveness and performance, while at the same time getting them to identify with the team effort, can be a challenge in some sports.

Of the two options for rules, option 1 indicates that athletes are simply expected to cooperate with each other. This might be self-evident in some sports and at some levels. Option 2 is more instructive about what "support" involves and expresses its points in both positive ("demonstrate concern") and negative ("avoid behavior that might hurt or injure") terms. You might supplement this rule by discussing examples at team meetings or in other relevant instances. For instance, you might point out and positively reinforce cooperative behavior

COACHING TIP

"I try to make contact with every athlete at every practice. I try to say hello or something similar to every athlete. I ask about the athlete's day, review his or her performance, and so on. Personal contact lets them know that I am watching all team members. For example, in a cross country meet, I have all our team members cheer until the last runner finishes, even if it's a runner from a different team. We want to win, but we also respect and have compassion for those who want to beat us."

—Mark Logan, track and field and cross country coach, RHAM High School, Hebron, Connecticut

such as helping a teammate up after a fall, persuading a teammate to walk away from a potential fight with an opponent, or encouraging a teammate to accept an official's decision without arguing. You might also point out and discuss uncooperative behavior such as hogging the ball, inciting teammates to aggressive behavior, or talking negatively about a teammate.

☐ *Coach A's rule*: The athlete will cooperate with his or her teammates in practice and games.

☐ *Coach B's rule*: The athlete will cooperate with his or her teammates in all team activities. He or she will actively demonstrate concern for and will support all teammates. The athlete will avoid any talk or behavior that might hurt or injure a teammate.

Contributing to Team Effort

Contributing to team effort should be a natural outcome of a caring team environment in which athletes support and cooperate with each other.

If you coach a team sport, you recognize how important it is to get the team to "click"—to think and work as one unit rather than as a collection of individuals. We tend to think of teamwork only in the context of team sports, but the concept also applies to sports in which the performances of individual athletes combine to determine the overall performance of the team, such as golf, swimming, track and field, and tennis. Whereas athletes might tend to focus on their own performance and effort individually, part of your job is to get them to think in the context of the entire team.

Option 1 is fairly minimal and may be self-evident in many sports. The term "team effort" could be interpreted in different ways. Consider this option if you can assume that your athletes understand what goes into the concept of team effort. The second option is more educational and emphasizes playing for the team.

☐ *Coach A's rule*: Each athlete should contribute to team effort.

☐ *Coach B's rule*: The athlete will be a committed member of the team and will put the needs of the team ahead of personal glory.

Encouraging Teammates

You expect your athletes to try their hardest and to support their teammates' efforts. In young people, acceptance by their peers can be a strong motivator, both positive and negative. Harsh criticism from a teammate can be even more detrimental to an individual athlete and to the team than similar comments by an adult.

Option 1 models only positive encouragement by teammates toward one another. The second option encourages positive actions and prohibits negative actions. This option is more educational because many young athletes are unaware of the effects of their negative words or actions on each other and on team cohesion. Consider this option for athletes who spend a lot of time training or traveling together.

☐ *Coach A's rule*: The athlete should praise the effort of his or her teammates.

☐ *Coach B's rule*: The athlete will praise his or her teammates' efforts and successes by applauding or through positive gestures such as giving high fives. The athlete should use positive words and should not harshly criticize a teammate or use negative words when talking with or about a teammate.

Caring goes beyond how athletes interact with and show respect for each other. Caring also concerns athletes' health, safety, and well-being. Over the long term, healthy athletes are more likely to perform their best, and a safe sports program is more likely to achieve its goals and be successful.

Leading a Healthy Lifestyle

There is no doubt that lifestyle factors such as sleep, diet, and other behaviors influence sport and academic performance, especially in young people who are still maturing physically and emotionally. Consider the time and effort you put into organizing and training your team. It is natural for you to expect your athletes to take care of themselves so they can perform their best.

Option 1 leaves it to each athlete to interpret what constitutes a healthy lifestyle. Option 2 clarifies that diet, sleep, and avoiding unhealthy behaviors are expected aspects of a healthy lifestyle. In choosing your option, consider the age of participants, their skill level and level of competition, and how much control you have over their lifestyle choices. Parents of high school athletes might appreciate the guidance provided by the second option, and your athletes might perform better if you clearly explain a "healthy lifestyle" and its relationship to good performance. On the other hand, some families might find this level of instruction intrusive.

☐ *Coach A's rule*: The athlete should seek to lead a healthy lifestyle.

☐ *Coach B's rule*: The athlete will lead a healthy lifestyle that includes getting enough sleep, eating a healthy diet, and avoiding unhealthy behaviors such as smoking, drinking alcohol, and using drugs or banned substances.

The previous rule focused on helping athletes remain healthy, but as a coach you also have a responsibility to ensure your athletes' health and well-being. In some states or conferences, athletes are required to obtain medical clearance before joining a team, whereas this might not be mandatory in other situations.

Obtaining Medical Clearance

Your athletes must be in good health to train hard and exert full effort day after day. You and your school or organization have a duty of care to ensure that your athletes are healthy and fit enough to train and compete at the expected level. A good place to start is to ensure that all athletes are considered medically fit to participate in competitive sport. Although medical conditions that might endanger a young person competing in sport are rare, some conditions can be dangerous or even fatal if left undetected or untreated.

Option 1 leaves it to the athlete to determine his or her fitness to participate. High-level sports require consistently good health and fitness, and the school might be held responsible if an unfit or unhealthy individual is injured participating above the level that he or she is physically capable of. Option 2 is more prescriptive and requires medical approval before an athlete may compete. When choosing your rule, consider the demands of the sport, the level of competition, and the likelihood of injury to the athlete.

☐ *Coach A's rule*: The athlete should be healthy and fit enough to participate in sport.

☐ *Coach B's rule*: Before an athlete can participate in practice or competition, he or she must have a physical examination by a medical practitioner who certifies that the athlete is medically fit to participate. Medical clearance is valid for one calendar year. The medical practitioner can be the student's usual doctor or one provided by the school. The school shall maintain a written record of medical clearance for all participants.

Handling Injuries and Illness

An injured or ill athlete cannot practice and compete at the expected level. Young athletes are sometimes reluctant to admit to minor illness or injury because of their enthusiasm for the sport, their sense of "invincibility," a fear of being sidelined, or a lack of understanding about when an injury or illness requires rest and treatment. If you are unaware that an athlete is ill or injured, you might misinterpret his or her poor performance as a lack of motivation or interest. Ideally, your team philosophy, policies on respect and responsibility, and leadership style will encourage your athletes to be honest and open about matters such as illness and injury. Nevertheless, you might consider whether you should have rules that require your athletes to inform you of all illnesses and injuries.

Communicating With the Coach About Illness or Injury

The first option relies on open communication between athletes and coaches or medical staff and encourages athletes to tell the coach about an injury or illness. This option leaves it to the athlete to decide if the injury or illness affects his or her ability to practice or compete. Option 2 requires the athlete to promptly inform the coach or medical staff of any injury or illness, regardless of whether the athlete believes the condition affects his or her performance. This option gives the coach and medical staff the power to make decisions about whether the athlete should practice or compete. You might choose this option if you want to limit the risk of exacerbating an injury or illness by allowing your athletes to train or compete.

☐ *Coach A's rule*: The athlete should tell the coach or team doctor (or physical therapist or trainer) about any injury or illness that might affect his or her ability to practice or compete.

☐ *Coach B's rule*: The athlete must report all injuries or illness, no matter how slight, to the coach and team doctor (or physical therapist or trainer) within 48 hours of the first signs of illness or injury. The coach, in consultation with the team doctor (or therapist or trainer), will determine if the athlete is fit to practice or compete.

Return to Play

For minor illness (e.g., common cold) or injury (e.g., mild muscle strain), the athlete usually misses only a few days of practice and perhaps one game or match. A young and fit athlete can quickly return to full training and competition after a few days off. However, an athlete with a more serious injury or illness needs longer to recover and a more gradual return to full training. Returning to full training and competition too quickly after a serious injury or illness can cause reinjury, injury of another part of the body, return of the illness, or other possibly serious complications.

The first option allows athletes to decide when they are ready to return to sport, provided the coach agrees. This option works well for athletes returning from minor illness or injury or when your athletes and their parents are well informed about the importance of a gradual return. Option 2 is stricter, requiring athletes to demonstrate full fitness in a fitness test or during practice before returning to competition. Requiring the athlete to complete the same number of sessions as those missed helps the athlete return to full fitness gradually and ensures that he or she is healthy before going all-out in competition. This option also distinguishes between minor or brief illness or injury and more serious or long-lasting illness or injury.

☐ *Coach A's rule*: An athlete who misses practice or competition because of illness or injury may return to sport when he or she feels ready, subject to approval by the coach or medical clearance.

☐ *Coach B's rule*: An athlete who misses practice or competition because of illness or injury lasting fewer than five days may return to practice as soon as the illness or injury is resolved, subject to approval by the coach. Any athlete who misses practice for five or more days because of illness or injury may not practice or compete until he or she receives written medical clearance from his or her own physician or the team doctor (for illness or injury) or physical therapist or trainer (for injury only). Before competing, the athlete must pass a fitness test or participate in as many practice sessions as the number he or she missed.

The school, community, and coach are responsible for ensuring that athletes practice and compete in a safe environment. Policies on providing a safe environment for athletes are covered in the next chapter. So far, this chapter has covered three of the six moral values—respectfulness, responsibility, and caring—and has offered many ideas for rules relating to each value. These moral values seem to flow naturally from one to the next. That is, helping athletes to achieve respect for themselves, others, and the environment provides a basis to guide them to translate that respect into responsible and caring behavior. Let's now discuss the fourth moral value, honesty, which can be considered a close cousin of respect and responsibility.

Coach's Exercise

Make a list of ways that your athletes demonstrate caring toward each other. Prepare a handout for your athletes and their parents to communicate your personal philosophy and team policy about how teammates can and should demonstrate caring.

POLICIES ABOUT HONESTY

Honesty involves being truthful and trustworthy and acting with integrity and loyalty to the team and sport. Honest athletes are good team players who recognize that success in most sports requires a team effort.

☐ *Coach A's policy introduction*: All team members should be honest in all team activities.

☐ *Coach B's policy introduction*: Our team believes that honesty and loyalty to the team are crucial aspects of sport. All athletes are expected to act with honesty and integrity and have the right to expect others to act similarly.

Being Truthful and Trustworthy

At the least, you should be able to assume that your athletes will be truthful and not lie to you about issues relating to their participation in sport. Young people might not necessarily recognize that you need to know certain facts about them to make decisions about the team. For example, you would probably not start a player you knew had been very ill a few days earlier, and you would not push an athlete in practice if you knew he or she was experiencing pain from an injury you thought had healed. You would rethink selecting an athlete for your varsity team if you knew that he or she was a member of another team whose schedule conflicted with yours. Honesty, like respect, runs both ways. This chapter discusses issues relating to honesty for athletes; the next chapter discusses these issues as they relate to coaches.

The first option requires the athlete not to lie. This rule might suffice for athletes whom you generally trust or when your school has a more general program about honesty for all students. Although some may view this option as expecting complete honesty, different people have different definitions of telling the truth and lying. For example, not everyone would consider withholding important information, whether intentionally or unintentionally, as the same as lying. The second option is based on a broader definition of honesty, one that includes not lying as well as being forthcoming about important information. You might consider this option when it is important for you to know more information about your athletes, or when some might be tempted to stretch the truth or intentionally withhold information. This option is also more educational in terms of its broader expectations about being truthful.

☐ *Coach A's rule*: The athlete should not lie to the coach, other team members, or medical and support staff.

☐ *Coach B's rule*: Athletes should be open and honest with the coach, teammates, and medical and support staff. Athletes should not lie or withhold information and should volunteer relevant information without being asked.

The moral value of honesty extends beyond telling the truth to also encompass loyalty. Just as you expect your athletes to be truthful and cooperative, you also expect them to be committed and loyal to your team.

Being a Loyal Team Member

Have you coached or encountered a talented athlete who sought only to further his or her own goals, sometimes at the expense of certain teammates or the entire team? The evidence is sometimes obvious (e.g., the ball hog who always wants to take the crucial shot) and other times subtle (e.g., the athlete who fails to give credit to his or her teammates for the team's success). It might even extend to an athlete whose attitudes and actions cause divisions within the team, whether unintentionally or through intentionally manipulative behavior.

Loyalty to the team is an essential part of team culture, team spirit, cooperation, and cohesion. Loyalty is also an important life skill that young people can and should learn through sport. Despite its importance, loyalty is often difficult to teach through rules and is probably best taught through consistent example.

Both options are relatively simple rules that expect athletes to be loyal to the team. Option 2 goes further in explicitly stating that athletes are to value the needs of the team above personal glory. This option might work best when you want to send a clear message about team loyalty. It might also be appropriate if your team or sport attracts a lot of attention from the media or local community. You might consider supplementing this rule by intentionally reinforcing positive behavior (unselfish play, giving credit where it is due) and steering athletes away from negative behavior (warning athletes not to play selfishly or to take credit for team achievement).

☐ *Coach A's rule*: The athlete should be loyal to the team.

☐ *Coach B's rule*: The athlete should be loyal to the team and put the needs of the team ahead of personal glory and goals.

This short section has discussed the fourth moral value of honesty, which includes being truthful, not lying or withholding information, and being a loyal team member. Although these might be among the more subtle aspects of participating in sport, they are nevertheless important life lessons for youth that should help your team achieve its goals. Let's now consider the fifth moral value, fairness, which is closely aligned with honesty and respect.

POLICIES ABOUT FAIRNESS

Everyone involved in sport has a right to be treated fairly. Your own personal or team philosophy likely includes a statement regarding the importance of good sportsmanship to the school, team, community, and the individual athlete's development.

Policies on fairness cover fair play, sportsmanship, and following due process when disciplining someone for infractions.

Fair play extends beyond simply following the rules of a game or sport; it encompasses an attitude and way of thinking, of playing within the spirit of sport. As we discussed previously, fair play is an important part of respect for the game. Fair play includes issues such as playing to the best of one's ability regardless of expected outcome, competing honestly, and avoiding gamesmanship, harassment, violence, substance abuse, and excessive commercialism.

Everyone involved in sport has a responsibility and role to play in ensuring fairness. As a coach, you probably spend a lot of time and effort teaching the concepts of fair play. If you work with different ages, you probably realize that teaching these concepts becomes more, not less, complex as athletes get older. Far more pressure is put on the older, skilled youths to excel than is placed on younger or less experienced groups.

☐ *Coach A's policy introduction*: The athlete should play according to the rules of the sport.

☐ *Coach B's policy introduction*: The athlete should represent the team and school with honor and display good sportsmanship in all team activities. The athlete is expected to follow the athlete's fair play code and general code of conduct, to respect the integrity of the sport, and to adhere to the concepts of sportsmanship and fair play in all team activities.

Immediately following this paragraph is an example of an athlete's "fair play" code. Some schools and clubs have a fair play code to clarify their philosophy and attitude about fair play and how athletes are expected to exhibit fairness. This code differs from the general athlete's code of conduct presented at the end of the chapter because it focuses specifically on the moral values of fairness and honesty. This fair play code is presented intentionally in positive terms (i.e.,

COACHING TIP

"It's important to be honest and fair with athletes, especially in situations that require judgment. Talk with your players about the decisions you make and the processes you take to make your decisions. Make every effort to obtain as much pertinent information when dealing with athletes. Never teach or use tactics that bend the rules to your advantage."

—Laura Sundheim, girls' volleyball and track and field coach, Hardin High School, Hardin, Montana

how athletes should act), rather than in negative terms (behavior to avoid) to be educational while also setting a standard of behavior and attitude.

Fair Play Code for Athletes

As a team member, I will strive to

- participate to enjoy the sport and to learn new skills,
- recognize that winning is not the only important aspect of sport,
- play by the rules and within the spirit of the game,
- respect myself, my teammates, and my opponents,
- be a true team player, placing team goals ahead of personal goals,
- acknowledge good performance of my teammates and opponents,
- accept decisions by officials without argument or expressing dissatisfaction,
- confine my competitiveness to practice and the field of play, and
- show dignity and respect for teammates and opponents in both victory and defeat.

We have covered a lot of ground on the first five moral values—respectfulness, responsibility, caring, honesty, and fairness. Respect covers the attitudes and behavior that athletes show toward themselves, other people, and the environment, and is the foundation of the other moral values. Athletes who truly respect themselves and others are more likely to feel and demonstrate a sense of responsibility, to care about their teammates and the sport itself, to be honest and loyal, and to act with fairness. Let's now move on to cover the final moral value, being a good citizen, which we defined earlier as being a good role model, being informed about lawful and ethical behavior, obeying laws and rules, cooperating and contributing to the community, and avoiding and discouraging substance abuse.

POLICIES ABOUT GOOD CITIZENSHIP

Athletes are expected to exert maximal effort and to compete all-out, but they are also expected to be good citizens. Occasionally, athletes will act as if they believe their sporting success entitles them to ignore or bend rules. Allowing such behavior can adversely affect team morale and does the athlete involved a disservice. You should expect your athletes to follow all school rules, both within and outside of sport, act lawfully, and cooperate with teammates and coaching and support staff. High-profile athletes are admired and

 COACHING TIP

"On our team, being a good citizen means polite manners and talk ('please' and 'thank you'), performing community service, helping without being asked, and dressing appropriately when traveling as a team. The athletes know that they represent the school. Here's one example: A blind athlete has a guide dog. At a regatta, the athletes, of their own initiative, went out and bought travel food and water bowls for this athlete's dog."

—Cassandra Cunningham, boys' rowing coach, Junipero Serra High School, San Mateo, California

emulated and are expected to be positive role models for young people in the community.

☐ *Coach A's policy introduction*: Athletes should be good citizens and act lawfully during the season.

☐ *Coach B's policy introduction*: Sport is an important part of the school and local community. Athletes representing the school are admired and emulated by many within and outside the school. Athletes have a responsibility to the school and local community to be good citizens and to act lawfully at all times.

Contributing to the Community

People who excel in sport often become role models and the focus of community attention, though the athlete may or may not seek or accept this attention willingly. You might consider whether you want to encourage your athletes to become actively involved in their community. Doing so can help them learn life skills such as public speaking, empathy, and how to interact with diverse people. Such attention can raise the profile of your sport, organization, or athletes in the local community and aid in recruiting new members. On the other hand, such a schedule might detract from the time the athlete has to focus on his or her sport or studies. Rules regarding contributing to the community might not suit every team or every sport. When deciding if you wish to create such a rule, consider

the age and maturity of your athletes, the demands on their time and attention, whether they might learn or benefit from participating in community activities, and the community's perception and expectation of your team.

Option 1 encourages but does not require athletes to become involved in their community. Young people often respond negatively to being forced to participate in activities for which they see no immediate or direct purpose (i.e., they might not see the connection between their participation in sport and contributing to the community). On the other hand, if you give your athletes the opportunity and a good reason for becoming involved, those who volunteer on their own will be more likely to have a sense of purpose in their community pursuits rather than acting only to fulfill an obligation.

☐ *Coach A's rule*: The athlete is encouraged to become active in a volunteer community activity.

☐ *Coach B's rule*: All athletes will participate in one or more volunteer community activity during the season.

Coach's Exercise

Identify local community events or other activities that your athletes could become involved with to fulfill the moral value of good citizenship. Suppose that your athletes are reluctant to volunteer. How would you select appropriate activities and convince them that they should become involved?

School Rules

Sport is all about playing by the rules, and most people accept the need and reasons for rules both within and outside of sport. However, some young people arrive at this acceptance later than others. For some talented athletes in high-profile sports, the attention and expectation they receive might give them reason to believe (consciously or otherwise) that they are somehow above the rules. This might be especially true for young athletes who feel their only role in life falls within the context of sport. Schools that bend the rules about eligibility for top athletes who are marginal students contribute to this problem. The media and local community can also play a part by focusing too much on performance and outcome and too little on the processes leading to achievement. If we expect athletes to play by the rules within sport, we should also expect them to follow the rules outside of sport.

Although the first option below seems to state the obvious—that athletes, like everyone else, must follow the school rules—it might be necessary to clearly state this expectation, at the very minimum. Option 2 expands on the expectation of following rules to place an obligation on the student athlete to know the rules (i.e., the athlete must be proactive and cannot claim ignorance). This option sets a higher standard of expectation and commitment on student athletes than does the first option.

☐ *Coach A's rule*: The student athlete should follow all school rules.

☐ *Coach B's rule*: The student athlete is expected to know and follow all school rules. A student found to have broken a school rule may be disciplined, suspended, or removed from the team.

Lawful Behavior

As we all know too well, the United States has among the world's highest rates of murder and violent crime; other unlawful behaviors, such as underage drinking and use of illicit substances among young people, are also much higher than average in the United States. Some of these statistics, such as murder of young people and the use of illicit substances, seem to be on the increase. Even if you set high standards of behavior for your athletes, odds are one or more of them will at some time be accused of unlawful behavior.

Option 1 allows the athlete who has been arrested to continue as a member of the team and is consistent with the concept of "innocent until proven guilty." Depending on the seriousness of the alleged crime, the involvement of the accused, and the presumption of innocence, you might wish to introduce some discretion in this option. It is possible that allowing an athlete to participate while defending a serious charge such as assault, rape, or another violent crime may cause dissention or morale problems among your athletes or in your community. This option also gives the coach the discretion to remove the athlete from the team if convicted—or, to allow him or her to continue as a team member after conviction, depending on the type and seriousness of the crime and the likelihood of the athlete's rehabilitation. Option 2 does not allow an athlete who has been arrested to continue to participate until the matter is resolved. To enforce this option, you might need to seek legal advice and clarify whether your rule applies to all infractions (i.e., misdemeanors as well as felonies) and if it can be applied to minors (whose court records may not be released) as well as to athletes who are considered adults.

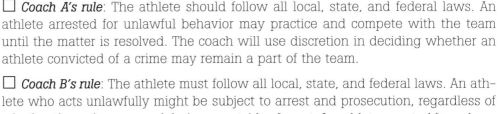

☐ *Coach A's rule*: The athlete should follow all local, state, and federal laws. An athlete arrested for unlawful behavior may practice and compete with the team until the matter is resolved. The coach will use discretion in deciding whether an athlete convicted of a crime may remain a part of the team.

☐ *Coach B's rule*: The athlete must follow all local, state, and federal laws. An athlete who acts unlawfully might be subject to arrest and prosecution, regardless of whether the action occurred during or outside of sport. An athlete arrested for unlawful behavior will not practice or compete with the team until the matter is resolved. An athlete found guilty of breaking the law will be removed from the team.

Tobacco

The health risks and addictiveness of tobacco use are well documented, and banning the use of tobacco products is consistent with a philosophy that values the athlete's health and well-being above all else. Most schools have a policy that expressly forbids use of any tobacco product by athletes. What varies among schools is the severity of penalties for breaking the rules and whether policies extend to activities outside of school. Option 1 is less restrictive and easier to enforce because it applies only to school events. Option 2 is harder to enforce but sends a clear message that tobacco use is unacceptable at any time.

☐ *Coach A's rule*: The athlete will not use any tobacco product at practice, games, or other team events.

☐ *Coach B's rule*: The athlete is forbidden to use, possess, distribute, or sell any tobacco product at any time.

If you choose to have a policy on tobacco use and possession, consider clarifying for your athletes the specific situations in which the rules apply. For example, "possess" in its strictest sense could include holding an unlit cigarette for a few seconds for a parent who is tying his shoes.

Drug and Alcohol Abuse

Drug abuse, including underage drinking, is a serious health risk to young people. Illicit drugs may include performance-enhancing substances, such as anabolic steroids or other hormones, and controlled substances such as marijuana, cocaine, and prescription drugs (e.g., amphetamines and barbiturates) not legally prescribed for the athlete.

Athletes choose to use illicit drugs or performance-enhancing substances for several reasons, including a real or perceived pressure to perform and win, real or perceived peer pressure, a belief that others are doing so and that it must be done for the athlete to remain competitive, and to escape emotional difficulties.

Most schools include a total ban on underage drinking, consumption of alcohol during school activities, and the use of illicit drugs. Similar to your policies on tobacco use, the main decisions about your drug policy relate to how far the policy should extend and the consequences for infractions.

Definitions

* A controlled substance is defined as any drug, obtained with or without a prescription, that can be used in a manner deemed dangerous to the user or that is illegal to possess or use without a prescription provided to the user by a medical practitioner.

* An illicit performance-enhancing substance is defined as any substance that enhances, or is purported to enhance, exercise capacity or sport performance that appears on the list of banned substances (the source of this list might vary by sport, school, club, or conference).

* Alcohol is defined as any beverage containing alcohol, including wine, beer, spirits, wine coolers, liquor, or nonalcoholic beverages to which alcohol has been added.

* Drug-related paraphernalia is defined as any equipment or materials to use or produce illicit drugs.

☐ *Coach A's rule*: Team members may not consume, use, be under the influence of, possess, distribute, or sell alcohol, any controlled substance, any illicit performance-enhancing substance, or drug-related paraphernalia at any school (or organization) event or activity.

☐ *Coach B's rule*: Team members may not consume, use, be under the influence of, possess, distribute, or sell alcohol, any controlled substance, any illicit performance-enhancing substance, or drug-related paraphernalia at any time during the competitive season.

Policies to help keep athletes drug free are discussed in the next chapter on coaching responsibilities. Establishing rules regarding the use (or misuse) of drugs, alcohol, tobacco, and other illicit substances of course does not guarantee 100 percent compliance. If your team has rules about the use and abuse of these substances, you should also consider how you will enforce the rules and how to penalize those who break them.

Enforcing Rules on Drug, Alcohol, and Tobacco Use

Young people are naturally inquisitive, and some might experiment with alcohol or drugs out of curiosity. Although you need to consistently enforce your drug, alcohol, and tobacco policies, you might also consider whether it could be counterproductive to punish an athlete heavily for a first-time offense. Involvement in school activities such as sport is one of the most powerful deterrents against drug use, and removing an athlete from the team may remove him or her from the very environment that will prevent further use.

Some school policies provide for a graded series of penalties, which combine suspension from some activities, counseling and drug education, and community service. In contrast, many schools or organizations have a zero-tolerance policy, which stipulates that any infraction, no matter how small or unintentional, carries an automatic heavy penalty. Although zero-tolerance rules have had some success in curbing abuse and making students feel safer, many have criticized these policies for being unnecessarily harsh, inflexible, and lacking common sense (and causing litigation). Such policies might not permit authorities to distinguish the generally good student who makes a single mistake from the habitually unruly student.

This discussion classifies infractions according to whether they are a first, second, or third offense; for each of these, we offer two options. These are presented only from the perspective of participation on the team (i.e., these rules might supplement or be independent of school rules on the consequences of substance abuse). The first offense is treated moderately, but consequences increase with subsequent infractions. In addition, for each set of rules, the first option is more general and the second more strict. If your school has a zero-tolerance policy, you might not have much choice in your team policies regarding the consequences of substance abuse. If you do have some choice, consider the best ways to balance the need to maintain discipline and ensure your athletes' health while recognizing that young people occasionally break rules out of curiosity or peer pressure.

First Offense

☐ *Coach A's rule*: An athlete found to have used or possessed alcohol or drugs or illicit substances for the first time will be given a warning and required to complete an alcohol or drug education program as approved by the school. The athlete may continue to practice and compete as a member of the team.

☐ *Coach B's rule*: An athlete found to have used or possessed alcohol or drugs or illicit substances for the first time will be suspended from the team for 20 school days. He or she will complete an alcohol or drug education program as approved by the school. The athlete may not practice or compete as a team member until the end of the 20 days and may then rejoin the team only if the coach and school are satisfied with his or her progress in the alcohol or drug education program.

Second Offense

☐ *Coach A's rule*: An athlete found to have used or possessed alcohol or drugs or illicit substances for a second time (even if for a different substance from the first) will be suspended from the team for 20 school days. The athlete will not be permitted to train with the team while suspended. The athlete may rejoin the team after the 20 days if the coach and school are satisfied that he or she will not make a third mistake.

☐ *Coach B's rule*: An athlete found to have used or possessed alcohol or drugs or illicit substances for a second time (even if for a different substance from the first) will be suspended from the team for the remainder of the season. The athlete will not be permitted to train with the team during the suspension. The athlete may rejoin the team for the next season if the coach and school are satisfied that he or she will not make a third mistake.

Third Offense

☐ *Coach A's rule*: An athlete found to have used or possessed alcohol or drugs or illicit substances for a third time (even if for a different substance from the first or second offense) shall be suspended from team participation for one year. The athlete will not be permitted to train with the team during the suspension. The athlete will not be permitted to rejoin the team until the one-year suspension is satisfied and the athlete has successfully completed a rehabilitation program.

☐ *Coach B's rule*: An athlete found to have used or possessed alcohol or drugs or illicit substances for a third time (even if for a different substance than the first or second offense) shall forfeit his or her right to participate in any school sport for the duration of his or her enrollment in school.

Depending on the school's policy, second and third offenses might also result in suspension or expulsion from school, further drug education and counseling, and police action.

Drug Testing

If we count alcohol as a drug, drug use is prevalent among young people, and schools, parents, and the community are understandably concerned about the possible impact on their children and the community. The United States Supreme

Court has ruled that a school may (i.e., has the right to) require athletes representing the school to participate in random, "suspicionless" drug testing. This does not mean that a school must or even should have a drug-testing program. "Suspicionless" means that testing is random and not aimed at individuals whose personal actions have raised suspicion of drug abuse (Bailey 1997). Some states expressly forbid random drug testing in schools.

Much controversy has arisen over the use of random, suspicionless drug testing in school sports. The American Academy of Pediatrics (1996) and others (Bailey 1997) have expressed concerns about the use of such drug testing as a requisite for sport participation in school sport. These concerns include

- the cost involved;
- the implied mistrust and adverse effects on morale inherent in such testing;
- the confidentiality of test results;
- practical concerns about sample collection and storage techniques to avoid contamination;
- the accuracy of the tests used;
- the potential misuse of information from tests (e.g., punishment rather than health referral).

It has been argued that participation in sport and other extracurricular activities is a strong deterrent against drug use and that there is a lower incidence of drug abuse among athletes compared to the general student population. Thus, drug testing might be unlikely to identify drug abusers. Some people have argued further that drug testing is not an effective deterrent to drug use in students. Moreover, a student excluded from sport and other extracurricular activities for drug use might not receive the necessary health care or counseling and might be left unsupervised after school. These are factors known to increase the risk of drug abuse and addiction.

If you decide to have a suspicionless drug-testing policy, it is recommended that you incorporate the following information:

- There is a sound reason behind your use of drug testing.
- Timing of tests should be random so athletes cannot predict when they will be tested.
- Timing of tests should be related to substances being tested (e.g., a midweek test will not detect weekend alcohol consumption).
- Selection of athletes for testing should be random so they cannot predict who will be tested.
- The most accurate tests available are used.
- A positive test is reassessed with a more sensitive test, if one exists.
- An athlete identified by testing is referred to a qualified health care professional for evaluation, counseling, and treatment.

- Informed consent is obtained from both the parent (or guardian) and athlete.
- Information is handled confidentially.

☐ *Coach A's rule*: Athletes may not be tested for drugs.

☐ *Coach B's rule*: An athlete may be tested for drugs at any time. The results of the drug test will be kept confidential and will be used only according to the team's rules on drug use and discipline for breaches of the rules.

Coach's Exercise

Research and identify the likely performance-enhancing substances your athletes might use. Identify the reasons that they would use each substance. Do your current rules cover all of these substances? If not, how could you modify your rules to include them all? How well do your policies and rules on substance abuse fit within the context of your other policies (e.g., about responsibility, caring, and good citizenship)? Prepare for a meeting with parents in which you clarify your team's rules about substance abuse and how they fit into the context of your other team policies and rules.

This completes our discussion of the six moral values as applied to athletes. In this chapter we have looked at several different views and options on rules to give life and practical applications to these values. You should now have a clear idea of the various types of policies and rules that many coaches and administrators employ. You should also understand how these rules fit with your personal philosophy and management style and with that of your team and school (or other organization). As comprehensive as your policies and rules might be, however, you should expect that things might not always run smoothly. When you are dealing with young people and their involvement in complex systems such as sport, it is inevitable that you will encounter different points of view as well as disagreement and conflict.

QUESTIONING A DECISION, CONFLICT RESOLUTION, AND APPEALS PROCEDURES

As a coach, you have probably had experiences when athletes questioned or even argued about your decisions. Think for a moment about your personal philosophy and management style. How do you feel about and handle a difference of opinion or a conflict with your athletes? The words "questioning" and "conflict" do not always need to have a negative connotation; if handled judiciously, these processes can help you and your athletes understand and appreciate different points of view, clarify issues, resolve problems, and prevent future problems. To better manage any conflicts that arise over your decisions, consider creating a rule about whether and to what extent athletes may question your decisions and what to do about issues that cannot be resolved easily.

The Athlete's Right to Question a Decision

The first option permits an athlete to question any decision and allows the athlete to expect the coach to be open to discussing his or her decisions. This option allows a process for dealing with questions or differences of opinion; the coach is the first stop, followed by an appeals process (which obviously requires your team, school, or organization to have an appeals process). This rule will work only if you have a relatively open management style and are willing to take the time to discuss all issues, including contentious ones, with your athletes. Some teenagers might appreciate this approach because it actively involves them in planning and decision making. You might also consider this option if you have a long-standing relationship with your athletes (e.g., if you have coached the same athletes through their school careers). Option 2 is much stricter and gives the coach the authority to make decisions without being questioned by athletes. You might choose this option for larger programs or those requiring you to make difficult or complex decisions. This option might also be best if you do not have the resources or time to discuss most decisions.

☐ *Coach A's rule*: An athlete may appeal decisions by the coach by discussing them with the coach; if problems are not resolved through discussion, athletes may appeal decisions through the team's appeals procedures.

☐ *Coach B's rule*: The coach's decisions on matters relating to team selection, strategy, training, discipline, and enforcement of rules are final, and no discussion is allowed.

Grievance and Appeals Procedures

Athletes have a right to be treated fairly in all aspects of their involvement in sport. The inclusion of fairness as one of the six moral values indicates the importance most people attach to it. Much is made about the concept of fairness, although we tend to think of fairness primarily in the context of the game itself—playing by the rules, respecting one's opponents, and not taking undue advantage. Thinking athletes, however, will quickly perceive the natural connection of the expectation that they should act fairly with the expectation that they should be treated fairly.

In chapter 2 we introduced the concept of due process. The glossary (page 195) also defines some terms relevant to due process. Due process is the legal process to ensure that an individual's rights are protected in any decision making or proceedings. The preceding section presented rule options regarding whether your athletes may question and appeal decisions. If you chose the first option, which allows athletes to appeal a decision after discussing the issue with the coach, you will need to have an appeals process to deal fairly with athletes who wish to appeal a decision. This appeals process must be objective and able to resolve disagreements and disputes fairly, quickly, and economically—and without the need to go outside the school (i.e., through legal action). For example, an athlete appealing his or her loss of eligibility who is forced to wait months for a decision effectively loses the decision in any case if he or she cannot practice or compete until the matter is resolved.

Rather than having a separate procedure for each team, many schools have a central appeals procedure to handle all disputes for all athletic teams. Limiting the coach's involvement in deciding the outcome of the appeal helps ensure objectivity and fairness for the athlete. Appeals procedures often restrict the types of issues that can be appealed. Allowing athletes to appeal each and every decision regarding such matters as game strategy or how to run a practice session could cause chaos for your team and program. Issues that athletes are permitted to appeal typically involve eligibility, harassment, discipline, or team selection.

Structuring Appeals Policies

This section presents a model of an appeals policy for athletes. This is a fairly minimal model of an appeals procedure, so we suggest you consult widely (with your school, athletes, parents, a legal representative, etc.) before adopting an appeals policy.

The purpose of this policy is to provide a process to hear and resolve disputes or disagreements objectively, fairly, quickly, and economically within the organization.

Whom Does This Policy Cover?

This policy applies to all athletes named to the team.

What Situations Does This Policy Cover?

This policy applies to athletes who appeal decisions regarding eligibility, discipline, harassment, or team selection. This policy does not apply to decisions about team strategy, the structure or elements of practice, the rules of the sport, or decisions not directly related to the athlete making the appeal or the team.

Appeals Process and Procedures

An athlete appealing a decision must submit a written appeal to the appeals committee (or person designated by the school or organization to handle appeals) no more than 21 days after he or she became aware of the decision. The written appeal must describe the decision being appealed and provide the grounds for the appeal as well as a summary of the evidence supporting the appeal.

Within five days of receiving the appeal, the president or chair of the appeals committee (or designate) will consider whether the athlete has a basis for the appeal.

Within two weeks of receiving the appeal, the chair or president will notify the athlete in writing whether the appeal will proceed or not proceed further. The president or chair must give reasons for disallowing an appeal to proceed further. The

(continued)

(continued)

president or chair's decision on whether the appeal will proceed is final and may not be appealed.

The appeals committee must consider the matter within 10 days of receiving the appeal and must arrange a hearing to take place within 15 days of receiving the appeal. An extension may be granted for good cause.

The committee that hears the appeal will be comprised of three or more individuals who have no significant relationship with the team, coach, or athlete involved or with his or her parents or any other party to the original decision.

The committee may organize an oral hearing or, if needed to resolve the appeal quickly, a telephone conference to hear the appeal. Any of the individuals involved may be accompanied by a representative or advisor, including a legal advisor.

The committee will consider evidence that was available to the person making the initial decision before or at the time of the decision. The committee may choose to consider other evidence that became apparent after the original decision.

Decision

The decision will be made by majority vote of committee members. The committee may decide in one of three ways:

1. To reject the appeal and uphold the original decision
2. To uphold the appeal and require the original decision maker to make a new decision
3. To uphold the appeal and alter the decision if the decision cannot be corrected by the original decision maker

Unless a procedure is in place for alternative dispute resolution or arbitration or mediation to resolve such disputes, the decision of the appeals committee is final.

SUMMARY

This chapter has covered a lot of ground regarding many of the important issues to consider when selecting your policies and rules to guide athlete attitudes, behavior, and effort. The options from which you can select your policies and rules were presented within the framework of the six moral values (respectfulness, responsibility, caring, honesty, fairness, and good citizenship). The six moral values are interrelated and ultimately based on self-respect and respect for others, which translates into responsible, caring, honest, fair, and lawful behavior.

In selecting and developing your team policies and rules, you first need to define and clarify your personal and team philosophies (see chapter 2) so that your policies and rules are consistent and fit logically with your philosophies. Your job will be much easier if your athletes can see how your team policies and rules extend naturally from your philosophies. This chapter has shown how you can provide both negative and positive modeling to frame your policies and rules in terms of the expected standard, including clear examples of acceptable and unacceptable attitudes and behaviors. Because they have educational value in teaching young people important values for sport and life in general, your policies can serve as more than a mere collection of rules. However, young people are neither angels nor automatons; despite your best intentions and efforts, some will not meet the expectations as detailed in your rules. One hopes that the policies and rules you select will enable you to deal effectively and fairly with lapses on the part of your athletes; this will allow the situation to become a life-learning experience for the athlete involved and for your team.

Of the options presented for each rule, none is intended as a "one size fits all" solution to problems. You are encouraged to adapt the rules to suit your philosophy, coaching style, school, team, and athletes. Expect to require some time to find the right mix for your situation. Please recognize that selecting and developing policies and rules is an ongoing process that is best served by consulting widely with all participants and keeping an open mind about what works and what does not work. Your ultimate goal is getting your athletes to achieve their potential, inside and outside of sport. Setting high but achievable standards for them is one of the best ways to help them succeed in this goal.

Sample Codes of Conduct for Athletes

Coach A's Choices

Participation as a team member is an honor and privilege. As a team member, I understand that I am expected to act with honor and dignity at all times and to recognize that my behavior both inside and outside of sport reflects on the team and the school.

As a member of the team, I promise to behave in ways consistent with the following values:

Respectfulness

- Speak respectfully at all times.
- Act respectfully toward opposing players and coaches in both victory and defeat.
- Not argue with an official's decision.
- Take proper care of my equipment and uniform.

Responsibility

- Exercise self-control during practice and games and not fight or display excessive aggression.
- Ensure that I meet the minimum eligibility standards to participate in sport.
- Attend all practices, or if I cannot attend a practice, inform the coach as soon as I know that I cannot attend.
- Give a full effort at all practices and games; if I do not feel physically capable of a full effort, inform the coach.

(continued)

(continued)

- Wear the team uniform for all games and dress neatly for all team events outside of practice and games.
- Get enough rest to perform to my ability both academically and athletically.
- Understand and follow all team rules.

Caring

- Cooperate with my teammates in practice and games.
- Contribute to team effort.
- Lead a healthy lifestyle.
- Tell the coach or team doctor (or physical therapist or trainer) about any injury or illness that might affect my ability to practice or compete.

Honesty

- Be truthful with the coach, other team members, and medical and support staff.
- Be loyal to the team.

Fairness

- Play according to the rules of the sport.

Good citizenship

- Follow all local, state, and federal laws.
- Not use any tobacco product at practice, games, or other team events.
- Not consume, use, be under the influence of, possess, distribute or sell alcohol, any controlled substance, any illicit performance-enhancing substance, or drug-related paraphernalia at any school event or activity.

Appealing decisions

- I may appeal decisions by the coach by first discussing these with the coach; if the problem is not resolved through discussion, I may appeal a decision through the team's appeals procedures.

Coach B's Choices

Participation as a team member is an honor and privilege. As a team member, I understand that I am expected to act with honor and dignity at all times. I recognize that my behavior both inside and outside of sport reflects on the team and the school.

Our team's success depends on discipline, cooperation, and each member giving a full effort. Our team is committed to providing a supportive environment in which all participants are treated, and treat others, with respect. As a team member, I promise to behave in ways consistent with the following values:

Respectfulness

- Show respect for opposing players and coaches before, during, and after the game by shaking hands and observing other pre- or postgame rituals.

- Show respect to teammates, opponents, officials, and spectators in all situations, regardless of the outcome of a game or match. I will not show excessive emotion in either victory or defeat.
- Use positive words and phrases whenever possible. I will not use offensive, profane, vulgar, or lewd language, cheers, comments, or gestures.
- Avoid participating in booing, heckling, taunting or name calling of anyone involved in sport, including teammates, coaches, opponents, officials, and spectators.
- Accept all officials' decisions without arguing and without displaying excessive emotion or sarcastic or offensive language or body language.
- Take care of my equipment and uniform and return them in good condition at the end of the season. I will be responsible for paying for any uniform or equipment that is lost or damaged beyond normal expected wear and tear.
- Respect the personal property of others (e.g., teammates, coaches, opponents), the sports facilities used in practice and games (whether home or away), and other public and private property not directly associated with sport (e.g., the school or local community).
- Keep locker rooms neat and clean.

Responsibility

- Exercise self-control during practice and games and in other sport-related activities.
- Avoid showing excessive emotion, anger, frustration, or physical or verbal aggression. I will not start a fight or become involved in a fight in any situation.
- Help my teammates avoid fights or other displays of aggression.
- Be responsible for understanding and making every effort to meet the eligibility criteria. If placed on academic probation for poor grades, I will fulfill the terms of that probation before I resume participation.
- Attend all scheduled practices; if I must miss a practice, let the coach know as soon as possible and give the reason for my absence. If I miss more than one practice in a given week, I accept that I will be ineligible to play in that week's game or match.
- Concentrate fully and exert myself to the expected level at all practices and during games and matches. If I do not feel capable of giving a full effort, I will inform the coach.
- Wear the prescribed uniform or attire for all games and team activities, including award ceremonies, publicity events, and travel to and from competition.
- Travel with the team to and from games or matches and other team activities.
- During the sport season, I will observe the following curfews:
    –Weeknights and nights before a game or match: 10:30 p.m.
    –Weekends, if no game or match the next day: 1:00 a.m.
- Follow all school and team rules and be responsible for and accept the consequences of my actions.

(continued)

(continued)

Caring

- Cooperate with my teammates and actively support and show concern for teammates in all team activities.
- Be a committed member of the team and put the needs of the team ahead of my own personal glory.
- Praise my teammates' efforts by applauding or through other positive gestures such as high fives. I will use positive words and will not criticize a teammate or use negative words to talk with or about a teammate.
- Lead a healthy lifestyle that includes getting enough sleep, eating a healthy diet, and avoiding unhealthy behaviors such as smoking, drinking alcohol, and using drugs or banned substances.
- Report any injury or illness I experience, no matter how slight, to the coach or team doctor (or physical therapist or trainer) within 48 hours.

Honesty

- Be open and honest with the coach, my teammates, and medical and support staff. I will not lie or withhold information and will volunteer relevant information without being asked.
- Be loyal to the team and put the needs of the team ahead of my own glory and goals.

Fairness

- Represent the team and school with honor and display good sportsmanship in all team activities.
- Play according to the rules of the sport and respect the integrity of the sport.

Good citizenship

- Participate in one or more volunteer community activity during the season.
- Follow all local, state, and federal laws. If I am arrested for unlawful behavior, I understand that I will not be permitted to practice or compete with the team until the matter is resolved. If I am found guilty of breaking the law, I will be removed from the team.
- Not use, possess, distribute, or sell any tobacco product at any time.
- Not consume, use, be under the influence of, possess, distribute, or sell alcohol, any controlled substance, any illicit performance-enhancing substance, or drug-related paraphernalia at any time during the competitive season.

Appealing Decisions

- I will accept that decisions on matters relating to team selection, strategy, training, discipline, and enforcement of rules are final.

Now that you've read the codes of conduct written by coach A and coach B, it's time to write your own! Visit www.humankinetics.com/CoachesGuideToTeam Policies/ to create a code of conduct. You will also find other helpful documents to use for your team.

Selecting Team Policies and Rules for Coaching

𝒜s head track and field coach, you are concerned that your club's top shot putter, Claire, normally a confident athlete, has been overly nervous about an upcoming competition. She has pushed herself harder than ever at practice. At the event, she finishes third and is distraught by her performance. You later find out that one of the assistant coaches had been telling Claire that her big chance to represent the school at state finals rested on the outcome of that one competition. She is now devastated for "letting everyone down." How would you deal with this situation? Do your team policies for coaches explain your philosophy about athlete encouragement?

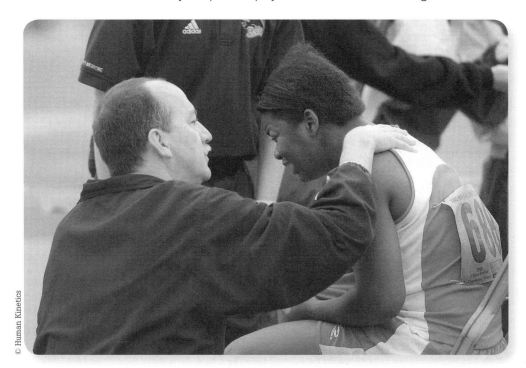

You know that coaching is sometimes much more than training athletes and planning team strategy. As a coach, you represent the team and sometimes the community; you need to act with tact and diplomacy in difficult and complex situations, despite your personal feelings. You are expected to be a role model, to help young athletes mature, and to teach them life skills and about the integrity of the game. These examples show that a coach's actions outside of competition might be as important as how he or she acts during a game or match.

Think about coaches you admire and respect. They might have been your mentors when you started coaching, or they might be your fiercest competitors. What qualities do these coaches have that have earned your respect and admiration? Is it an indomitable spirit of never giving up? integrity? the ability to act honorably, win or lose? How about the way they treat their athletes and supporters or how they talk to the media? Is it their ability to teach young people life skills and inspire them to perform their best?

Consider what initially attracted you to coaching and why you continue to coach. Do you thrive on seeing your athletes mature into responsible individuals? Do you love witnessing their excitement at performing at a level they never thought possible? Is your competitive nature a driving force? What is it about you and your coaching style that has earned your players' respect and confidence?

Respect, integrity, positive role model, confidence, tenacity, inspiring—these are terms we associate with the best coaches. Parents, schools, communities, and the government encourage and support sporting opportunities for young people because of the many benefits associated with sport participation. Fair play, teamwork, sportsmanship, and character are important life skills that parents and communities hope their children learn through involvement in sport. Implicit is the expectation that the coach is a positive role model who helps young people acquire important life skills.

Of course, it's impossible to write policies and rules that govern every action or that guarantee impeccable behavior in all instances. However, we can create a set of guidelines outlining the community's expectations of the coach's attitudes and behavior. Having team policies about how you (and your school or organization) expect coaches to act, both inside and outside of sport, is a good start to ensuring that coaches act in the best interests of their athletes, organization, profession, and community.

In chapter 2 we discussed six moral values, and in chapter 3 we used these values as a framework for developing team policies and rules about athletes. In this chapter we will continue to apply this framework as we present choices for team policies and rules about coaches.

In this chapter, you will learn about sports policies relating to the following moral values:

- Respectfulness: interacting respectfully with athletes, other coaches, parents, officials, property, and the environment
- Responsibility: being responsible to yourself and your team, maintaining self-discipline, and enforcing team rules
- Caring: being cooperative, compassionate, generous, and forgiving; creating a safe environment; caring about athletes' health and well-being
- Honesty: being truthful, trustworthy, and reliable; acting with integrity; doing the right thing; demonstrating loyalty to the team and encouraging team spirit and unselfish play; playing within the spirit of the rules
- Fairness: competing fairly and within the spirit of the rules, demonstrating good sportsmanship, being tolerant and open with your athletes, acting fairly when selecting the team and making awards
- Good citizenship: being a good role model, acting lawfully and encouraging athletes to act lawfully, avoiding and discouraging substance abuse, contributing to the community

Coach's Exercise

Think about your own personal philosophy about coaching and sport. Are there any aspects of the six moral values that seem inconsistent with your personal philosophy? How would you reconcile this inconsistency?

POLICIES ABOUT RESPECT

Think about people you respect. How do you convey your respect for these people? Is it in your choice of words, tone of voice, body language, and actions?

What way do your athletes and their parents act toward you that makes you feel respected? Can you recall an instance when you felt you were not treated with respect? Perhaps you have seen a coach acting disrespectfully toward an athlete or official or witnessed parents act disrespectfully toward a coach or official. Consider the effect that disrespectful behavior had. Did it help resolve the problem or make things worse?

Policies on respect involve coaches' interaction with athletes, parents, officials, opponents, support staff, and others involved in sport. Class, a component of respect, is acting with dignity in both victory and defeat, despite disappointment or disagreement. Class is probably one of the most difficult qualities to teach, but its importance cannot be overemphasized. Young people learn to act with class by example, through observing others and receiving positive feedback.

As discussed in chapter 3, respect works on different levels. For the coach, different levels of respect include

* self-respect;
* respect for those whom the coach is responsible for (athletes, assistant coaches, support staff);
* respect for opponents (athletes and coaches);
* respect for others involved in sport (parents, officials);
* respect for the game and its rules and traditions.

☐ *Coach A's policy introduction*: The coach should show self-respect and respect for others and for the game.

☐ *Coach B's policy introduction*: Our team believes that respect is an integral part of sport. The coach should demonstrate self-respect and should act respectfully at all times toward everyone involved in sport, including athletes, other coaches, parents, support staff, officials, opponents, spectators, volunteers, the media, and members of the public. All coaches have the right to expect others to treat them with respect.

When selecting your team rules about respect, you might consider whether it is helpful to clearly define respectful behavior by the coach and to give specific examples of respectful and disrespectful behavior. If your coaching staff is large or inexperienced, this might help to clearly communicate your expectations about coaching behavior to your coaches, athletes, parents, and the community. On the other hand, experienced coaches might view such lists as unnecessarily prescriptive.

Here are some examples of respectful behavior by a coach:

* Using positive words even when discussing an opponent or an unfavorable situation or event
* Avoiding unnecessary or hostile confrontations
* Shaking the opposing coach's hand sincerely before and after the game, regardless of outcome
* Standing and participating sincerely in pregame rituals

- Refraining from disagreeing with or reacting emotionally to an official's decision
- Taking the time to meet and talk respectfully with parents
- Answering questions from the media with sincerity

Here are some examples of disrespectful actions by a coach:

- Vulgar or offensive talk about opponents (see section on language below)
- Offensive or obscene gestures aimed at opponents or spectators
- Excessive aggression or violence in any form directed at athletes, other coaches, opponents, officials, spectators, or others involved in sport
- Obvious displays of emotion, anger or sarcasm (verbal or nonverbal) directed at officials, opponents, athletes, other coaches, or spectators
- Blaming individual team members or others outside the team (e.g., officials) for the team's poor performance
- Refusing to participate, or doing so reluctantly, in established rituals, such as shaking an opposing coach's hand after the game or standing respectfully during player introductions or during the national anthem
- Intentionally damaging property
- Treating the media with disdain or sarcasm or not answering their questions sincerely

Respect for Athletes and the Team

Respect is an essential component of sport. You know that as a coach you automatically receive a certain level of respect. With young people, respect goes two ways—they respect someone whom they feel respects them, and they quickly lose respect for someone who does not act accordingly.

Here are two rule options regarding how coaches show respect to athletes. The first rule option simply asks coaches to avoid harsh treatment of their athletes. The word "harsh" is open to interpretation. For example, some might consider publicly criticizing an athlete as harsh, whereas others might consider this part of the "toughening up" process for athletes. Option 2 requires coaches to act positively and to avoid punishment or negative words. This option probably requires more effort and creativity from coaches but in the long run might result in a more cooperative team effort. This option might be appropriate if you wish to instill a culture of cooperation and selflessness within your team or club.

☐ *Coach A's rule*: The coach should treat athletes with respect and avoid treating athletes harshly.

☐ *Coach B's rule*: The coach should treat athletes respectfully, praise the athletes' efforts, and actively encourage athletes to work cooperatively through positive words and examples.

Young people are still learning about themselves, their abilities and limitations, and their relationships with others. Young people learn through trial and error, and our responses to their mistakes can have a major impact on their attitudes. Let's now turn to the issue of respect when criticizing athletes.

Young people can be especially sensitive to criticism or ridicule, especially in front of their peers, even when in the context of humor. As a coach, you might have witnessed how devastating it can be for a young athlete to be publicly berated or ridiculed. We're not suggesting that athletes should never be criticized, because constructive criticism is important to their learning new skills and meeting challenges. Instead, We're suggesting that young people respond best to criticism expressed in positive rather than negative terms and when expressed with humor and warmth, with no trace of anger or sarcasm.

Option 1 asks the coach not to publicly yell at or insult an athlete. Have you ever observed a team of youngsters motivated by fear rather than inspiration? They often play a restricted, unimaginative, and defensive game that rarely leads to a successful or enjoyable season. Option 2 expects the coach to be more sensitive to the athlete's reactions and to use positive rather than negative language. This option clarifies the types of language that are unacceptable. This option might require more effort and creativity by the coach but is probably better for developing individual athletes.

☐ *Coach A's rule*: The coach should not yell at or insult an athlete.

☐ *Coach B's rule*: The coach should use constructive criticism and positive language and avoid excessively harsh criticism when coaching or disciplining an athlete.

Coach's Exercise

In a recent practice after an embarrassing loss, one of your assistant coaches became frustrated and loudly berated four athletes. Athletes on other teams and several parents heard his comments, and now the entire community knows about the incident. The event has caused a loss of morale on the team because the four players involved feel they were unjustly singled out for the team's poor performance. Does your current code of conduct for coaches address this issue? If yes, how would you use the code to (a) rebuild team morale, (b) restore confidence and trust of the four athletes in the assistant coach, and (c) help your assistant coach find other ways to deal with frustration? If your current code does not address this issue, how can you revise your code so that it does?

Athletes are not the only people whose performance you might feel warrants criticism.

Respect for Officials

In *Coaching for Character*, Clifford and Feezell make a compelling argument about respect for officials: "In organized sport, officials are 'part of the game.' They are part of the tacit agreement that makes the game possible" (page 52). If we accept that one of sport's important functions is to teach young people to play by the rules, then we should also accept that respecting the game extends to respecting the officials and their decisions. Consider creating rules regarding how coaches act toward officials and deal with athletes' actions toward officials. When deciding on these rules, consider the degree of consistency you wish to achieve between your rules for athletes (discussed in chapter 3), coaches (discussed here), and parents (discussed in chapter 5).

Accepting Officials' Decisions

You know that you do not always agree with the decisions of officials. Sometimes the official is right, but sometimes—because officials are human, too—an official makes a poor decision. Some coaches have almost a trademark reaction when they disagree with an official's decision. However, you know that protesting at the time will probably not have much effect on the decision itself and might work against the team, say, if the coach is ejected. Consider how you react when an official makes the "wrong" decision and the example your reaction sets for your young athletes.

Option 1 lets the coach show some emotion within reason. Reacting "emotionally" and "not disrupting the game" are open to interpretation. There are times when a coach's reactions inspire a team to perform better. Option 2 restricts the coach to accepting all officials' decisions. Strict interpretation of this rule requires the coach to avoid any indication that he or she disagrees with a decision. Your choice might depend on the level of your athletes, how much an official's decision might influence the outcome, how closely you expect athletes and coaches to control their emotions, and whether your sport or conference permits dissent.

☐ *Coach A's rule*: The coach may question or react emotionally to an official's decision provided this reaction does not disrupt the game or show disrespect to the official or opposing team.

☐ *Coach B's rule*: The coach should cooperate with an official's decision and should not argue with, question, or indicate disagreement with any official's decision.

Commenting on Officials' Decisions

Officials don't always make the right call, and occasionally poor officiating at the wrong time can affect the outcome of a game. Opinions about a decision can also vary depending on your particular bias (i.e., which team you are supporting) and how much detail of the play you saw or missed. After a

COACHING TIP

"I find that the best way to approach an official is at a break in the competition, as calmly as possible and without anger. After the competition, I think it's important to let the official know you appreciate that he or she listened to your concern. This shows respect and the will to communicate like adults about differences of opinions. I think officials are more likely to respond to this type of approach."

—Tim DeBerry, cross country and track and field coach, Von Steuben High School, Chicago, Illinois

contest, your athletes, their parents, or the media might ask you to comment on the quality of officiating or whether you think a certain call influenced the game. This situation might require you to find a balance between saying what you really believe and maintaining respect for the officials' authority.

Option 1 allows the coach to express an opinion as long as he or she is respectful. You would probably want to consider the message this leeway sends to your athletes. This option would probably suit sports with professional and experienced coaches. If you choose this option, you might consider giving examples of what is and what is not appropriate language or topics. For example, coaches might be permitted to comment on the game's overall officiating but not on specific calls or officials. Option 2 does not permit the coach to comment on the officials. Professional coaches might find this option unnecessarily restrictive.

☐ *Coach A's rule*: The coach may comment publicly on the quality or effectiveness of the officials provided he or she does so with respect.

☐ *Coach B's rule*: The coach should not comment publicly on the quality or effectiveness of the officials.

Allowing Athletes to Comment on Officiating

Athletes invest a lot of energy and emotion in their sport. It is easy to see how an athlete might comment on the officiating during a game, when emotions are high, or after a game, when he or she might not have fully thought through the consequences. Depending on the type of rule you choose about athletes' acceptance of officials' decisions, you might also consider a rule about the coach's role in encouraging or discouraging athletes from commenting on officiating.

Option 1 asks the coach to avoid encouraging athletes to be critical of officials; this rule stops short of expecting the coach to discourage criticism or to reprimand athletes who criticize officials. Option 2 expects the coach to be proactive in discouraging and punishing athletes' criticism of officials. In making your choice, consider how strict your athletes' code is on this point and how much control you have over your athletes' actions.

☐ *Coach A's rule*: The coach should discourage athletes from criticizing officials.

☐ *Coach B's rule*: The coach should actively discourage athletes from criticizing or talking negatively about officials. The coach should discipline athletes who publicly criticize officials.

After discussing rules about respect for athlete and officials, let's continue our discussion of respect and apply it to respect for opponents, an ideal that is not always easy to convey.

Respect for Opponents

Respect for opponents can be considered an extension of respect for oneself and for the game. If we expect our athletes to display self-respect and respect for the game, we also expect them to show respect for their opponents. Defeating a respected opponent increases your feelings of achievement; it's a hollow victory to defeat an opponent you don't respect. Respect for one's opponents is reflected in pre- and postgame rituals, such as shaking hands, and in other interaction that occurs before, during, and after a game or match, such as at press conferences or interviews.

© Human Kinetics

Interacting With Opposing Coaches

Option 1 is the bare minimum expected of a coach—to simply go through the motions of shaking hands with the opponent. With bitter rivalries, you might find that this is the most you can expect. Option 2 is more in tune with the ideals of sportsmanship and respect for the game; this option calls for a higher level of respectful behavior and might require coaches to hide their true feelings about each other.

☐ *Coach A's rule*: The coach should shake the opposing team coach's hand before and after the game.

☐ *Coach B's rule*: The coach should show respect for opponents by speaking cordially with and shaking the hand of the opposing coach before and after the game. The coach should speak positively of the opposing team's play, regardless of outcome, and should not make negative comments to or about the opposing team.

Interacting With Opposing Teams

You might strive to treat your athletes and opponents with respect, but there is no guarantee that your opponents will reciprocate. You can probably think of times that your opponents provoked you, whether intentionally or unintentionally. Have you encountered opposing coaches or athletes whom you just couldn't stand losing to? Did you have to consciously stop yourself from reacting emotionally to their arrogance?

The first option is fairly minimal and assumes some agreement about what is disrespectful talk and action. You might choose this option when it's unlikely that your coaches would be provoked by the opposition. Option 2 clearly defines unacceptable talk and behavior. You might consider this rule in the context of the detail included in your rules on respectful behavior by athletes, as discussed in chapter 3. Some professional coaches might find this too prescriptive.

☐ *Coach A's rule*: The coach should talk respectfully to or about opposing teams.

☐ *Coach B's rule*: The coach should avoid taunting, trash talking, boasting, booing, vulgar language, jeers, or gestures aimed at the opposing team or coach. The coach should actively discourage athletes from exhibiting these behaviors and discipline any athlete who does so.

Respect can take many different forms, verbal and nonverbal. Language and body language can be subtle or overt means to express respect or disrespect, intentionally or unintentionally. Let's continue to discuss rules about respect by focusing on offensive language and gestures.

Coach's Exercise

Your next game is against your arch rival, who has beaten your team in the conference championship in each of the past three years. Their players and fans have a reputation for taunting and trying to incite the opposing team, which often works by distracting the players and coaches. The media is aware of the rivalry and has given your upcoming game a lot of publicity, mainly negative. Prepare your team strategy to help your athletes deal with this situation.

Offensive Language and Gestures

Young people model their behavior, both positively and negatively, on the actions of adults who are important to them. The concept of respect includes both language and gestures. Modern sport is replete with examples of coaches, athletes, parents, and fans using language and gestures in different ways to show respect or disrespect for their team and their opponents.

Offensive or abusive language is a sign of disrespect. Think about the last time you heard a coach use offensive language in the context of sport. What was the reaction of the person or people hearing this? Have you ever observed the effect on a young athlete or even an entire team when an adult uses offensive language to berate them, perhaps for making a simple mistake or not performing up to expectations?

Chapter 3 defined disrespectful language in the context of the athlete; many organizations expect these definitions also to apply to coaches. To reiterate, disrespectful language is profanity, vulgar words, chants or gestures, booing, heckling, and taunting; these sometimes go under the broad category of "trash talk." If we want our athletes to always speak respectfully, it makes sense that coaches should lead by example.

You might consider whether your team needs specific rules on language, or if your more general rules on respect and responsibility are enough to discourage disrespectful language. Here are some suggestions for specific rules on language.

Option 1 is minimal and asks only that coaches avoid profanity around athletes. Option 2 applies more generally to all sport situations and sets a higher standard of behavior for the coach. In choosing your rule, you might consider it in the context of your rules about offensive language and gestures for athletes, parents, spectators, and others, as discussed in chapters 3 and 5. For example, it might be inconsistent to have a strict rule preventing athletes and spectators from using offensive language in any situation yet permit coaches more latitude.

☐ *Coach A's rule*: The coach should avoid using profanity or abusive language or gestures around athletes.

☐ *Coach B's rule*: The coach should use positive words, even when being critical, and should avoid using vulgar or offensive language or gestures and aggressive or taunting actions or language when involved in any sport activity.

Respect for Parents

You recognize that parents can be an asset—they volunteer for many unrewarded tasks and can greatly influence their children's attitudes toward sport. You might even coach in a sport in which strong parental support is necessary to run a successful team. Most parents are helpful and unobtrusive, but you have no doubt encountered a parent who didn't recognize the line between being supportive and meddling. These parents try your patience. However, if we expect our athletes to show respect for everyone involved in sport, it is reasonable to expect the coach to treat parents with respect.

The first option requires the coach simply to speak respectfully to parents. This option does not oblige the coach to be accessible to parents. Option 2 sets a higher standard of expectation that the coach will, first, meet with parents and, second, answer their questions honestly and respectfully. Your choice might depend on the age and level of your athletes, your philosophy and management style, your relationship with the athletes' families, and how much time and effort you wish to devote to meeting with parents.

☐ *Coach A's rule*: The coach should speak respectfully to parents.

☐ *Coach B's rule*: The coach should take the time to meet with parents as needed. The coach should willingly and respectfully answer questions from the parent(s) (within the rules about parental access to the coach; see chapter 5). The coach should speak honestly and positively about an athlete to his or her parent(s).

Respect for Property

Sport is expensive, and schools and athletes usually invest heavily in facilities, equipment, and uniforms. Properly functioning equipment is essential to a safe and effective sport program. The school expects that the coach will respect the facilities, equipment, and uniforms and teach athletes to do the same.

☐ *Coach A's rule*: The coach should demonstrate care in using the facilities, equipment, and uniforms.

☐ *Coach B's rule*: The coach should ensure that facilities, equipment, and uniforms are treated with respect and care by athletes and others involved in sport. The coach should ensure that equipment is in working order, that broken equipment is fixed or replaced, and that athletes have suitable uniforms.

The focus so far has been on respect for other people and their property. In sport, the concept of respect also extends to respect for the sport itself and its traditions.

Respect for the Game: Winning and Losing Graciously

Think about the emotions you feel at the end of a close game. These might include resigned acceptance or extreme disappointment if you lost, or, if you won, relief, satisfaction, or elation.

Regardless of outcome, everyone closely connected with sport feels some type of emotion at the end of a game or match. Think about how you and your athletes react after a close game. Are you demonstrative or restrained? Does your reaction influence your athletes' reaction? Your school and community probably have some expectations regarding how you and your athletes will react in both victory and defeat. While you're not expected to be an emotionless automaton, you might be expected to display some level of restraint and to act as a role model for your athletes and fans.

Option 1 allows the coach to react emotionally yet modestly. Option 2 clearly expects the coach to control his or her emotions, regardless of outcome. This option might work when there is a history of emotional overreaction that has sparked controversy or emotional outbursts from the team or fans. Sport is all about control. Think of the amount of discipline required to excel.

☐ *Coach A's rule*: The coach may react emotionally at the end of a contest. He or she should accept victory with modesty and defeat with dignity.

☐ *Coach B's rule*: The coach should contain his or her emotions both in victory and defeat.

Chapter 2 defined harassment, and chapter 3 presented policies on preventing athletes from exhibiting harassing behavior. Briefly, harassment is any behavior that is cruel, intimidating, harmful, humiliating, or offensive to an individual or a group. An element of subjectivity and perception enters into any discussion or assessment of harassment. Let's look at some rules to guide coaches in developing professional relationships with their athletes and avoiding behavior that could be construed as harassment.

Harassment and Professional Relationships

You may or may not choose to have a specific policy for coaches on harassment. Your school might already have a policy that covers all employees, including coaches. If you decide to create a policy on harassment for coaches, you might consider whether you need to clearly state the definition and give examples of harassment. Consider also the best ways to communicate the policy to your coaches. Definitions and examples of harassment were provided in chapter 3.

Sexual harassment is a particular type of harassment involving unwelcome remarks, advances, or actions of a sexual nature. The example at the start of this chapter, the rumor about the underperforming tennis star who was troubled by a coach's sexual advances, if true, is an example of sexual harassment. Sexual harassment is both a legal and ethical issue. Sexual harassment or contact between a coach and athlete can be especially difficult for three reasons: because of the inherent difference in power between the coach and athlete, because sexual contact between a coach and athlete at an education institution or between an adult and a minor might be subject to criminal law, and because a personal relationship can interfere with the objectivity needed by the coach to treat all athletes fairly.

The coach's duty of care extends beyond his or her direct relationships with athletes. The coach is also responsible for ensuring that sexual harassment does not happen between others involved with the team, for example between or among assistant coaches, support staff, and athletes. Ignoring or not being aware of signs of sexual harassment is not a valid excuse, and coaches are expected to be proactive in creating an environment that prevents sexual harassment from occurring, or if it does occur, taking a leadership role in reporting and addressing the issue.

As a coach, some of the things you can do to prevent sexual harassment include the following:

- Ensure that your behavior is appropriate at all times.
- Be clear in your mind about the definition of sexual harassment and communicate this information clearly to everyone involved with your team through your policies, rules, and everyday actions.
- Be aware of interactions among your staff (coaching and support) and athletes.
- Let athletes and staff know that you are receptive to them expressing their concerns about or reporting any instances of sexual harassment.
- Guard against false accusations by avoiding situations or relationships that could be misinterpreted and by having others present when you or other staff members are interacting closely with athletes.

You might consider whether your team would benefit from a specific rule on sexual harassment and contact between a coach and athlete. Such a rule might not be needed if you believe that sexual harassment is already covered by other rules.

Rule option 1 is fairly general and assumes that everyone knows and accepts the definition of "professional relationship." This option might suit schools with clear policies on harassment and professional relationships. Option 2 is more explicit in defining the expectations about acceptable and unacceptable behavior. This option requires the coach to be proactive in discouraging others from acting inappropriately and in reporting unacceptable behavior. You might choose this option if your school does not already have clear policies on harassment and professional relationships.

☐ *Coach A's rule*: The coach should maintain a professional relationship with all athletes.

☐ *Coach B's rule*: The coach should maintain a professional relationship with all athletes. The coach should not engage in conduct, gestures, actions, or comments of a sexual nature with any athlete. The coach should actively discourage athletes from behavior that could be construed as sexual harassment. The coach should report any incident of alleged sexual harassment to the appropriate authorities.

Maintaining a professional relationship between the coach and athletes is probably easier within the context of practice, meetings, and games. The ability to maintain a professional relationship can be tested, however, in social settings outside of strictly defined team contexts.

Socializing With Athletes

Although coaches can become very close to their athletes, defined boundaries must be maintained between coach and athlete. This is important if the coach is to remain objective and treat all athletes equally. Such boundaries are also important to ensure that athletes recognize and understand the coach's role as authority figure and teacher and to maintain the athletes' respect. If parents and the community are to trust a coach to supervise and teach their children, the coach must establish and maintain a dynamic in which everyone feels comfortable.

Option 1 gives the coach some discretion and flexibility about socializing with athletes. In some small communities, the coach is an integral part of the community (and might even be a parent or relative of athletes), so it might be impossible to restrict the coach from interacting socially with athletes. You might consider the age of the athletes, the size of the community, and how close-knit the community is. Option 2 restricts the coach from socializing with athletes outside of sanctioned team or community events.

☐ *Coach A's rule*: The coach will use discretion in deciding whether to socialize with athletes outside of official team events.

☐ *Coach B's rule*: The coach will not socialize with athletes except for official events (e.g., team awards banquets) or other community events (e.g., charity fundraisers).

Personal or Sexual Relationship Between Athlete and Coach

Sometimes an athlete might attempt to initiate a personal or sexual relationship with the coach without encouragement. Not actively discouraging such behavior may be misinterpreted by the athlete as encouragement. Moreover, sexual involvement with an athlete, regardless of who initiates the relationship, is illegal in many situations.

The first option is more subtle and low key, leaving open to interpretation what an appropriate boundary might be. Option 2 is more explicit in defining inappropriate behavior and the expectation that the coach will actively discourage the athlete. Parents and administrators might support option 2 for larger programs, especially if coaches spend a lot of time with athletes.

☐ *Coach A's rule*: The coach should maintain appropriate boundaries between him- or herself and the athletes.

☐ *Coach B's rule*: The coach should refrain from initiating a personal or sexual relationship with an athlete and will actively discourage an athlete from initiating a personal or sexual relationship.

Close Physical Contact and Touching

Some sports require close physical contact between a coach and an athlete. Examples of activities that might involve physical contact include spotting, taping or strapping, massage, or assisted stretching. Spontaneous physical contact can occur in other situations, especially emotional reactions to victory or defeat—think about how you and your athletes might embrace after winning a close match or how you might place a consoling arm around the athlete disappointed with his or her performance.

Although such contact is, in most instances, an innocent part of sport, there are enough cases in which coaches have been accused of inappropriate behavior, sexual harassment, or even sexual assault to cause concern. You might need to consider whether you should have rules regarding when and how coaches may touch their athletes.

Option 1 leaves open the option for appropriate physical contact and makes clear that such contact is to occur only when necessary. Making sure others are present should, one hopes, prevent abuse or unfounded accusations. Option 2 is quite restrictive but if closely followed is likely to prevent any allegations of impropriety. On the other hand, this option might not be appropriate for all sports or all situations and might feel unnaturally restrictive. You might consider the age of your athletes, whether touching is a frequent and required part of your sport, and the situations in which touching might occur.

☐ *Coach A's rule*: Coaches should touch athletes only in appropriate ways to ensure athlete safety and when instructing certain skills, such as when spotting, instructing, applying first aid, or encouraging athletes. Coaches should touch athletes only when others are present.

☐ *Coach B's rule*: Coaches should avoid touching athletes in any situation.

Entering the Locker Room

Depending on the degree of informality and your facilities, the coach may sometimes enter the locker room. You might consider the age and sex of your athletes; the level of supervision needed by the coach; whether others, such as parents, are available; and if the coach has reason to be in the locker room.

Option 1 leaves it to the coach to decide if and when to enter the locker room. Option 2 is more restrictive and gives athletes the most privacy. Option 2 would work when there are other facilities available to meet with athletes.

☐ *Coach A's rule*: The coach may enter the locker room to meet with athletes.

☐ *Coach B's rule*: The coach should not enter the locker room at any time, except in the case of an emergency.

Maintaining a professional relationship with your athletes extends to the issue of how you treat personal or confidential information. The moral value of respect also includes an assumption that you would respect the athlete's privacy and the need to handle such knowledge sensitively and confidentially. This is an example where two moral values overlap: respect for the athlete as a person and the trust between an athlete and coach.

Confidentiality

As a coach, you might become aware of personal information about an athlete or his or her family. Judging by a sudden change in motivation or attitude, you might suspect an athlete is having personal problems. An athlete troubled by personal difficulties, such as family or relationship breakdown, might confide in you. If the athlete does confide in you, you have a responsibility to treat that information confidentially. Think about how damaging it could be if an athlete discussed with you very personal information, only to find him- or herself the subject of rumors or ridicule because you discussed the issue with others. You would not only have lost the trust and respect of that athlete but would probably have added to the athlete's problems. You should encourage the athlete to seek assistance if you believe the problem is very serious or the athlete is not coping with the problem (e.g., talk of suicide or unhealthy behavior). Also, please note the following exception to the confidentiality rule: If you suspect an athlete or other student is the victim of child abuse or neglect, you are required *by law* to report that information.

Option 1 is probably the bare minimum in expecting the coach to treat all personal information confidentially. The second option is stricter and has a higher level of expectation of the coach, particularly that the coach who becomes aware of an athlete's personal problems will require the athlete to seek help. This option also gives the coach the option of consulting with others who might be able to help the athlete (e.g., counselor or psychologist), provided that the coach has the athlete's permission to do so.

☐ *Coach A's rule*: The coach should treat all personal information about an athlete confidentially.

☐ *Coach B's rule*: The coach should treat all personal information about an athlete confidentially and should not discuss the information with anyone else without permission from the athlete. The coach should be alert for signs of personal problems in an athlete that might affect his or her school or sport performance and should require the athlete to seek assistance for significant personal problems.

To summarize, this section has argued that respect is multidimensional and includes respect for oneself and others, property and the environment, and the ideals of sport. Respect is translated into action through the way you treat your athletes and others involved with your team. Your athletes' actions—and the level of respect they show for themselves and toward others—will be modeled to a large degree on your attitudes and actions. Let's now consider the moral value of responsibility, a natural extension of respect.

POLICIES ABOUT RESPONSIBILITY

You know that being a coach entails an enormous amount of responsibility to your athletes and their parents, your school or organization, your supporters and local community, and your sport and profession.

Consider your various responsibilities. First and foremost, you are responsible for the health and safety of the athletes you supervise. Think about the steps you take to ensure your athletes' health and safety while under your care. Consider the amount of time you spend teaching them proper skills and technique, and how closely you watch athletes for signs of injury or illness.

Parents and the community expect you to act as a role model while creating an enjoyable and positive environment for your athletes. How do you teach your athletes to strive to perform at their best or guide them to develop good character while also helping them avoid serious pitfalls, such as substance abuse or eating disorders?

You have a responsibility to lead the team, to create a sense of team loyalty and cooperation among your players. Think about how you plan your team's training and strategies to nurture individual talent and ambition while also getting your athletes to work together for the good of the team.

Your athletes, school or organization, and local community expect you to inspire your athletes to perform their best and to win. Your sport and coaching association expect you to play by the rules, to nurture talented athletes, and to advance the sport's standing in the community.

Policies and rules about coaching responsibilities cover a wide range of topics, including the following:

- Ensuring athlete eligibility
- Acting as a positive role model for athletes to develop life skills
- Developing good character and encouraging responsible behavior in athletes
- Ensuring the health and safety of athletes
- Acquiring proficiency to coach your sport and staying current with new techniques and equipment

- Encouraging athletes to maintain a healthy lifestyle and avoid substance abuse
- Making decisions, enforcing rules, and administering discipline as needed

☐ *Coach A's rule*: The coach should act responsibly in all activities relating to sport.

☐ *Coach B's rule*: The coach should act responsibly in all activities relating to sport and create a positive environment for athletes that values playing with honor, self-control, effort, good character, health, and learning life skills.

The following section discusses rules about the coach's responsibilities to athletes, to parents, to the school, and to the profession.

Responsibility to Athletes

As mentioned above, responsibility to your athletes is probably one of your most important, complex, and time-consuming tasks as coach. Your responsibilities extend to providing a safe environment for your athletes, teaching them the required sport skills, fostering team spirit, helping each individual develop to his or her potential, encouraging academic progress, teaching life skills, and, of course, trying to win.

Some of your responsibilities may be dictated by law (e.g., your duty of care to provide a safe environment) or the terms of your employment (e.g., coaching certification). Others might be based on tradition or community expectation (e.g., parents expect you to be a positive role model).

Here are two rules about a coach's responsibility to be a positive role model. The first option simply states the minimal expectation by parents and the community about the coach. The second option expects more of the coach and expands on what being a positive role model entails, in particular that the coach should be actively involved in his or her athletes' character development.

☐ *Coach A's rule*: The coach should be a positive role model for athletes.

☐ *Coach B's rule*: The coach should be a positive role model for athletes, should strive to teach them important life skills, and should foster their development of good character. The coach should always act in the best interests of athletes' health, safety, and well-being.

🏆 COACH'S HIGHLIGHTS

1. That I am still in contact with 80 percent of my players
2. That some of my players want to be coaches
3. That 90 percent of my players have attended college

—Annette Scogin, multisport coach, Springdale High School, Springdale, Arkansas

Part of acting responsibly toward your athletes also involves the example you set regarding commitment and fulfilling obligations.

Punctuality and Fulfilling Obligations

You expect your athletes to be reliable and punctual and to do what they say they will. In turn, your school and your athletes and their parents expect you to set an example of reliability and carrying through on your promises.

Of the two rule options below, the first requires simply that the coach will be where he or she is supposed to be when needed. This is probably the minimum requirement to ensure that your program is viable and that the team can complete the season. Although much of practice for sport can be routine, the coach is needed to supervise and instruct athletes, and in some instances this might be required by the organization's insurance or by law. The second option sets a higher level of expectation regarding the coach's obligations beyond simple supervision and, importantly, makes the coach responsible for finding a suitable replacement if he or she cannot attend practice or a game. This option also includes the expectation that agreeing to coach implies that the coach will remain with the team until the season's end to prevent a situation in which a team lacks guidance and supervision.

☐ *Coach A's rule*: The coach should be punctual and attend all practices and games.

☐ *Coach B's rule*: The coach should fulfill his or her commitments. The coach should be punctual, attend all practices and games, arrange for alternative supervision or coaching if he or she cannot attend a practice or game, and, except in cases of extreme or unpredicted difficulty, should remain in the position through the end of the contract.

In addition to being reliable and a good role model, a coach is generally expected to maintain order and ensure that athletes are not harmed by their experiences in sport. This area includes the issue of physical discipline—whether physical work is part of the coach's repertoire for exerting control and maintaining discipline.

Physical Discipline

Do you use physical means to discipline your athletes? Some coaches consider that making athletes do extra laps or other exercise as a form of punishment or discipline helps the athletes or establishes the coach's authority. Others feel that young people respond better to other forms of discipline and means of establishing authority. The American Sport Education Program believes strongly that discipline should be corrective rather than

© Human Kinetics

punitive—that is, that it should be aimed at educating the athlete to correct the problem rather than punishing the athlete.

Consider the situations in which extra exercise might be useful and when it might be counterproductive. Let's say the athletes on your soccer team were expected to maintain their fitness in the off-season, but several players start the season very unfit and admit that they haven't exercised regularly since the previous season ended. Would it be reasonable to make these athletes spend an extra 15 minutes after each session working on their fitness to bring it up to the other athletes' level and read an article about the importance of maintaining fitness between seasons? What about making them run continuously for two hours without a water break every day after practice? There is a clear difference between the corrective, educational discipline in the first example (15 minutes is a reasonable amount of extra work to regain fitness coupled with an explanation about the importance of maintaining fitness) and the obvious punishment inherent in the second example (two hours without a break is an excessive amount of exercise that places the athletes at risk of injury and heat stroke).

Option 1 allows the coach discretion but indicates that the discipline cannot be excessive or harmful. Option 2 bans coaches from using physical means to discipline athletes. You might wish to consider this option in the context of your sport or team's objectives, other policies and rules, as well as the parents' and community's expectations.

☐ *Coach A's rule*: The coach may use a reasonable amount of physical exercise to discipline athletes only to allow the athlete to regain fitness or catch up on lost sessions. The exercise must be within the athlete's capacity and must not place the athlete at risk of illness or injury.

☐ *Coach B's rule*: The coach may not use physical exercise (e.g., push-ups, extra laps) as a form of punishment or discipline in any situation.

In addition to your responsibility to your athletes while they are in your care, you also have some level of responsibility to their parents and your school, and possibly to the wider community. Beyond simply ensuring that your athletes' parents feel comfortable with your supervising and instructing their children, they also expect open communication and to be informed about their children's involvement.

Responsibility to Parents, the School, and the Community

Young athletes devote considerable time and effort to sport, and their participation often depends on input from their parents as well. Parents pay for their children's equipment, lessons, uniforms, and travel expenses. They ensure that their children attend (and usually drive them to) practice and games. Parents volunteer as timers, officials, scorers, record keepers, and managers. Parents and families might form a large proportion of your audience each week. Perhaps most important, parents influence their children's attitudes toward sport and the team. Can you recall an athlete whose participation was influenced, either positively or negatively, by his or her parents' attitudes or behavior?

Meeting With Parents

Getting parents to work together to achieve your and the team's goals can be a complex task, but it is vital to the team's success. Being open and receptive to parents' questions and clearly communicating your expectations of parents can help you organize your team, especially if your team depends on parent cooperation. Clear communication with parents can help you achieve your goals and might prevent some of the problems associated with parental interference (policies and rules for parents interacting with coaches are discussed in chapter 5). If you have ever had any problems dealing with parents of your athletes, consider what might have caused these problems and whether better communication might have prevented or helped solve the problem.

Option 1 invites parents to seek a meeting with the coach at any time in the season. This might work when the coach has an open and consultative managerial style and the time to meet with parents, or when the coach, athlete, and his or her parents develop a close relationship (e.g., personal coach). Option 2 restricts parental access to the coach and makes it clear that the coach is expected to meet with parents only to discuss certain decisions. You might consider this option in larger, more structured programs, when you have professional staff, or when there is a history of parental interference.

☐ *Coach A's rule*: The coach should meet with parents to discuss their concerns at any time in the season.

☐ *Coach B's rule*: The coach should meet with parents who make an appointment to discuss selected issues, excluding team awards and selection, playing time, team strategy, and other athletes on the team.

Not all parents will wish to meet with you during the season, but most will expect you to be proactive in communicating with them about the requirements of their children's participation in sport. This is especially important at the start of a new season, if you are a new coach, or when the athlete is new to the team.

Communicating With Athletes and Their Parents

We have emphasized the importance of clearly communicating your policies and expectations to athletes and others involved with your team. Being open and direct will help your athletes and their families understand what you expect of them and likely make your team run more smoothly. Think about a recent misunderstanding or conflict involving your team. Did poor communication play any role in causing the problem? Would better communication have helped prevent or solve the problem?

Option 1 is the more reactive option—parents and athletes must make the effort to ask the coach for information. Option 2 requires the coach to be more proactive, to provide information in writing, and to organize a preseason meeting with parents. This option might be more suitable for sports with long seasons or when travel is involved.

 COACHING TIP

"When I talk about rules with my athletes, I always discuss why and how the rules impact on the team and the responsibility athletes have to themselves, our team, and their families. I do the same thing for parents when I meet with them."

—Arnie Miehe, cross country coach, Darlington High School, Darlington, Wisconsin

☐ *Coach A's rule*: The coach should answer questions by athletes or their parents before and during the season.

☐ *Coach B's rule*: The coach will provide athletes and parents a written description of expectations at the start of the season and will meet with athletes and parents before the season starts to discuss these expectations.

Communication is one important aspect of responsibility. Another is helping ensure that your athletes achieve and maintain their eligibility. One viewpoint is that athletes and their families should be responsible for achieving the eligibility standards. This might be suitable if your program is well established and most parents are actively involved, or if you have little control or input into their eligibility. Another way of thinking is that young people and their families do not always understand the intricacies of eligibility standards and that your active encouragement will help them. Let's now turn to rules about the coach's role in monitoring athlete eligibility.

Athlete Academic Eligibility

In chapter 3 we discussed issues and rules relating to athlete eligibility. Most schools with rules on academic eligibility require the athlete to be responsible for his or her academic progress. However, the coach can, and is sometimes expected to, take an active role in monitoring the athlete's academic eligibility.

Encouraging Academic Achievement

In deciding the extent of your role in academic eligibility, you might consider several issues:

- How rigorous are the academic eligibility requirements? (More rigorous requirements might require a more active role by the coach.)
- Does the school's policy require or expect you to take an active role?
- Are you involved in decision making about academic eligibility?
- What other support does the school offer to student athletes to help them meet academic eligibility requirements (e.g., counselors to monitor grades, tutoring, study sessions, summer school)?
- Does the school permit failing students to participate in sport through a probation period?

Option 1 simply indicates that the coach should encourage his or her athletes to do well in school. You might choose this option when academic eligibility is not an issue or is generally beyond your control. Option 2 requires the coach to be proactive in encouraging athletes to do well in school and in monitoring academic progress. This option would work only when the athlete's participation depends on academic eligibility, as in high school sports programs.

☐ *Coach A's rule*: The coach should encourage student athletes to achieve academically.

☐ *Coach B's rule*: The coach should take an active role in ensuring that all student athletes meet the minimum academic eligibility requirements. The coach should actively monitor grades of struggling student athletes or those on academic probation. Together with the school counselor, the coach will be responsible for reinstating an athlete after completing the terms of his or her academic probation.

Coach's Exercise

You have recently been hired as a new varsity coach in a school that prides itself on both academic and sporting success. Prepare what you would say to parents at your first meeting with them to demonstrate how your personal philosophy fits with their expectations.

Influencing Teachers' Grading of Student Athletes

Student athletes have many demands on their time and might not always achieve at the level needed to maintain academic eligibility. As discussed in chapter 3, on average, athletes tend to achieve academically, although some may struggle, especially if your school requires a higher than usual level of grades to maintain eligibility. Depending on your school's size and the level of support (e.g., counselors), part of your mentoring role might include monitoring your athletes' academic progress. Although this might help you identify athletes needing help before they lose eligibility, it could also be interpreted by some teachers as trying to influence their evaluation of the student.

Option 1 permits the coach to discuss each student athlete's progress with teachers. You might choose this option in small schools, in settings with little support by counselors to monitor athletes' grades, or when coaches are expected to keep an eye on athletes' grades. Option 2 is more restrictive and would avoid any appearance that the coach is trying to influence grades. However, it requires either a liberal academic eligibility policy or an established process for someone else to monitor athletes' academic progress (e.g., a school counselor).

☐ *Coach A's rule*: The coach may discuss an athlete's academic progress with teachers to help ensure that athletes maintain academic eligibility.

☐ *Coach B's rule*: The coach may not discuss an athlete's grades with teachers.

When selecting rule(s) for coach responsibility toward academic eligibility, you'll need to also consider the rules for athletes presented in chapter 3 to make sure these are consistent.

Besides the responsibility to your athletes and their families, you also have a responsibility to the school that you work for. These responsibilities might be governed by your contract, by your relationship with the school (e.g., employee or consultant), or by tradition. Let's look at some rules relating to the coach's responsibility to the school and wider community.

Responsibility to the School, Community, and Spectators

Think about what your school or community expects of you: to teach and develop your athletes' skills, to be successful (i.e., to win), to represent the school and community with honor, to adhere to the rules, to instill in your athletes and their parents a positive attitude toward the sport, and to enhance the school's or community's reputation. That might seem like a heavy burden, but all of it is consistent with the ideals of sport for young people and the reasons why schools and communities invest in youth sport.

Option 1 asks only that coaches avoid acting in a way that might reflect badly on the organization. It does not state or even imply that the coach should strive to promote a positive image of the school and community. The second option reflects a much higher expectation of the coach to both follow the rules and to actively promote the school and community in a positive way. This option may be appropriate when the team or organization has a higher profile and the local community associates the coach with the organization.

☐ *Coach A's rule*: The coach should act in a way that reflects positively on the school and community.

☐ *Coach B's rule*: The coach should act in the best interest of the school and community and should actively promote a positive image of the school and community in all team activities. The coach should follow and enforce all school rules relating to athletics. The coach should actively encourage athletes, their parents, and others involved in sport to promote a positive image of the school in all team and community activities.

In some sports or schools the coach might occasionally interact with spectators. The outcome of such interactions can influence the public perception of the coach, and by extension, the community he or she represents.

Coach's Interaction With Spectators

In many sports, the fans sit quite close to the team; the smaller the venue, the more likely that fans will be seated close to the team and coach. Spectators can sometimes inappropriately express their particular views about your coaching and players. Can you recall a time when fans, maybe even your own, made inappropriate comments or gestures that unsettled you or your athletes?

Option 1 allows the coach discretion in deciding whether to speak with spectators or others during a game but requires the coach to be respectful. This option might work in more informal settings. The second option gives the coach no discretion and thus decreases the chance of a confrontation between coach and spectator. Of course, this option does not prevent a spectator from trying to initiate a confrontation (rules about this are discussed in chapter 5).

☐ *Coach A's rule*: The coach may speak to spectators, parents, or the media during a competition, provided he or she does so respectfully.

☐ *Coach B's rule*: The coach may not speak or gesture to spectators, parents, or the media during a competition.

As coach, you might be expected to interact with the media by providing information about the team or an athlete or by participating in an interview or news conference. Based on the expectation that the coach has a responsibility to avoid portraying his or her organization negatively, the school can expect the coach to be respectful and cooperative when dealing with the media.

Communicating With the Media

The rules for communicating with parents could also apply to dealing with the media. You might consider whether your team has a high profile in your community. Does the public have a keen interest in your team's activities? If so, consider your relationship with the media. Has the media portrayed your team positively and honestly? If not, consider the possible benefits to establishing a good relationship with the local media. On the other hand, the media can sometimes distort issues or be a distraction for your athletes and fans. Your school might already have a policy in place about dealing with the media.

Option 1 leaves it to the coach to decide whether to speak to the media. This option gives you the chance to avoid commenting on some issues or to allow your team to focus at certain times without the distraction of media reports. Option 2 requires the coach to be available for interviews. You might consider this option if your team is often reported on and the community expects regular stories about your team, or if you already have an established relationship with the media. Ideally, the coach who is required to be available for interviews has the skills and experience to interact positively with the media.

☐ *Coach A's rule*: The coach may use his or her discretion in deciding whether to speak to the media about the team's activities. The coach may refuse to speak to the media about any team activity at any time.

☐ *Coach B's rule*: Coaches should maintain a positive relationship with the local media. The coach has a responsibility to promote a positive image of the school (or organization) and to regularly provide the media with accurate relevant information about the team's activities. Within reason, coaches are expected to be available for interviews when requested by the media.

Policies about the media's relationship with the team are discussed in chapter 5.

Part of the coach's responsibility to the athletes and their parents, and to the school and community, is ensuring that the coach is qualified and competent to work and to instruct young people.

Professional Responsibility and Competency

To teach sport skills and train athletes safely and effectively, you need a certain level of expertise in your sport. Part of your credibility and the trust and respect you earn from your

 COACHING TIP

"I try to do as much as possible for our local paper. The morning after a meet, I drop off a complete set of results with our runners' names highlighted. I list the runners who ran their best times and write down a few sentences about the boys' races and girls' races. The easier I can make it for them, the better the coverage. I find that it's better to give them quotes than to answer questions."

—Arnie Miehe, cross country coach, Darlington High School, Darlington, Wisconsin

athletes is based on your ability to demonstrate and share your expertise. You might consider some of the following issues when developing your team policies and rules relating to coach competency:

- How important is technical competency in a particular situation?
- What is the minimum or optimal level of competence needed by the coach? How is this level obtained?
- How important is continuing education to update the coach's knowledge and competency?
- Is it important for the coach to be a member of a professional sport or coaching organization?
- How risky is the sport? (High-risk sports require a higher level of competence to coach safely.)
- Are there any rules regarding first aid or CPR qualifications required by the sport, school, club, or insurer?

In some instances, your insurance policy or conference or school rules may dictate if the coach needs to have a certain level of competency.

Option 1 acknowledges that volunteer coaches are sometimes needed who might not have competency in specific sport skills or coaching but encourages them to acquire these skills during the season. This could be accomplished through coaching courses or by working with a more experienced coach. Option 2 requires the coach to have the necessary competence and accreditation. This option would work when there is an element of risk in a sport (e.g., gymnastics, diving, football) or when there is an expectation that the coach will teach athletes the specific skills needed to improve performance. Insurance issues might also influence your choice of rule.

☐ *Coach A's rule*: The coach may coach without formal qualifications provided he or she follows the school and conference rules. The coach is encouraged to further develop his or her coaching skills.

☐ *Coach B's rule*: A coach should have technical competency and the minimal level of accreditation required to coach the sport at the level required. The coach is responsible for ensuring that assistant coaches have the relevant expertise to coach. The coach must be a member of a relevant coach or sport association and must complete one or more continuing education courses every three years.

The coach is also expected to act as a positive role model in other areas. Just as the coach can be a role model for language, he or she can also play an important role in preventing athletes from displaying inappropriate physical aggression or violence.

Aggression and Violence

Excessive aggression and violence can be viewed as extreme outcomes of disrespect. Someone who truly respects himself or herself and his or her opponents would find it difficult to condone or encourage violent behavior as a result of a sporting event.

Option 1 disallows the coach from acting violently during practice and games. One assumes that avoiding violent behavior will help prevent or stop others from acting violently. Option 2 expects the coach to avoid acting violently or inciting others and also to actively discourage such behavior. When choosing your rule, you might consider the likelihood of violent behavior by athletes and others involved in your sport. You might also consider whether others in your school are responsible for preventing violence (e.g., if your school has security guards at games) and the number and type of spectators your sport attracts.

☐ *Coach A's rule*: The coach should not display violent behavior during practice or games.

☐ *Coach B's rule*: The coach should not participate in or display violent behavior or incite athletes or spectators to act violently during any sport activity. The coach should discourage and try to prevent violent behavior and should discipline athletes who act violently.

In addition to the coach's responsibilities to act as a positive role model and to communicate effectively, there are other, perhaps less obvious, responsibilities the coach might have to fulfill.

Other Responsibilities of the Coach

You might consider expanding your rules to include responsibilities of the coach on issues such as appropriate dress, travel, conflicts of interest, and accepting gifts.

The Coach's Appearance

The coach's appearance gives an impression to the team's athletes, opponents, and the community. If you have watched a recent professional game, you will recall seeing the coaches professionally attired, either in a suit or a team uniform. Of course, not all schools or clubs can afford to or wish to provide uniforms for their coaches. Your choice of rule will depend on your team's resources, community expectations, and level of competition.

The first option expects the coach to dress neatly and appropriately, which probably seems obvious but might still need to be stated in some situations. This option suits smaller programs that do not provide a uniform for the coach. The second option is stricter and more explicit and might suit larger, more structured programs.

☐ *Coach A's rule*: The coach should dress neatly, as appropriate for the activity and weather.

☐ *Coach B's rule*: The coach should dress professionally during official team activities. The coach should wear a suit or coaching staff uniform (comprising the team's colors) for games.

Travel

For teams that do not have managers, the coach might be responsible for arranging travel and supervising athletes at away contests, which might involve overnight travel. For larger organizations that have managers and parents to supervise the athletes, or when athletes stay at the host school or with families in the host city, it may not be essential for the coach to be with the athletes at all times.

Coach Traveling With the Team   Depending on the program and the nature of the competition, the coach may be required to travel and stay with the team. The first option permits the coach to travel separately and would suit programs in which the parents or school arrange and supervise the athletes' travel. For example, athletes might travel with their parents or by school bus to after-school or weekend games in nearby towns, and the coach could drive separately. The second option expects that the coach will travel and stay with the team, which suits situations in which the coach's presence is needed.

☐ *Coach A's rule*: When the team travels, the coach may choose to make separate travel and accommodation plans, provided that he or she maintains regular contact with the team.

☐ *Coach B's rule*: When the team travels, the coach must travel and stay with the team.

Coach Supervising the Team During Travel   Depending on whether there are others traveling with the team, the coach might be expected to supervise the athletes when traveling.

Option 1 requires the coach to supervise the athletes at all times, which might be suitable for small teams or short trips or when other adults are not available. Option 2 requires the coach to supervise athletes only during official team functions. This option would work for longer trips on which constant supervision might be tedious or impossible or when other adults can supervise the athletes during their leisure time.

☐ *Coach A's rule*: When the team travels, the coach should supervise the athletes during all activities, both inside and outside of sport.

☐ *Coach B's rule*: When the team travels, the coach is responsible for supervising athletes during team activities (practice, games, and other official functions). The coach may permit athletes to select their own activities outside of sport provided that athletes attend all required practice and competition.

Another subtler and often overlooked area of coach responsibility relates to conflict of interest. Conflict of interest might apply in a coaching situation if a coach has competing concerns, for example, if a coach acts in different roles for different groups or organizations.

Conflicts of Interest

In sports, conflict of interest is defined as a situation or relationship in which there may be a conflict between the team or club's interests and an individual's interests. One example might be if a coach of a high school team is also a recruiting agent for a college. Acting as a recruiting agent, the coach has recommended an athlete from another school for a scholarship to the college. However, if that athlete's team competes against the coach's own school team, the coach then has competing (conflicting) interests: He has an interest in the athlete performing well so the college offers a scholarship, but he also has an interest in his school's team winning. We hope that the coach would act objectively and professionally. However, when thinking about conflict of interest, we are equally concerned with the appearance of conflict as much as the reality. That is, the coach must be seen to be acting without bias; his or her motivation should be beyond question.

Pursuing Other Interests

The first option gives the coach leeway in pursuing other interests but leaves the coach to identify and avoid the appearance of conflict of interest. This option would suit situations involving volunteer coaches and situations in which conflict of interest issues are unlikely to arise or cause difficulty. The second option is more restrictive and explicit in defining conflict of interest and the situations in which it might arise. You might choose this option for larger programs involving professional coaches or when coaches work in more than one area of sport.

☐ *Coach A's rule*: The coach may pursue other sport interests provided he or she avoids any conflict of interest.

☐ *Coach B's rule*: The coach should act in the best interests of the athletes and the team. The coach should avoid any real or apparent conflict of interest by avoiding commitments, contracts, or relationships with others that might prevent the coach from effectively performing his or her coaching obligations, or conflict with the interests of the athletes or team. The coach should declare any possible conflict of interest in advance and should avoid involvement in decisions in which a potential for conflict of interest exists.

One potential area of impropriety or conflict of interest is accepting gifts.

Accepting Gifts From Athletes or Their Families

Giving a gift to a coach could be construed as trying to buy influence or to affect a decision, even when that is not the intention. For example, a grateful parent might show appreciation for a coach helping his or her child master a sport by giving the coach a gift. This gift could be interpreted as the parent trying to influence the coach's decision about playing time or team selection. On the other hand, coaches often develop close relationships with their athletes and families, which might involve the exchange of gifts without an ulterior motive.

When deciding on whether to include a rule about gifts, consider the type of relationship a coach usually has with his or her athletes and their families. Option

1 leaves open the possibility that coaches may accept or give gifts. You might consider this option when it is normal for coaches and athletes to develop a close relationship and there is no reason to expect impropriety. Option 2 avoids uncertainty by simply prohibiting the exchange of gifts.

☐ *Coach A's rule*: The coach may accept a personal gift from an athlete or family provided this does not involve a conflict of interest or influence the coach's decisions.

☐ *Coach B's rule*: The coach may not exchange (accept or give) personal gifts with athletes or their families.

Coach's Exercise

Plan or prepare an information sheet for two new assistant coaches joining your team who have never worked with athletes at your team's level or age. Focus on the expectations for how they would show respect and responsibility toward your athletes and officials.

Let's take a moment to recap. This chapter has discussed the issues to consider when selecting policies and rules for coaches relating to the first two moral values of respect and responsibility. Leading and coaching a team commands respect from the athletes, their parents, and the community; however, respect runs two ways: Athletes respect and model their behavior on those who treat them respectfully. Coaching also carries many responsibilities to athletes and their families, to the school or organization, to the local community, and to the sport and its traditions. We have also covered rules about coaches acting as role models of respect for oneself and others, self-discipline, effort, reliability, and appropriate language and actions. Clearly worded rules about how coaches are expected to show respect and take responsibility will help you communicate your vision, run your program effectively, and fulfill your team's objectives. Let's now turn to the third moral value of caring.

POLICIES ABOUT CARING

As mentioned in chapter 3, caring is related to fairness and respect; people who respect others will also care about them and treat them fairly. In sport, caring involves giving priority to developing team spirit and to the safety and health of athletes—both physical and psychological—above everything else, even the desire to win. Caring means that athletes and coaches play for the team rather than for themselves. It is possible to satisfy both demands—that is, to strive for excellence in performance while also caring about the health and safety of your athletes. After all, athletes who are physically and mentally tired, injured, or preoccupied with other issues rarely perform to their ability.

Consider the many ways that you ensure the health and safety of your athletes: Do you watch them carefully for signs of excessive fatigue, injury, or illness? Have you ever taken a player out of a game or adjusted training because you were concerned about an athlete's health? Do you listen to your athletes for signs of how they are coping with training demands? Do you teach them to look out for each other? Each of these shows your athletes that you care about them as individuals.

☐ *Coach A's policy introduction*: The coach should care about his or her athletes and encourage them to remain healthy and fit and to support their team and teammates.

☐ *Coach B's policy introduction*: Our team is committed to a caring environment. The team values team effort and the safety, health, and personal development of athletes above everything else.

The coach should give highest priority to athlete health and safety. All coaches should

- ensure that athletes perform activities suitable for their age and skill level;
- teach and actively encourage athletes to care about and look after their teammates;
- monitor athletes for signs of injury or illness or difficulty coping with training;
- prevent athletes from performing dangerous or reckless acts that might injure themselves or others;
- encourage athletes to maintain a healthy lifestyle.

Teaching Athletes to Work Cooperatively and for the Good of the Team

You can probably recall times when you chose an action for the good of the team rather than for the good of just one athlete. For young people, this is an important and sometimes difficult life lesson to learn. Your athletes might not understand why you made a certain strategic decision in a close match. Think about how you teach your star athlete that he or she needs to pass the ball more to spread out the opposition's defense, or how you get them to think about their individual efforts in the context of the team effort.

Option 1 might be self-evident in some sports or at some levels of sport. Option 2 is more descriptive and prescribes disciplinary action for athletes who play selfishly.

☐ *Coach A's rule*: The coach should encourage all athletes to work together as a team and to contribute to a team effort.

☐ *Coach B's rule*: The coach should teach athletes to cooperate with and to care about teammates. The coach should actively encourage athletes to play for the good of the team. The coach should help athletes correct their own selfish behavior and create instructive examples of selfish behavior that might occur.

Caring about your athletes and team also extends to creating an environment that encourages athletes to demonstrate caring toward each other and toward sport in general.

Creating a Caring Environment

The first option is a bare minimum of the expected level of concern coaches should show toward athletes; most would assume that any coach involved in sport would accept this rule. The word "concern" has different meanings for different people, however, and only experienced or very perceptive coaches would understand all that "concern" entails. The second option defines concern in terms of athlete health, safety, and well-being and advises the coach to teach and encourage concern for one another to the team. This rule would work when athletes and coaches spend significant time together in practice and games.

☐ *Coach A's rule*: The coach should demonstrate concern for athletes.

☐ *Coach B's rule*: The coach should consider the athletes' health, safety, and well-being as top priorities. The coach should actively encourage athletes to look out for each other.

Caring about your athletes' health and well-being also involves making decisions about their fitness to practice and play and how to handle an ill or injured athlete. Looking after your athletes' health is part of caring and is also an important strategy for winning because ill or injured athletes cannot train and compete effectively.

 COACH'S HIGHLIGHTS

1. Caring relationships with players and parents
2. Seeing my players mature and excel on other teams
3. Enjoying friendships with players years later
4. Giving players a solid skill and knowledge foundation
5. Influencing their lives in a positive way beyond soccer

—Jim Caputo, boys' soccer coach, Blue Ridge High School, Farmer City, Illinois

Medical Clearance and Return to Play

Chapter 3 presented policies and rules about medical clearance for athletes. In most schools and in many clubs, the coach is responsible for ensuring that athletes have received the necessary medical clearance to participate and that injured or ill athletes have recovered sufficiently to return to play.

Injured or Ill Athletes

Injury and illness are part of sport, especially in contact sports and those with high training demands (e.g., gymnastics, competitive swimming, long-distance running). Young people often view themselves as indestructible or are so enthusiastic about their sport that they ignore or hide illness or injury. But in keeping with a caring philosophy and the duty of care, coaches have a responsibility to try to prevent or limit injury and illness in their athletes.

Option 1 asks the coach to encourage the athlete to seek advice; the decision to practice or compete remains with the athlete. Option 2 gives the coach control and allows him or her to decide whether an athlete may play when ill or injured. This option might work best in sports associated with significant or frequent injury and when continued training can exacerbate minor illness or injury.

☐ *Coach A's rule*: The coach should encourage an injured or ill athlete to seek medical advice.

☐ *Coach B's rule*: The coach should not permit an injured or ill athlete to practice or compete unless cleared by the physician or athletic trainer.

Return to Play

As a coach, you are sometimes faced with a decision regarding when an injured or ill athlete has recovered enough to resume practicing and competing. For minor illness or injury requiring a few days or weeks of rest (e.g., flu or strained muscle), you might find that it is obvious when the athlete is ready to return. The decision is more complex for more serious illnesses (e.g., mononucleosis, hepatitis) or injuries (e.g., ligament tear, stress fracture).

The first option gives the athlete the decision to return to play, assuming that he or she will consult the coach and team's health professionals before making the decision. Athletes who are used to working closely with health professionals might appreciate being given the responsibility for making this type of decision; however, it does allow the athlete to disregard the advice. Option 2 gives the coach and health professionals the final decision on whether an athlete can return to play. This option might suit more physically demanding sports when reinjury could have devastating consequences for an athlete.

☐ *Coach A's rule*: The coach should allow the athlete, in consultation with the coach and team physician or athletic trainer, to decide when he or she is healthy and fit enough to resume practice and competition.

☐ *Coach B's rule*: The coach will permit an injured or ill athlete to return to practice and competition only after the athlete has been cleared to return by a physician or athletic trainer.

This short section has discussed rules to help the coach demonstrate caring and to create a caring environment for the team. Let's now move on to present policies and rules about the fourth moral value, honesty, which is interrelated with respect, caring, and fairness (the fifth moral value). Coaches who respect and care about their athletes generally strive to be honest and fair and to ensure that their athletes are treated honestly and fairly.

POLICIES ABOUT HONESTY

Honesty involves trustworthiness, reliability, loyalty, and integrity. Parents and the community have high expectations for coaches in terms of trust, honesty, and integrity. Consider how much time you spend with your young athletes and how important it is for their parents and the school or club to trust that you are providing a safe learning environment for these young people. The community also expects you to be a positive role model for young people and to teach them important life skills, including integrity and honesty.

Think about the people you trust and the people who trust you. What expectations do we have of people we trust? Policies relating to a coach's honesty include expectations that he or she will act honorably (e.g., pursuing victory with honor) and honestly (e.g., playing by the rules), display good sportsmanship and loyalty to athletes and the team, and be reliable (fulfill commitments).

When selecting your policies and rules relating to honesty, you might consider some of the following questions:

- What personal qualities do athletes, parents, and the community value in their coaches?
- What personal qualities are important to success in coaching?
- How do you try to translate these personal qualities to sporting situations?

☐ *Coach A's rule*: The coach should act honestly in all activities related to sport.

☐ *Coach B's rule*: The community values trustworthy behavior and attitudes, such as integrity, honesty, reliability, and loyalty. The coach should display and promote honest and trustworthy behavior.

When selecting your rules on honesty for coaches, consider whether to address some or all of the following areas:

- Honesty with athletes, parents, and others
- Loyalty to the team
- Playing by the spirit of the rules and cheating
- Gambling
- Reliability
- Scouting and recruiting

We will look at these areas in more detail in upcoming sections.

Honesty With Athletes, Parents, and Others

Athletes, parents, and others involved in sport rely on coaches to provide accurate information about a range of issues, including playing time, team selection, eligibility, college entrance requirements, and the athlete's potential as a college recruit or in higher-level competition. Honesty involves not only information you give but also information that is intentionally withheld.

Option 1 expresses the minimal expectation that coaches will try to be honest but leaves the interpretation of "honesty" open. Option 2 expects not only that coaches will tell the truth but that they will check their facts and correct any falsehoods. The second option requires the coach to tell the full story without withholding any relevant information.

☐ *Coach A's rule*: The coach should be honest in all verbal and written communication with athletes, parents, and others involved in sport (e.g., volunteers, media, community).

☐ *Coach B's rule*: The coach should check all facts discussed or included in written communication with athletes, parents, and others involved in sport. The coach should not withhold any relevant information from an athlete or parent and should make a reasonable effort to correct any false statements.

COACHING TIP

"I try to be honest and open with the players about why they aren't playing, why I took them out of a game. In turn, I ask them to be honest if they are hurt or not feeling well, because that can hurt their performance, and in turn, let down the team. Be honest at all times—it avoids problems."

—Mark Jones, softball coach, Mahomet–Seymour High School, Mahomet, Illinois

Honesty About Eligibility

Eligibility rules are sometimes complex. An ineligible athlete might join your team without you or others realizing it. If your conference penalizes a team for playing an ineligible athlete, it is in the interests of your team that you or another responsible person check each athlete's eligibility.

In option 1, the coach can rely on others to check eligibility. This option would work in large programs in which the school or organization checks eligibility. This option leaves open the possibility that the coach could turn a blind eye and not delve too deeply into the question about an athlete's eligibility. Option 2 requires coaches to actively check the eligibility of their athletes. You might need this option if you don't have another system to check eligibility or if your team would be penalized (e.g., stripped of conference championship or suspended from the conference) should an infraction be discovered.

☐ *Coach A's rule*: The coach should not knowingly allow an ineligible athlete to play.

☐ *Coach B's rule*: The coach should check the eligibility of each athlete on the team and not permit any ineligible athlete to join the team.

In some sports, recruiting is a part of the coach's job and recruiting the best athletes makes a difference in a team's performance and a program's success.

Honesty in Recruiting

In some sports and situations, recruiting is low key and there is little reason to expect that a coach might not act honestly. In other situations, a coach might feel pressured to recruit new talent to quickly improve a team's performance. The community and school expect the coach to deal as honestly with potential recruits as he or she does with current athletes and their families.

Option 1 expects honest recruiting within the league rules and would work if your league already has a well-articulated and enforced policy on recruitment.

Option 2 prevents the coach from actively approaching a potential athlete. This option prevents any appearance of undue influence.

☐ *Coach A's rule*: The coach will comply strictly with league rules about recruiting athletes and will use honest means to recruit athletes. The coach should not make insincere or unrealistic promises or use undue influence or inducement to recruit an athlete.

☐ *Coach B's rule*: The coach should not actively recruit athletes from another team.

Loyalty to the Team

Loyalty is central to the concept of trustworthiness. As a coach, you might occasionally find yourself in situations with competing or conflicting demands. In theory, anything that makes your team perform well should also enhance your career, but it might not always work that way in reality.

Option 1 puts loyalty in the context of prioritizing needs and asks the coach to consider whose needs come first: the team's or the coach's. There might be times when the coach decides that his or her needs come first. Option 2 makes it clear that the coach is expected to be loyal and to always attend to the team's needs, even if it means his or her own personal interests go unfulfilled. Ideally, the team's and coach's interests are one and the same, but this is not always the case.

☐ *Coach A's rule*: The coach should be loyal to the team and consider the team's needs ahead of his or her own.

☐ *Coach B's rule*: The coach should be loyal to the team and organization (school) and should put the team's interests ahead of personal interests and glory.

Playing by the Spirit of the Rules and Cheating

As a coach, you might sometimes feel torn between the pressure to win, the expectations to play by the rules, and the temptation to occasionally bend the rules to your advantage. There is sometimes a fine line between working within the rules and spirit of the rules and using trickery to gain an advantage. For example, in a basketball game, calling a time-out to interrupt your opponents' momentum and refocus your team's defense at a critical time in the game is a legitimate strategy. In contrast, ordering one of your players to fake an injury or start a fight when you have used up all your time-outs would be considered outside the spirit of the rules.

Option 1 takes a minimalist approach and leaves the coach some flexibility as long as he or she does not actually violate a written rule. Some might argue that this in not in keeping with the spirit of the game, which can be open to different interpretations. Option 2 makes it clear that the coach is to respect both the written and unwritten rules of the game and always to seek to play fairly.

☐ *Coach A's rule*: The coach will observe the written rules of the game.

☐ *Coach B's rule*: The coach will play strictly by both the written and unwritten rules and will not bend or knowingly break a rule to gain an advantage.

Let's now turn to the issue of gambling on sport, which might be relevant to a small but significant segment of sport at the highest level (e.g., varsity and elite teams).

Gambling on Sport

Gambling is pertinent to honesty if it calls into question or divides a coach's loyalty to the team or places the coach in a position that might be construed as conflict of interest.

Option 1 allows the coach to bet only on sports and teams not directly related to the coach's team. Option 2 is more restrictive and avoids impropriety by disallowing betting entirely. In choosing your policy, consider whether anyone ever bets on your team(s), whether you have a policy on gambling for athletes and others involved in sport, your conference's rules on gambling, and your local community's views about gambling. The second option is more suitable for teams that feel strongly about coaches being role models for young people.

☐ *Coach A's rule*: The coach will not gamble or bet on the outcome of a match or game involving his or her team.

☐ *Coach B's rule*: The coach will not gamble or bet on the outcome of any sporting activity, game, or match, regardless of sport or level (i.e., amateur, school, community, professional).

To summarize, honesty involves being trustworthy, reliable, and loyal, not lying or withholding information, and acting with integrity in all activities relating to sport. These concepts are not always evident and might sometimes be difficult to convey but are nevertheless important to showing respect and developing a caring environment that values excellence and teamwork. Let's now move on to discuss the fifth moral value, fairness, which gives life to the other moral values of respectfulness, responsibility, honesty, and caring.

POLICIES ABOUT FAIRNESS

Fairness involves playing by the rules, both written and unwritten, and acting fairly and openly in all situations. Although fairness might seem at the surface a simple concept, in reality it is complex. Different people have different perspectives on what is fair. The parents of an athlete who starts the game on the bench might not think it is fair that another player is in the starting lineup. Some athletes might not always agree with your selection of most valuable player at the end of the season. Others might not agree with your method of discipline for a particular athlete. You might think that an opposing coach's tactics border on being unfair.

It goes without saying that not everyone will agree with and understand every decision you make, but you can create policies that make your actions and the reasons for your decisions more consistent and transparent, and thus easier for people to understand. One hopes this understanding would lead people to believe you are acting fairly.

☐ *Coach A's policy introduction*: The coach should act fairly and should play according to the rules of the sport.

☐ *Coach B's policy introduction*: Our team believes that fairness is an integral part of sport. The coach should act fairly and openly in all team activities and should follow all team, school, and sport rules. The coach should follow the coach's code of conduct and respect the integrity of the sport. The coach should actively teach and encourage athletes to demonstrate sportsmanship.

Consider the diverse situations you encounter that require you to act fairly and openly. These might include obvious issues, such as following a sport's rules, but it might extend to acting fairly in making decisions in complex situations (e.g., discipline) and to acting openly when selecting teams and giving awards.

When trying to decide the best ways to ensure that you act fairly, consider your own personal decision-making style and the team's traditions. For example, if athletes have always voted to award most valuable player, you might find it difficult to suddenly change the tradition and make the decision yourself. If you are normally a very open person who discusses all major decisions with your assistant coaches, they might be confused if you suddenly made decisions without consulting them or explaining your reasons.

Following Rules

Following rules is one of the central tenets of sport. Consider how chaotic and dangerous sport would be without strict enforcement of rules. Can you recall a game or match in which officials did not adequately control the players? Chances are the game degenerated into frustrating, sloppy, and perhaps even dangerous play that might have yielded an unfair outcome.

The expectations about following rules extend beyond the rules as written to also encompass the spirit of the rules and respect for the game.

Option 1 requires the coach simply to follow the written rules but implies the option of "bending" the rules or of different interpretations of the rules. Some might infer that this option encourages coaches to bend the rules, whereas others might accept that rule-bending is part of sport and that everyone does it. Option 2 clarifies that coaches are expected to follow both the written and unwritten rules and to actively seek to play honestly within the spirit of the game. This option is more consistent with the ideals of the six moral values, but some skeptics might argue that it is unrealistic to expect coaches to act this way in every situation.

☐ *Coach A's rule*: The coach should play by the written rules of the sport.

☐ *Coach B's rule*: The coach should play by the written rules of the sport. The coach should ensure that competition is fair and should never evade or bend rules to advantage the team. The coach should also ensure that his or her athletes do not bend the rules to create an advantage.

Good Sportsmanship

Good sportsmanship is an ideal behavior many people expect of coaches and athletes. Putting this ideal into practical expectations can be complex. Some say that sport is more about achievement and winning than developing sportsmanship in athletes. However, as Clifford and Feezell say in *Coaching for Character*, "It's a mistake to think that teaching and requiring good sportsmanship is inconsistent with the pursuit of victory. . . . There have been fine coaches who demand both athletic excellence and moral excellence from their players." (page 7)

What emphasis do you place on demonstrating good sportsmanship? Is this something you are constantly aware of in your own actions and in those of your athletes? Do you teach sportsmanship actively, or do you think your athletes can develop sportsmanship through observing your leadership and example? Can you recall times when your athletes witnessed good sportsmanship and what you did to acknowledge this behavior? What about bad sportsmanship?

The first option expects the coach simply to demonstrate good sportsmanship and implies that doing so will help teach sportsmanship to athletes. More prescriptive and expansive, option 2 expects the coach to demonstrate sportsmanship and also to actively teach sportsmanship to his or her athletes and to discipline athletes who violate the concept of sportsmanship.

☐ *Coach A's rule*: The coach should demonstrate good sportsmanship in all team activities.

☐ *Coach B's rule*: The coach should act as a role model for athletes to develop good sportsmanship. The coach should actively encourage athletes to demonstrate good sportsmanship by acknowledging sportsmanlike behavior. The coach should use positive discipline to correct an athlete's unsportsmanlike behavior.

Coach's Exercise

Can you recall an incident in which a coach seemed to bend the rules to his or her team's advantage? How could you use this example to teach your athletes about playing within the spirit of the rules?

Team Selection and Awards

Young athletes have many reasons for participating in sport. We hope that these reasons are motivated by love of the game, a desire to excel, and personal satisfaction. Although young people are rarely motivated solely by external recognition, such as awards, it is sometimes important to formally recognize their effort and achievement.

Obviously, if you are coaching a highly competitive team of skilled athletes with a winning tradition, your team selection criteria will focus on performance and the demands of being competitive at your level. You would make very different decisions, however, when coaching a young group of novices who are participating in sport to learn skills, improve, and have fun.

Team Selection

Teams have various rules and traditions for selecting teams, starting lineups, and playing time, and it is impossible to write specific rules to cover every team. When determining your own team's rules, consider these issues:

- The age and skill level of the athletes
- The team's philosophy and objectives (e.g., to win a conference championship, to teach sport skills, to ensure that everyone plays)
- The expectations of the athletes, school or organization, and community (e.g., to win, to develop talent, or to have fun)
- Whether it is necessary to "cut" players or if you have enough resources for everyone to play

Option 1 is consistent with an "everyone plays" team philosophy and is most appropriate for teams for which the focus is on fun and learning skills. Choosing option 2 gives you the option to cut some players and to allot playing time according to ability and contribution to the team.

☐ *Coach A's rule*: The coach will not cut any athlete from the team. The coach will assign each athlete to play a similar amount of time each game, regardless of outcome.

☐ *Coach B's rule*: The coach will select the best athletes for the team and starting lineup and will base playing time on giving the team the best chance to win. Some players may be cut from the team.

Awards

The arguments for team selection also apply to giving awards. Think about the reasons for awards: to recognize achievement while encouraging further participation and development. Regardless of the number and types of awards, you need to have a clear and fair process that you can explain to your athletes and that your athletes will recognize as being fair.

Option 1 acknowledges that other factors are important to a team's performance and that sometimes the player who is most valuable to the team is not the best performer but one who contributes to the team in other ways. You might choose option 2 if you coach a highly competitive team with a tradition of awards, such as an MVP award based only on performance.

☐ *Coach A's rule*: The coach will consider a range of factors including performance, effort, dedication, and leadership when deciding on awards. The coach may consult athletes or others involved in the team when deciding on awards.

☐ *Coach B's rule*: The coach will decide on awards based on performance only.

The Selection Process and Communicating Your Decisions

How do you communicate the process to decide team selection and awards? Do you announce the team selection at practice one day, post the team list outside your office, or send a letter to each athlete? Do you consider how those who miss out might react?

When reflecting on your process for team selection, consider factors such as your team philosophy and the age and experience level of your athletes. You might also think about discussing the reasons for your decision or if you expect your decisions to be final and remain unquestioned.

Option 1 allows you to meet individually and privately with each athlete. This option might soften the disappointment for those not selected, especially if you can suggest ways for them to improve or other places they might play (e.g., a community club). This option requires more of your time and an open communication and management style. Option 2 is the stricter option and gives complete control and responsibility to the coach. This option might be appropriate if athletes know in advance that making the team is not automatic and understand the process of team selection.

☐ *Coach A's rule*: To inform athletes of team selection, the coach will meet individually with each athlete to explain the reasons the athlete was or was not selected.

☐ *Coach B's rule*: The coach will post a list of names of athletes selected for the team. The coach's decision is final.

Besides making decisions about awards, your starting lineup, and playing time, you will at some point have to make decisions about disciplining your athletes. Sometimes these decisions will be difficult.

Disciplining Athletes

An important part of sport is teaching young people important life skills, such as taking responsibility and facing consequences for their actions. Sometimes a young person might not know that he or she has broken a rule or acted inappropriately. It might be unwise to jump to conclusions before exploring what happened with the athlete(s) involved. Think of a recent situation on your team that you did not witness, such as a fight or disagreement between two athletes. Did the two involved have different perspectives on what happened? Think of an athlete who might have unintentionally broken a rule without realizing it. Allowing the athlete to explain his or her perspective might help you see the incident in a different light. If disciplinary action is warranted, explaining clearly to the athlete the reasons that action is being taken helps reinforce and link actions to consequences. One hopes this would help the athlete avoid repeating the same actions in the future.

Option 1 requires the coach to consider the facts and different viewpoints before acting. This option requires the coach to clarify to the athlete how and why his or her action was inappropriate. Because this option requires the coach to take the time to investigate infractions and discuss the matter with the athlete, your school must have a discipline committee. Option 2 gives all the power to the coach and none to the athlete, who must accept the coach's decision. You might choose this option if strict control is essential on your team or if there is no mechanism for appeal. This option, however, might violate school rules and the expectation of due process. This option might also discourage athletes who feel unjustifiably punished.

☐ *Coach A's rule*: The coach should not take disciplinary action against athletes without first discussing the situation with the athletes and any witnesses (if relevant) to hear their viewpoints. If disciplinary action is warranted, the coach should explain to the athlete the reasons for such action and how the athlete can remedy the situation that required disciplinary action to be taken.

☐ *Coach B's rule*: The coach is responsible for enforcing team rules and for disciplining athletes who break the rules. The coach's decision about disciplinary action is final.

To summarize, thus far in this chapter we have discussed rule options relating to the five moral values of respectfulness, responsibility, caring, honesty, and fairness. As in the last chapter on athletes' attitudes and behavior, this chapter started with the moral value of respect and offered examples to help you develop policies and rules to clarify your team's and community's expectations about self-respect, respect for athletes and others involved in sport, and respect for the environment and for the rules and traditions of the game. A coach who respects his or her athletes and their families, as well as the game's rules and traditions, is usually one who acts responsibly, cares about his or her team and its members, and acts with honesty, loyalty, fairness, and integrity in most of life's endeavors, including sport. Let's now discuss rules for coaches relating to the final moral value, being a good citizen, which we defined earlier as being a good role model, being informed about lawful and ethical behavior, obeying laws and rules, cooperating and contributing to the community, and avoiding and discouraging substance abuse.

POLICIES ABOUT GOOD CITIZENSHIP

Good citizenship involves following rules, both written and unwritten, and playing within the spirit of the game. Some aspects of good citizenship overlap with other moral values (e.g., respect and responsibility). Because athletes, coaches, and others involved in sport are role models and are often idolized or emulated by young people, communities expect good citizenship from athletes and coaches.

Consider the aspects of good citizenship that you value in your athletes and in other coaches. Whom do you consider to be good ambassadors for your sport? These people are probably those who live up to the expectations of the other moral values but who also add an extra dimension to their involvement in sport. Examples of that extra dimension might be demonstrating good sportsmanship regardless of outcome, being active in charity or community work, taking time to talk with fans and work with young athletes, cooperating with the media, and actively promoting the sport. Sometimes members of the media focus on the bad behavior of athletes and coaches and ignore the "good news" stories. Good citizenship is often quiet in its methods but goes a very long way toward respecting one's sport and building personal development.

☐ *Coach A's policy introduction*: The coach should be a good citizen and role model.

☐ *Coach B's policy introduction*: Sport is an important part of the school and local community, and coaches are admired and emulated by many in the community. The team values striving for excellence, good citizenship, and contributing to the community. The coach should exhibit good citizenship and should actively encourage good citizenship among athletes.

Striving for Excellence

Although some say that sport is about winning, most acknowledge that sport is really about striving for excellence, the best performance possible regardless of the outcome. Consider some of your team's or athletes' best performances—did they always result in a win? How do you acknowledge excellence in your athletes? How do you encourage your athletes to recognize excellence among their peers?

The first option might be assumed for most coaches. The second option underscores the expectation of the coach to establish a team atmosphere in which all athletes are encouraged to strive for excellence and continue to improve, regardless of the level of competition or skill and the team's objectives. You might consider the best ways for your athletes to acknowledge their teammates' efforts (e.g., informally during and after games or more formally during a team meeting).

☐ *Coach A's rule*: The coach should encourage all athletes to strive for excellence.

☐ *Coach B's rule*: The coach should encourage athletes to continually improve and to strive for excellence. The coach should acknowledge effort and outstanding performance regardless of outcome (i.e., winning or losing).

Continually striving to improve is an accepted part of sport and is an often-mentioned life skill many offer as justification for public support of sport. Sometimes a community asks or expects a coach to contribute to the community or to "give something back" in return for its support.

Contributing to the Community

Coaches can build on their recognition and standing in the community to advance community ideals or projects. Being a positive role model for young people is one of the most powerful ways to give something back to the community. You might wish to include a rule that encourages or requires coaches to become involved in community activities. In a small community, most coaches probably become involved through their own families. In larger communities or large schools, community involvement might be part of the coaching contract.

Option 1 simply suggests that coaches should consider becoming involved in community activities. If you are a volunteer coach or one who receives only nominal remuneration, you are already contributing to the community, and the community might not expect much more from you. The second option is more of a requirement and might best suit teams with professional coaches or when the coach is well known or influential in the community. Communities that support sport (through taxes, sponsorship, facilities, etc.) might expect the coach (and athletes) to demonstrate an appreciation of their support by becoming involved in community activities.

☐ *Coach A's rule*: The coach is encouraged to become active in voluntary community activities.

☐ *Coach B's rule*: The coach will participate in one or more voluntary community activities during the season.

Many schools and clubs have policies restricting or banning tobacco use and substance abuse by their athletes and (sometimes) coaches. These policies are consistent with a general philosophy that values healthy behavior as an integral part of sport.

A Coach's Use of Tobacco, Alcohol, or Controlled Substances

If we accept that a coach has a responsibility to act as a positive role model, it makes sense that at least some of the team rules on tobacco use and substance abuse will also apply to the coach.

Consider possible problem areas that might require you to take action in regard to tobacco use or substance abuse. First, you might be expected to enforce your team's policies on athletes' use of these substances. Second, you might have to consider your own habits—if you smoke cigarettes or consume alcohol, for example—and ask yourself how appropriate they are for someone viewed as a role model for young athletes.

The Coach's Role in Enforcing Team Rules About Controlled Substances

First, consider what role a coach should play in enforcing rules and discouraging use of tobacco and substance abuse in athletes. The first option is minimal and implies that the coach will act consistently with and support the team's rules. Because it leaves open the issue of who is responsible for enforcing the rules, this option places the coach in a somewhat neutral position. You might choose this option if abuse is unlikely or if your team or organization has a system to enforce rules regarding controlled substances. The second option requires the coach to take a more active role in enforcing the rules, helping to educate athletes, and preventing them from abusing controlled substances.

☐ *Coach A's rule*: The coach will support the team's rules on tobacco use and substance abuse.

☐ *Coach B's rule*: The coach is responsible for enforcing the team's rules on tobacco use and substance abuse. The coach should take an active role in discouraging athletes' use of tobacco and controlled substances and in ensuring that athletes using such substances are enrolled in preventive counseling or educational programs. The coach is responsible for reporting any infringements of the school's (or organization's) rules on tobacco or substance abuse by athletes to proper authorities.

Tobacco and Alcohol

Consider whether you want to have rules to guide the behavior of the coaching staff. Your decision might depend on the community's expectation of coaches as role models and the general perceptions and acceptance of smoking, drinking alcohol, and using other substances.

Option 1 allows coaches to use tobacco or alcohol in the presence of athletes only as permitted for other adults. For example, the coach might smoke in designated smoking areas. This option would also permit the coach to smoke or drink in school or team events not involving students. Option 2 limits the coach's use of substances to legal and responsible consumption in the social context outside of practice, competition, and other organized events. This option might be most appropriate in communities with high expectations of the coach as a positive influence on young people.

☐ *Coach A's rule*: The coach may use tobacco products or alcohol in designated areas and according to venue rules in the presence of athletes.

☐ *Coach B's rule*: The coach should not use tobacco products or consume or be under the influence of alcohol in the presence of athletes or when involved in any team or school (organization) activity.

Controlled Substances

A controlled substance was defined in chapter 3 as any drug that can be used in a manner deemed dangerous to the user or that is illegal to possess or use without a prescription provided to the user by a medical practitioner.

Option 1 restricts the coach from using or possessing controlled substances in team or school activities. Because this rule does not apply to the coach's own time, it is easier to enforce than the second option. You might choose this option when the coach is unlikely to encounter athletes in social activities outside of sport. Option 2 is stricter and forbids the coach from using controlled substances at any time, both in and out of organized activities. You might find this option difficult to enforce. It might best suit a smaller community where there is a chance that athletes and coaches could encounter each other outside of organized sport. You might also consider your contractual arrangements with coaches. Does your school or organization consider substance abuse as grounds for dismissal? Also consider the legality of restricting the coach's behavior when he or she is not directly involved with the team.

☐ *Coach A's rule*: The coach should not consume, use, be under the influence of, possess, distribute, or sell any controlled substance, any performance-enhancing substance, or drug-related paraphernalia at any school (or organization) event or activity.

☐ *Coach B's rule*: The coach should not consume, use, be under the influence of, possess, distribute, or sell any controlled substance, any performance-enhancing substance, or drug-related paraphernalia at any time during the competitive season. The coach who supplies a controlled substance to an athlete will be disciplined.

Coach's Exercise

Does your team currently have a code of conduct (or ethics or behavior) for coaches? If so, look closely at the code. Does it include at least one statement that relates directly to each of the six moral values? If not, suggest additions to your code of conduct to include the moral value(s) not currently addressed. If your team does not have a code of conduct, write a draft and decide how you will circulate it and obtain feedback (see suggestions in chapter 2). Then get feedback and incorporate it as appropriate.

SUMMARY

Continuing to build on the framework of the six moral values (respectfulness, responsibility, caring, honesty, fairness, good citizenship), in this chapter we have discussed options for your team policies and rules relevant to coaches.

When choosing your policies and rules for coaches, you need to consider your team's philosophy and your own personal philosophy about sport as well as your team's situation (e.g., athletes' ages, level of skill and competition, resources). In some situations, coaches play an important role in teaching athletes both sport skills and life skills. Coaches can be prominent figures within a community, leading to higher expectations of them as role models and specialists in their sport. In other situations, a community might have lower expectations regarding their coaches' behavior, expertise, and role in developing talent in young athletes. Your team's philosophy, focus, and objectives, as well as the role of the coach, should be reflected in your policies and rules about coaches.

You should also consider how well your policies and rules regarding coaches match your policies and rules for athletes, as discussed in chapter 3, and for others involved in sport. As mentioned before, good policies have a sense of consistency or logic that makes it easy for people to see the reasons behind the rules you adopt.

Sample Codes of Conduct for Coaching

Coach A's Choices

As a coach, I will display the highest ethical and professional standards in all situations. As coach of the team, I promise to behave in ways consistent with the following values:

Respectfulness

- Treat athletes with respect; avoid treating athletes harshly.
- Question or react emotionally to an official's decision only if this reaction does not disrupt the game or show disrespect to the official or opposing team.
- Discourage athletes from criticizing the officials.
- Shake the opposing team's coach's hand before and after the game.
- Talk respectfully to and about parents, athletes, and opposing teams.
- Accept victory with modesty and defeat with dignity.
- Maintain a professional relationship with all athletes.
- Treat all personal information about an athlete confidentially.

Responsibility

- Be a positive role model for athletes.
- Be punctual and attend all practices and games.
- Use a reasonable amount of physical exercise within the athlete's capacity as discipline only to allow the athlete to regain fitness or catch up on lost sessions.
- Encourage student athletes to achieve academically.
- Act in a way that reflects positively on the school and community.
- Dress neatly, as appropriate for the activity and weather.
- Pursue other sport interests only if they do not cause a conflict of interest.

Caring

- Encourage all athletes to work together as a team and contribute to team effort.
- Encourage an injured or ill athlete to seek medical advice.

Honesty

- Be honest in all verbal and written communication with athletes, parents, and others involved in sport.
- Comply strictly with league rules about recruiting athletes; use only honest means to recruit athletes.
- Be loyal to the team and consider the team's needs ahead of my own personal interests.

(continued)

(continued)

Fairness

- Play by the written rules of the sport.
- Demonstrate good sportsmanship in all team activities.

Good citizenship

- Encourage all athletes to strive for excellence.
- Support the team's rules on tobacco and alcohol use and substance abuse.

Coach B's Choices

Coaches have a strong influence on young athletes and should act as positive role models for the young people they come in contact with.

As a coach, I will display the highest ethical and professional standards in all situations. I will remember that sport is a game and that young people participate to have fun, develop social and physical skills, and learn important life lessons. As coach of the team, I promise to behave in ways consistent with the following values:

Respectfulness

- Treat athletes respectfully, praise their efforts, and actively encourage athletes to work cooperatively through positive words and examples.
- Use constructive criticism and positive language; avoid excessively harsh criticism when coaching or disciplining an athlete.
- Cooperate with officials' decisions and not argue with, question, or indicate disagreement with any official's decision.
- Actively discourage athletes from criticizing or talking negatively about officials; discipline athletes who publicly criticize officials.
- Show respect for opponents by speaking cordially with and shaking the hand of the opposing coach before and after the game.
- Use positive words, even when being critical, and avoid vulgar or offensive language or gestures and aggressive or taunting actions or language when involved in any sport activity.
- Speak positively of the opposing team's play, regardless of outcome.
- Meet with parents as needed and answer parents' questions respectfully and honestly.
- Ensure that facilities, equipment, and uniforms are treated with respect and care by the athletes and others involved in sport.
- Contain my emotions both in victory and defeat.
- Maintain a professional relationship with all athletes; avoid engaging in conduct, gestures, actions, or comments of a sexual nature with any athlete; report any incident of sexual harassment to the appropriate authorities.
- Treat confidentially all personal information about an athlete and not discuss it with anyone else without permission from the athlete.

Responsibility

- Be a positive role model for athletes and always act in the best interest of athletes' health, safety, and well-being.
- Fulfill my commitments by being punctual, attending all practices and games, arranging for alternative supervision or coaching if I cannot attend a practice or game, and except in cases of extreme or unpredicted difficulty, remain in the position through the end of my contract.
- Not use physical exercise as a form of punishment or discipline in any situation.
- Provide athletes and parents a written description of expectations at the start of the season and meet with athletes and parents before the season starts to discuss these expectations.
- Take an active role in ensuring that all student athletes meet the minimum academic eligibility requirements; monitor grades of struggling student athletes.
- Act in the best interest of the school and community; actively promote a positive image of the school and community.
- Maintain a positive relationship with the local media and provide the media with accurate information about the team's activities.
- Not participate in or display violent behavior or incite athletes or spectators to act violently; discourage or prevent violent behavior during any sport activity.
- Dress professionally at all team activities and wear a suit or team uniform for games.
- Avoid any real or apparent conflict of interest by avoiding commitments or relationships that might prevent me from effectively performing my coaching obligations; declare any possible conflict of interest in advance.

Caring

- Teach athletes to cooperate with and to care about teammates, actively encourage athletes to play for the good of the team, and discipline athletes who act selfishly.
- Consider my athletes' health, safety, and well-being as top priorities; encourage athletes to look out for one another.
- Not permit an injured or ill athlete to practice or compete unless cleared by a physician or athletic trainer.

Honesty

- Check all facts discussed or included in written communication with athletes, parents, and others involved in sport; not withhold any relevant information from an athlete or parent.
- Be loyal to the team and school and put the team's interests ahead of personal interests and glory.
- Play strictly by both the written and unwritten rules without ever bending or knowingly breaking a rule to gain an advantage.

(continued)

(continued)

- Not gamble or bet on the outcome of any sporting activity, regardless of sport or level of play (i.e., amateur, school, community, professional).

Fairness

- Play by the written rules of the sport, ensure that competition is fair, and never evade or bend rules to the team's advantage (or allow athletes to do so).
- Act as a role model of good sportsmanship and encourage athletes to demonstrate good sportsmanship by acknowledging sportsmanlike behavior.

Good citizenship

- Encourage athletes to continually improve and to strive for excellence; acknowledge effort and outstanding performance regardless of outcome.
- Participate in one or more voluntary community activity during the season.
- Enforce the team's rules on tobacco use and substance abuse; play an active role in discouraging athletes' use of tobacco and controlled substances and in ensuring that athletes using such substances are enrolled in preventive counseling or educational programs.
- Not use tobacco products or consume or be under the influence of alcohol or any controlled substance in the presence of athletes, or provide these to athletes, when involved in any team or school activity.

Now that you have read the codes of conduct written by coach A and coach B, it is time to write your own. Visit www.humankinetics.com/CoachesGuideToTeam Policies to create a code of conduct. You will also find other helpful documents to use for your team.

Selecting Team Policies for Parents, Spectators, Staff, and the Media

© Human Kinetics

The last few seconds of a basketball game are ticking off the clock at the finals of a major tournament. It has been a close, hotly contested game since the starting buzzer with both teams matching baskets throughout. The two teams have played beyond anyone's expectations, and the atmosphere is electric. Your key player—your go-to guy at crunch time—has fouled out, and your team is down by one point. The replacement has just been fouled and now has two free throws, which can tie the game and send it into overtime or give your team the lead. The player misses both shots, and your team goes home with a tough loss.

Let's stop now and consider how various people—the parents, other spectators, volunteers, and the media—might react to this outcome. Sitting in the crowd with your ears open, what comments might you hear? "He choked." "Even I could have made one free throw. How could he miss them both?" How many people in the crowd would you hear saying things like, "Tough spot. He tried his best" or "It must be rough to make free throws under such pressure" or "What a game! Both teams should be proud of how they played."

How do you think the local media might report the game? Would they report simply on one player's failure in the final few seconds, or would they focus on the skill and spirit of both teams throughout the entire game?

If that were your son or daughter who missed those free throws, what would you say to him or her after the game?

The way that parents, spectators, volunteers, and the media interact with sport varies widely and can be a powerful positive or negative force depending on their expectations of "their" team. You might not be able to dictate or control how these people think and talk about your team, but you might be able to communicate a certain expectation about their behavior when involved in sport.

In chapter 5 you will learn about creating and choosing sport policies for parents, volunteers and support staff, and the media. This chapter continues using the framework of the six moral values: respectfulness, responsibility, caring, honesty, fairness, and good citizenship.

SELECTING POLICIES AND RULES FOR PARENTS

Parents can be your greatest allies; they help your team in many ways: encouraging their children, paying their children's expenses, providing transportation, organizing awards functions, fund-raising, and serving as fans, assistant coaches, or managers. Their attitudes toward sport, both positive and negative, can make a big difference to team cooperation, spirit, and discipline.

Think about the parents of some of the athletes you have coached and how their attitudes and willingness (or lack thereof) to help affected your athletes and team. Can you recall a parent whose optimism or encouraging words persuaded a discouraged athlete to keep trying despite setbacks? How many of your athletes' parents regularly volunteer for demanding but unrewarded roles such as laundering uniforms, transporting athletes to tournaments, assembling team records, keeping score in games, or soliciting sponsorship?

Most parents are cooperative and have balanced and positive attitudes toward sport, but the occasional disruptive or abusive parent (sometimes called the "ugly parent") focuses attention on the inappropriate behavior of a few. You can probably recall parents who questioned your team selection criteria or felt compelled to share their ideas about team strategy, or whose overeager commentary at games verged on abuse of officials and opponents. How about the parent who seems to take the sport more seriously than his or her child does? Have you ever observed the devastating effect of a parent's negative comment about his or her child's performance? There are even extremes of parental behavior, such as parents from opposing teams who physically fight with each other, sometimes with disastrous consequences, over the outcome of a game.

In selecting your team policies for parents, you might consider the following:

- The age and skill level of your athletes.
- How much time do you want to spend meeting with parents?
- How important is parental input into your team's activities?
- Is there a history of strong parental support or inappropriate parental behavior in your sport or organization?
- Do parents in your school have particular expertise that might be useful?

Respectfulness

To be consistent with policies on respect for others such as athletes and coaches, you might have a general policy statement about the team's expectations of respectful behavior by parents.

☐ *Coach A's policy introduction*: Parents should show self-respect and respect for athletes, coaches, officials, and others involved in our sport.

☐ *Coach B's policy introduction*: Our team believes that respect is an integral part of sport. All parents are expected to act with respect and dignity and have the right to expect others to treat them similarly. Parents should demonstrate self-respect and act respectfully at all times toward everyone involved in sport, including athletes, coaches, other parents, support staff, officials, opponents, volunteers, and spectators.

Parents' Respect for the Game

Just as athletes and coaches become emotionally involved in a contest, parents too can feel the highs and lows of close competition. It sometimes seems that some parents react with more emotion than the athletes or coaches do. Expecting parents to show respect and dignity in both victory and defeat can go a long way in setting an example of restraint and decorum for your young athletes and for the community.

Option 1 is fairly minimal. The word "respectful" carries different meanings for different people. Although you might assume that most parents would understand what respectful behavior involves, you might consider defining or giving simple examples. Option 2 more clearly defines respectful behavior and the situations in which it applies. This option also gives responsibility to parents for teaching respect to their children.

☐ *Coach A's rule*: Parents should act respectfully in both victory and defeat.

☐ *Coach B's rule*: Parents should show respect to their team and to the opposing team, officials, and spectators in all situations and regardless of the outcome of a competition. Parents should avoid excessive displays of emotion, both when winning and losing. Parents should teach their children to respect their opponents and to "pursue victory with honor" by emphasizing the importance of character, sportsmanship, and the six moral values of respectfulness, responsibility, caring, honesty, fairness, and good citizenship.

Parents' Respect for Their Children and Other Athletes

Do you know parents who seem to live vicariously through their children's sporting achievements and always demand that their children perform at a higher level? Have you ever observed the devastating effect of a parent's negative comments about his or her child's performance? This parent rarely praises performance, choosing rather to focus on what the child didn't do or achieve.

Or how about the opposite—the parents with such low expectations that they deflate their children's self-esteem and confidence?

Think about your team leaders, the athletes who not only perform well under pressure but who encourage their teammates and lead by example. Did they learn any of these skills from their parents' approach to sport?

Organizations such as Mom's Team (MomsTeam.com) and the CHARACTER COUNTS! Coalition (charactercounts.org) emphasize the importance of parents using positive words, praising efforts rather than focusing on outcomes, being a good listener, and empathizing with their children when discussing their sport participation. Although you cannot dictate how parents talk about sport, you can offer some suggestions to help parents have constructive conversations with their children.

Parents' Comments About Their Children's Performance   Think about why adolescents participate in sport. They are mainly in it for fun, social aspects, and to test themselves. The overzealous parent who overemphasizes performance and winning at the expense of self-improvement and enjoyment exhibits many traits contrary to the concept of "pursuing victory with honor." Such a person can make your task much harder.

As mentioned in the previous section, it's difficult to dictate or restrict how parents talk about their own children's performance. Similarly, you cannot strictly enforce rules about how parents talk about others involved in sport. However, you can convey that negative comments are counterproductive and contrary to the concepts of respect and victory with honor.

Obviously, changing the habits of some parents is difficult, perhaps impossible, to enforce. Option 1 is a simple suggestion about avoiding harsh parental criticism. Option 2 is more prescriptive but also presents suggestions about constructive ways to talk about sport. Some parents might find this option too prescriptive or intrusive. If you include such a rule, you might think about the best way to explain why you've included it and to give some examples, perhaps in a preseason meeting or in a newsletter to parents.

☐ *Coach A's rule*: Parents should try to use positive words when discussing their children's performance.

☐ *Coach B's rule*: Parents should listen to their children's views and use positive words when discussing their children's participation in sport. Parents should avoid using negative words to criticize performance and outcome and instead should praise effort and encourage their children's enjoyment and improvement.

COACHING TIP

"I allow parents to attend practice, but they must relinquish the role of parent. They must take on the role of a student manager and help the team. This often involves running and monitoring and being actively involved."

—Tim DeBerry, cross country and track and field coach, Von Steuben High School, Chicago, Illinois

Parents' Comments About Other Athletes, Coaches, and Officials   Have you ever observed the parent whose actions or attitudes seemed to undermine your efforts to instill respect and discipline among your athletes? Imagine the conflict of emotions that an athlete might feel if he or she had to listen to a parent constantly disparage your coaching skills, team strategy, player selection, or the abilities of other athletes.

Option 1 is simpler and only expects that parents will not show disrespect in front of their children. Parents who understand the concepts of victory with honor, fair play, and the spirit of the game will understand the subtle message behind this rule. This option might work in programs where parents have few opportunities to interact with coaches and officials. Option 2 is more prescriptive and clearly states that parents should show respect by accepting decisions without arguing. This option might work better in large programs or when a history exists of parents making negative comments to their children.

☐ *Coach A's rule*: Parents should speak respectfully about the athletes, coaches, and officials in front of their children.

☐ *Coach B's rule*: Parents should speak respectfully about and should not criticize athletes, coaches, or officials. Parents should accept decisions without arguing and support the efforts of coaches, officials, and other athletes.

Parents' Respect for the Coach

Even with the highest level of respect and support of parents, coaching can be a complex endeavor. Think how difficult it would be to maintain discipline and help your team achieve its objectives and potential if parents constantly disparaged, questioned, or undermined your efforts. Although you might hope that most parents would intuitively understand the need to trust and respect the coach, you might consider whether having a rule about this would help avoid the occasional parent who doesn't.

The first option is fairly minimal and understated. This option might suit programs in which parents do not have much opportunity to question the coach's decisions. Option 2 is more instructive and links respect with trust. It makes it clear that parents should trust the coach and not question his or her decisions about specific aspects of coaching (e.g., training, strategy, discipline).

☐ *Coach A's rule*: Parents should respect the coach.

☐ *Coach B's rule*: Parents should respect the coach and should trust his or her decisions about training, game strategy, team selection, and discipline.

Even if you have such a rule, some parents will want to meet with you to discuss any number of issues.

When Parents May Meet With the Coach   Parents might have useful skills or experience; a parent who was a former athlete might even become an assistant coach. On the other hand, have any parents tried to second-guess your decisions about playing time, team lineup, strategy, or your training plan for your athletes? You might consider whether you need rules about when and what parents may discuss with coaches. As a coach, you have many things on your mind before, during, and immediately after a practice or game. In a casual or impromptu meeting, you might not be able to give the parent the attention or answers he or she is seeking. You might consider how available you want to be for your athletes' parents: Do you want to always be accessible for informal chats, or would you rather maintain a more formal relationship with your athletes' parents?

Option 1 encourages parents to approach you any time that you're not directly supervising athletes. This option might be appropriate for less formal sport or when a close relationship exists among the coach, athlete, and parents (e.g., a personal tennis coach). This option might not work at more competitive levels or with larger programs. Option 2 is more restrictive, requiring the parent to seek a prearranged meeting and to state in advance the issues of concern. This option allows you to prepare for the meeting (e.g., assemble some statistics) and might diffuse or prevent any emotional responses. Your personality and management style might dictate which of these options would work best in your situation.

☐ *Coach A's rule*: A parent may talk with the coach at any time that the coach is not supervising practice and games.

☐ *Coach B's rule*: A parent wishing to talk with the coach must make an appointment in advance and state the reason for requesting the meeting.

What Parents May and May Not Discuss With the Coach   What do parents discuss with you when they ask to meet with you? Parents might have questions about their children's participation in sport or observations that may help the team. For example, a parent of a top high school athlete might want to know more about the college recruiting process and his or her child's chances of winning a scholarship. The parents of an injured athlete might want to know more about helping their child recover quickly. On the other hand, have you had to deal with parents who seem to want to offer you suggestions on how to coach or select your lineup?

Option 1 is minimal and openly invites parents to approach the coach about any issue. This option might work in small, informal programs or if you have infinite patience and a very open managerial style. Option 2 is much more restrictive, setting clear boundaries regarding what is appropriate for parents to question.

Again, in selecting your rule, you might consider how much time you have to devote to meeting with parents and whether such meetings are more likely to be helpful (i.e., considerate and positive parents) or counterproductive (i.e., parents constantly questioning your coaching decisions). If you are able to anticipate the questions and issues that parents might raise, you might provide this information to the parents through a preseason meeting or regular newsletters. For example, if each year your team has several athletes recruited by colleges, you might assemble an information packet for parents about the recruitment rules and process. If in a preseason meeting you can clearly state your philosophy and methods for starting team selection, parents might be less likely to question your decisions throughout the season.

 COACHING TIP

"I want parents to come to practice to see how hard we work, the skills we work on, and to gain a better understanding of the game. I find parents are less apt to complain when they witness the effort we put forth to improve."

—Jim Caputo, boys' soccer coach, Blue Ridge High School, Blue Ridge, Illinois

☐ *Coach A's rule*: A parent may discuss any issue with the coach.

☐ *Coach B's rule*: A parent may discuss with the coach only issues relating to his or her children. Issues that are inappropriate for a parent to discuss with a coach include playing time, team selection, game strategy, training drills, and other team members.

Parents Attending Practice

Some parents like to attend practice. Some have an active interest in the skills their children learn. For others, attending practice might be a way to connect with their children or to maintain control over them. A parent who regularly attends practice can better understand his or her child's experience with sport. On the other hand, parental presence can sometimes distract a child or even interfere with practice. Have you coached athletes who seem to lose concentration when their parents are watching?

Option 1 allows parents to take a direct interest and volunteer to help in practice. If you choose this option, however, you should be prepared for the possibility of attracting the occasional meddlesome or overprotective parent. Option 2 is restrictive and might be appropriate when there is a history of parental interference or children being distracted by their parents' presence.

☐ *Coach A's rule*: Parents may attend practice.

☐ *Coach B's rule*: Parents may not attend team practice.

Parents' Language and Actions During Sports Activities

Young people model their language and behavior on how they see adults act in various situations, especially those charged with emotion. You have probably coached athletes whose behavior was explained immediately on meeting their parents.

Chapter 3 provided some examples of disrespectful language, such as profanity; lewd chants, cheers, or gestures; booing or heckling of opponents or officials; and taunting or name calling. If we expect athletes and coaches to act and talk respectfully, then it's logical that we should expect the same of parents, the most important role models for young people.

Option 1 is probably the bare minimum if you expect your athletes themselves not to use profanity and abusive behavior. The word "abusive" might be open to interpretation in different situations. Whereas most understand what profanity means, you might need to give specific examples of abusive language or gestures to avoid. Option 2 includes both positive ("use positive words") and negative phrasing ("avoid using vulgar or offensive language"). Your choice might depend on the severity of your rules on offensive language and actions for athletes (discussed in chapter 3) and coaches (discussed in chapter 4). You might also consider how many parents attend practices and matches and how noticeable and influential their comments or actions are likely to be.

☐ *Coach A's rule*: Parents should avoid using profanity or abusive language or gestures at games or matches.

☐ *Coach B's rule*: Parents should use positive words, even when being critical, and should avoid using vulgar or offensive language or gestures and aggressive or taunting actions or language at any game or match.

Parents' Behavior During Competition

The vast majority of parents act appropriately during competition. However, enough appalling incidents of parents overreacting either verbally or physically have occurred to cause concern for anyone involved in youth sport. Closely contested matches can ignite emotions among both teams and parents. Think of how distracted or embarrassed your athletes would be if their parents acted disrespectfully or violently during a game. Would such behavior affect your team morale? How would it reflect on the image of your school?

Parents Coaching From the Sidelines   Have you ever coached a team with parents who constantly shouted instructions during a game? Young athletes can find this kind of interference confusing and distracting; they might not realize the instructions are coming from someone other than the coach, or the instructions might contradict your strategy. Done to excess, parental commentary can undermine your authority with the team.

Option 1 allows parents to instruct from the sideline (assuming that this is permitted by the rules of the sport). It is natural to shout "Shoot it!" or "Catch it!" in the heat of a game, and you probably don't want to make parents afraid to cheer their team. Option 2 makes it clear that only you are to give instructions to athletes, especially if the rules of the sport do not permit parental coaching from the sideline. Some parents might find this option overly intrusive, say if their child is injured or ill. If you choose to include such a rule, you might consider ways to let parents know what is and is not acceptable. For example, you might permit parents to ask their injured or ill child about whether he or she can continue playing or to make general encouraging comments such as "Rebound!" In contrast, you might limit parents making specific comments about strategy or plays, such as "Guard player X" or "Hit the ball deep" and calls normally made by the official (e.g., calling ball four).

☐ *Coach A's rule*: Parents may encourage their children from the sideline during the game.

☐ *Coach B's rule*: Parents are not permitted to talk directly to or give instructions to any athlete, including their own child, at any time during a game.

Coach's Exercise

Consider how you would approach an overeager parent who constantly shouts out instructions to his child during a match or game. What would you discuss with this parent? What approach would you take to modify this parent's behavior during games? Write a list of items you would discuss with this parent and the outcomes you would like to see result from this meeting.

Parents' Contact With Officials and Opponents   There probably aren't many reasons why parents would need to speak with officials or members of the opposing team. Whether you think it is appropriate for parents to speak to officials and opponents probably depends on the venue and the level of competition.

Option 1 allows the parent some discretion in speaking with officials and coaches but makes it clear that any contact should be respectful. Option 2 might be more appropriate in larger programs or when a history of parental overreaction exists. Limiting parents from speaking with officials or others on the opponent's side might prevent spontaneous emotional responses and confrontation. It is probably impossible, though, to prevent all confrontations if a parent is determined to ignore the guidelines and rules.

☐ *Coach A's rule*: Parents should speak to officials or opposing players, coaches, parents, and fans only if needed and should do so respectfully.

☐ *Coach B's rule*: Parents may not talk directly with officials or opposing players or coaches at any time before, during, or after a game or match.

 COACHING TIP

"I say to parents, 'On a 100-problem test, if you missed only 2 questions, your score would be 98 percent, a solid A. So, if an official misses only 2 of 100 calls in a game, what should his or her grade be?'"

—**Phil Robbins, football and boys' track coach, Powell Valley High School, Big Stone Gap, Virginia**

What to Do About Disruptive Parents?

You may or may not have authority over the parent who acts inappropriately or who flouts the team's rules. If an athlete is performing well and follows team rules, it would be unfair to drop that player from your team because of his or her parent's behavior. Chances are, that athlete is embarrassed and would like his parents to keep quiet. There are many instances from international sport of overzealous parents who became disruptive and were ejected or barred from attending competition (professional tennis provides several examples).

Option 1 makes it clear that disruptive behavior is not welcome and that the parent is expected to exercise restraint. Option 2 is more explicit and clearly spells out the consequences of unruly behavior. If you are going to bar parents from attending, however, you and your school might have to think about enforcement if the parent decides to ignore your decision. Is hiring a security guard a realistic option?

☐ *Coach A's rule*: A parent who disrupts practice or games will be given a warning and asked to refrain from such behavior in the future.

☐ *Coach B's rule*: A parent who disrupts practice will be ejected from practice and barred from attending practice for the rest of the season. A parent who disrupts competition (e.g., by verbally or physically abusing any athlete, official, or any member of the opposing side or by using obscene language or gestures) will be ejected from the match and barred from attending the next two matches. A second incident of disruptive behavior will result in that parent being barred from matches for the remainder of the season. Incidents of physical violence will be referred to the police for further action.

Responsibility

An athlete participating in sport has both rights and responsibilities. Active, positive role modeling by parents helps to teach young people to recognize and accept responsibility. In some instances, parents must accept some aspects of responsibility toward sport, for example, by making sure their children attend class and maintain academic eligibility, have the necessary equipment and uniforms, and show up on time for practice and competition. Beyond that, parents can also do a lot to help athletes understand and accept the consequences of failing to accept responsibility.

☐ *Coach A's policy introduction*: Parents should act responsibly and encourage their children to act responsibly in all aspects of sports participation.

☐ *Coach B's policy introduction*: We believe that it is an honor and a privilege to participate in sport. Parents should be good role models, act responsibly, and actively teach their children to act responsibly in all aspects of sport.

Encouraging Academic Achievement

Parental support is important to academic success for student athletes, especially those struggling to maintain academic eligibility. Schools can provide some support in the form of counseling, tutoring, and summer school, but the student athlete's home environment can be a major influence, either positive or negative. If your program emphasizes education as the primary goal ahead of sports participation or has fairly high expectations for academic eligibility, you might consider a rule that reflects the importance of academic achievement.

Option 1 asks parents simply to encourage their children. Many parents understand the subtleties involved (e.g., checking that homework is done, monitoring grades) in promoting academic progress. You might choose this option for sports that have no rules about academic eligibility or in school districts that clearly emphasize academic achievement in other ways. Option 2 is more prescriptive and clearly defines ways that parents can help their children achieve academically. You might consider the wording of this rule in the context of your rules about academic eligibility (discussed in chapter 3), the emphasis placed on academic achievement in your school, and the history of parental involvement in academic programs at your school.

☐ *Coach A's rule*: Parents should encourage their children to attend school and to maintain academic eligibility.

☐ *Coach B's rule*: Parents should actively support their children's education and encourage their children to be students first and to achieve academically. Parents should support the enforcement of team rules on academic eligibility, including rules on attendance and grades.

Communicating About Changing Circumstances

Except when an athlete is ill or injured, you expect all players to attend all practices and games. You know, however, that sometimes a change in family circumstances (e.g., parental separation, illness, or change in a parent's work schedule) can influence an athlete's punctuality or commitment. Ideally, your athletes and their families are conscientious and considerate and would tell you of any changes that might affect the athlete's ability to be there when needed. Just in case, you might consider making this request during your preseason meeting with parents or through a written communication.

Option 1 is more general and requests that parents consider whether they should tell you about any changes in family circumstances that might make it difficult for the athlete to participate. Parents might be reluctant to share personal and family information unless necessary, and you will want to balance your need to know about these issues with their desire for privacy. This option allows the parent to decide if and how much to discuss with you. Option 2 is more explicit, and while it might help your program run efficiently, this option could be seen as intrusive by parents. Your choice might depend on the level of trust among you and your athletes and their families.

☐ *Coach A's rule*: Parents should consider whether the coach should be aware of any change in family circumstances that might affect their child's punctuality or attendance at practice or games.

☐ *Coach B's rule*: Parents must inform the coach of any change in family circumstances that might affect their child's punctuality or attendance at practice, games, matches, or meets.

Responsibility for Equipment and Uniforms

Sport is an expensive pastime that families, schools, and sponsors donate considerable funds to. Young people are not always aware of the costs of sport and the financial sacrifices that parents make to allow them to participate. You probably expect your athletes to be responsible for taking care of their equipment and uniforms (discussed in chapter 3). For sports involving expensive equipment, you might also expect parents to assume responsibility because they are legally and financially responsible for their children.

The first option is only a suggestion that parents should be aware of the need for athletes to care for their uniforms and equipment. This option says nothing about who is responsible for the uniform. This option might work in situations in which the athlete provides his or her apparel and equipment (e.g., swimming, golf, tennis) or if the athlete uses the team uniform and equipment only briefly and in controlled situations (e.g., one game per week). In the second option, athletes and parents are responsible for the uniforms and equipment issued to them. You might choose this option if your school has invested in expensive uniforms or equipment, which the athletes use extensively or keep for the entire season. Your choice will depend on factors such as whether athletes provide most or all of their own uniform or equipment, if athletes pay a fee to use the equipment or uniform for the season, and the cost and expected lifetime of the equipment and uniforms.

☐ *Coach A's rule*: Parents should encourage their children to take care of the team uniform and equipment.

☐ *Coach B's rule*: Parents and athletes are responsible for caring for the team uniform and equipment used during the season. Parents or athletes must pay the cost of repairing or replacing uniforms or equipment lost or damaged beyond that expected by normal use.

Discipline and Self-Control

As mentioned in previous chapters, sport would not exist without control. If we expect athletes and coaches to exercise self-control, then we should also expect parents to support the concept and, ideally, to act as positive role models.

The first option simply implies that parents can influence their children's behavior during sport and should act as positive role models of self-control. The second option has a higher expectation of parents to both teach their children appropriate self-control and to model control in their own behavior. This option also clarifies what is considered unacceptable behavior and implies that parents are responsible for ensuring that their children avoid behaving inappropriately.

☐ *Coach A's rule*: Parents should exercise self-control during practices and games.

☐ *Coach B's rule*: Parents should actively teach their children to exercise self-control in all sport-related activities. Parents themselves should exercise self-control and actively discourage their children from displaying excessive emotion, anger, or physical or verbal aggression.

Accepting Disciplinary Actions   It's a challenge to teach young people self-control and to enforce discipline, even with the support of parents and your club or school. Think of how difficult it would be if parents didn't actively support you and your policies or if they even sabotaged your efforts.

Option 1 allows parents to question your decision about discipline. You would have to be willing to take the time to meet with parents and feel comfortable explaining your decisions. Option 2 is more restrictive. You might consider your options in the context of your general policies on discipline and appeals. For example, if your discipline policy permits athletes to appeal your decisions, option 1 might allow you to explain your decision without the need for an appeal; option 2 would be inconsistent with a policy that permits appeals.

☐ *Coach A's rule*: Parents should support the coach's decisions on disciplinary action. A parent may make an appointment with the coach to discuss any disciplinary action involving his or her child.

☐ *Coach B's rule*: Parents should accept the coach's decisions on disciplinary action without question.

Caring

One would think that rules about caring would be self-evident to most parents. However, with all the pressures on athletes to perform and the possibilities of financial or other types of reward for star athletes, it's easy to see how some parents might lose sight of the importance of a caring environment for the entire team.

☐ *Coach A's policy introduction*: Parents should actively support the team and all athletes on the team.

☐ *Coach B's policy introduction*: Our team is committed to a caring environment in which each team member is a valued part of the team and parents encourage all team members to support each other.

Encouraging Cooperation

A caring environment is characterized by cooperation among all participants. Although working cooperatively seems natural for some, it requires a conscious effort to get all participants to contribute. Parents can be a major influence, both positively and negatively, in your success in building a sense of cooperation among your team members. Can you recall an uncooperative athlete whose behavior seemed entirely consistent with his or her parents' inability to understand the importance of cooperation in sport? Think of athletes you have coached who were very cooperative. They likely learned this attitude and behavior at home.

Option 1 is the minimum you might expect of your athletes' parents. Although they might not necessarily act cooperatively themselves, you hope they will at least support your efforts to build a cooperative team environment. You might select this rule if your sport is primarily an individual sport that requires little teamwork. The second option expects more of parents: that they support your efforts and actively teach their children about cooperation. Importantly, this option directly involves the parents in teaching their children about the balance between personal and team needs. This option might suit sports in which athletes spend a lot of time together in practice, games, and other activities.

☐ *Coach A's rule*: Parents should encourage their children to cooperate with their teammates in practice and games.

☐ *Coach B's rule*: Parents should teach their children to cooperate with, to demonstrate concern for, and to support all teammates. Parents should teach their children to look out for one another and to put the needs of the team ahead of personal glory.

 COACH'S HIGHLIGHTS

1. Coaching for over 25 years and enjoying it
2. Giving female athletes at our school more athletic opportunities
3. Having several of my former athletes become coaches
4. Establishing our programs as models for others in this state

—**Mark Logan, track and field and cross country coach, RHAM High School, Hebron, Connecticut**

Health and Well-Being

You might think that parents would always consider the health and well-being of their children as paramount. Despite their best intentions, however, parents themselves do not always recognize the importance of a healthy lifestyle or the best way to achieve good health for themselves and their children, as evidenced by the recent epidemic of overweight and obese children in developed countries, especially the United States.

Option 1 is a simple recommendation about health and assumes that parents understand what a healthy lifestyle does and does not involve. Option 2 defines more completely what a healthy lifestyle entails and places the obligation on the parents to monitor and influence their child's lifestyle. Some families might find this option instructive, while others might find it intrusive. You might also consider this rule in the context of your rules about smoking and alcohol and substance abuse (discussed in chapter 3).

☐ *Coach A's rule*: Parents should encourage their children to lead a healthy lifestyle.

☐ *Coach B's rule*: Parents should ensure that their children lead a healthy lifestyle, which includes getting enough sleep; eating a healthy diet; allowing time to recover from illness or injury; and avoiding unhealthy behaviors such as smoking, drinking alcohol, and using drugs or banned substances.

Medical Clearance

Most of us tend to think of adolescence as a healthy time, free from serious illness and disease. Some parents might not understand the medical implications of their children's participation in sport or might not be aware that an unknown condition might put a child at risk during sport. Some conditions are common (e.g., asthma) or temporary (e.g., viral infection), and others are rare but serious enough to require medical attention (e.g., Marfan syndrome).

Option 1 is a simple recommendation and would apply when medical clearance is not required for participation. You might choose option 2 for high-level sport or when your sports program requires medical clearance and the school does not pay for or provide the medical examination. Your insurance or risk-management policies might require you to adopt this option.

☐ *Coach A's rule*: Parents should encourage their children to be healthy and fit enough to participate in sport.

☐ *Coach B's rule*: Parents should ensure that their children are medically fit before joining the team. Parents are responsible for arranging and paying for medical clearance and a physical examination of their children by a medical practitioner, who must certify that the athlete is medically fit to participate.

Honesty

Sport for young people is built on honesty and integrity. Parents and the community place their trust in the coach's honesty, integrity, and competence to provide a safe learning environment for their children. You would hope that this trust is reciprocated, that you are able to trust your athletes' parents to act honestly and with integrity and to actively teach these qualities to their children.

☐ *Coach A's policy introduction*: Parents should be honest when dealing with the coach, team, school, and recruiters.

☐ *Coach B's policy introduction*: Our team believes that honesty and loyalty to the team are crucial aspects of sport. Parents are expected to act with honesty and integrity and have the right to expect that others will act similarly.

Honest Behavior

Imagine how difficult your job would be if you couldn't rely on your athletes' parents to be truthful about their children's health, experience, capabilities, and commitment. Perhaps you have had to work with such parents. For example, you might form your team on the assumption that all your athletes are eligible, only to discover later that you have been misled by parents about a certain player's residency.

The first option articulates the simple expectation that parents will be honest with you and your organization. You might choose this option if it's unlikely that parents will be dishonest or withhold information, or if it's unlikely to make much difference if they do. Option 2 requires a higher level of parental expectation and equates withholding information with lying. This option makes it clear that parents are expected to be honest and to volunteer relevant information. If you choose this option, you might also consider how to let parents know what information is relevant (health, residency, attendance, absences, etc.).

☐ *Coach A's rule*: Parents should be honest with the coach, school, medical and support staff, and recruiters.

☐ *Coach B's rule*: Parents should be open and honest with the coach, the school, medical and support staff, and recruiters. Parents should not lie or withhold information and should volunteer relevant information.

Loyalty to the Team

Loyalty to the team is an essential part of team culture and an important life skill that young people learn in sport. Loyalty, like integrity, is best learned through appropriate role models and positive reinforcement. You might consider having a rule for parents to get them to think about how they can contribute to teaching their children about the importance of loyalty to the team.

Option 1 simply asks parents to encourage loyalty in their children. The second option defines loyalty more explicitly in terms of the parents' role in teaching their children about the balance between personal glory and the team's needs. You might find this option better suited to team sports at a higher level or when you want your rules to help educate parents about the more subtle aspects of moral values.

☐ *Coach A's rule*: Parents should encourage their children to be loyal to the team.

☐ *Coach B's rule*: Parents should teach their children to be loyal to the team and to put the needs of the team ahead of personal glory and goals. Parents should model this behavior.

Fairness

Playing by the rules means different things to different people. Some might think they are playing by the rules as long as they are following the written regulations. Others realize that there are both written and unwritten rules and such a thing as playing within the "spirit" of the rules. The latter viewpoint acknowledges the more subtle aspects of sport, which not all parents understand. Some parents can be so focused on their child's success that they fail to see the wider perspective of the game's traditions and the spirit of the rules. Part of your job might be to educate parents about the importance of respecting the game's traditions, which may extend beyond adherence to the written rules.

The first option states a simple expectation that parents will support your effort to have athletes respect both the written and unwritten rules of their sport. Some parents, especially those unfamiliar with your sport, might not understand what the "unwritten rules," are and you may need to give examples in a meeting or in a written correspondence. Option 2 expects more of parents, both in their own behavior and in teaching their children about playing according to unwritten rules. This option might suit larger schools or sport at a higher level, in which athletes might be tempted to bend the rules to their advantage.

COACHING TIP

"Student athletes want someone to be in charge; they want to know what is acceptable and not acceptable. They don't want to be responsible for something an adult should do."

—Beth Sarnacki, outdoor track and field and cheer coach, Cromwell High School, Cromwell, Connecticut

☐ *Coach A's rule*: Parents should encourage their children to play fairly within the written rules of the sport.

☐ *Coach B's rule*: Parents should actively encourage their children to play by both the written and unwritten rules and within the spirit of the rules. Parents should encourage their children to avoid bending or knowingly breaking a rule or cheating to gain an advantage. Parents should applaud fair play and excellent performance of all players, even those on the opposing team. Parents should discourage gamesmanship, or using questionable means to win games.

Good Citizenship

We have defined "good citizenship" in the context of striving for and encouraging excellence, acting lawfully, and avoiding and discouraging abuse of substances such as tobacco, alcohol, and performance-enhancing and illicit drugs. Research shows that parental attitudes and behavior are the most important factors influencing risk-taking behavior by young people.

Striving for Excellence

Adolescents participate in sport for various reasons. Having fun, participating with their friends, and learning and mastering new skills are often more important than winning. It's easy for adults to forget the values of their children and focus too much on an outcome (i.e., winning, getting a scholarship) rather than the process (i.e., learning and improving). Helping parents acknowledge and understand that their children are motivated by factors besides winning might help your athletes achieve their own goals and be more satisfied with the outcome. This in turn is more likely to translate into a positive and cooperative attitude that helps your team achieve its goals.

The first option simply acknowledges the importance of helping athletes strive for excellence. It does not define excellence, and some parents might interpret the word only within the narrow context of winning. If you choose this option, you might consider explaining what excellence means to you personally and to the team. Option 2 is more educational because it explains what striving for excellence means in sport and gives constructive examples of how parents can support this value with their children. You might choose this option if your team has a history of parents taking sport too seriously.

☐ *Coach A's rule*: Parents should encourage their children to strive for excellence.

☐ *Coach B's rule*: Parents should encourage their children to continually improve and to strive for excellence. Parents should focus on and acknowledge their children's efforts, improvement, and outstanding performance regardless of outcome (i.e., winning or losing).

Parental habits strongly influence whether an adolescent or young adult smokes or consumes alcohol. Previous chapters have discussed the importance of role models and sport as a way to encourage healthy behavior in young people. If the health aspects of sport feature prominently in your team's objectives, you might consider whether you want to also have policies on parental smoking and drinking around your athletes.

Parents Supporting the Team's Policies on Tobacco and Controlled Substances

It's not always easy to enforce rules about tobacco and substance abuse in young people, many of whom are testing the limits of their independence and maturity. Parental support can make a big difference in the effectiveness of your policy. Think of how difficult it would be to enforce a zero-tolerance policy if parents do not support your rules. Regardless of parental behavior (i.e., whether they smoke or consume alcohol or other substances), one hopes they would support your team's policies about the use of substances by athletes.

Option 1 is fairly minimal. You might consider this approach if your rules for athletes and coaches are more liberal. Option 2 is stricter and expects more of parents. Parents should both support the coach and take an active role in keeping their children away from controlled substances. If you choose this option, you might consider holding meetings and distributing handouts to clarify your rules about tobacco and substance abuse.

☐ *Coach A's rule*: Parents should support the team's rules on tobacco use and substance abuse.

☐ *Coach B's rule*: Parents should support the enforcement of team rules on tobacco use and substance abuse. Parents should take an active role in discouraging their children's use of tobacco and controlled substances. Parents should accept the coach's disciplinary actions in breaches of the team's policies on tobacco and substance abuse.

Coach's Exercise

During a game last year, some parents of your players got into a fight with parents from an opposing team. Prepare for a preseason meeting with parents this year in which you want to try to prevent a repeat of this behavior.

This ends the discussion about rules for parental involvement in your sport. Before progressing to discuss rules for spectators, let's look at two sample codes of conduct for parents, one that coach A might choose and another that coach B might select.

Sample Codes of Conduct for Parents

Coach A's Choices

Parental support is important; parents are encouraged to become actively involved in their children's sport activities.

As a parent of a team member, I understand that I am expected to act with honor and dignity at all sporting events and to show self-respect and respect for athletes, coaches, officials, and others involved in sport. I will behave in ways that are consistent with the following values:

Respectfulness

- Act respectfully in both victory and defeat.
- Try to use positive words when discussing my child's performance.
- Respect the coach.
- Speak respectfully about athletes, coaches, and officials in front of my child.
- Avoid using profanity or abusive language or gestures at sport activities.
- Speak to officials or opposing players, coaches, parents, and fans only if needed and with respect.

Responsibility

- Encourage my child to attend school and to maintain academic eligibility.
- Consider whether the coach should be aware of any change in family circumstances that might affect my child's punctuality or attendance at practice or games.
- Encourage my child to take care of the team uniform and equipment.
- Support the coach's decisions on disciplinary action; seek to discuss with the coach any disciplinary action involving my child.

Caring

- Encourage my child to cooperate with teammates in practice and games.
- Encourage my child to lead a healthy lifestyle and to be fit and healthy enough to participate in sport.

Honesty

- Be honest with the coach, the school, medical and support staff, and recruiters.
- Encourage my child to be loyal to the team.

(continued)

(continued)

Fairness

- Encourage my child to play fairly within the written rules of the sport.

Good citizenship

- Encourage my child to strive for excellence.
- Support the team's rules on tobacco use and substance abuse.

Coach B's Choices

Sport is an important part of a young person's development and education. Our team values the development of good character through sport and the principles espoused in the six moral values: respectfulness, responsibility, caring, honesty, fairness, and good citizenship.

As a parent of a team member, I will act with respect and dignity and will demonstrate self-respect and act respectfully at all times toward everyone involved in sport, including athletes, coaches, other parents, support staff, officials, opponents, volunteers, and spectators. I will behave in ways that are consistent with the following values:

Respectfulness

- Show respect to athletes, opponents, officials, and spectators regardless of the outcome of a competition. I will avoid excessive displays of emotion and will teach my child to respect opponents and to pursue victory with honor.
- Listen to my child's views and use positive words when discussing his or her participation in sport. I will avoid using negative words to criticize performance and outcome and will instead praise effort and encourage my child's enjoyment and improvement.
- Speak respectfully about and avoid criticizing athletes, coaches, and officials. I will accept decisions without arguing and support the efforts of coaches, officials, and other athletes.
- Respect the coach and trust his or her decisions about training, game strategy, team selection, and discipline.
- Make an appointment with the coach if I wish to speak with him or her.
- Discuss with the coach only issues relating to my child and recognize that it is inappropriate for me to discuss playing time, team selection, game strategy, training drills, and team members other than my children.
- Not attend practice.
- Use positive words, even when being critical, and avoid using vulgar or offensive language or gestures or aggressive or taunting actions or language at any sport activity.
- Not talk directly to or give instructions to any athlete, including my own child, at any time during a game.
- Not talk directly with officials or opposing players or coaches at any time before, during, or after a game or match.

- Be ejected from practice or games and barred from attending practice or games if I disrupt practice or games by being abusive or using obscene language or gestures.

Responsibility

- Actively support my child's education and encourage him or her to be a student first and to achieve academically. I will support the enforcement of team rules on academic eligibility, including rules on attendance and grades.
- Inform the coach of any change in family circumstances that might affect my child's punctuality or attendance at practices, games, matches, or meets.
- Share responsibility with my child for caring for the team uniform and equipment and pay the cost of repairing or replacing uniforms or equipment lost or damaged beyond that expected by normal use.
- Actively teach my child to exercise self-control in all sport-related activities; discourage my child from displaying excessive emotion, anger, or physical or verbal aggression; exercise self-control myself when watching competition.
- Accept the coach's decisions on disciplinary action without question.

Caring

- Teach my child to cooperate with teammates, to demonstrate concern for them, and to support them. I will teach my child to put the needs of the team ahead of personal glory.
- Ensure that my child leads a healthy lifestyle, which includes getting enough sleep; eating a healthy diet; allowing time to recover from illness or injury; and avoiding unhealthy behaviors such as smoking, drinking alcohol, and using drugs or banned substances.
- Ensure that my child is medically fit before joining the team; arrange and pay for medical clearance and a physical examination of my child by a medical practitioner, who must certify that my child is medically fit to participate.

Honesty

- Be open and honest with the coach, the school, medical and support staff, and recruiters. I will volunteer relevant information and will not lie or withhold information.
- Teach my child to be loyal to the team and to put the needs of the team ahead of personal glory and goals. I will model this behavior myself.

Fairness

- Actively encourage my child to play by both the written and unwritten rules and within the spirit of the rules. I will encourage my child to avoid bending or knowingly breaking a rule or cheating to gain an advantage and will applaud fair play and excellent performance of all players, including those on the opposing team.

(continued)

(continued)

Good citizenship

- Encourage my child to continually improve and strive for excellence. I will focus on and acknowledge my child's efforts, improvement, and outstanding performance regardless of outcome (e.g., winning or losing).
- Support the enforcement of team rules on tobacco use and substance abuse. I will actively discourage my child's use of tobacco and controlled substances and will accept the coach's disciplinary actions in breaches of the team's policies on tobacco and substance abuse.

SELECTING POLICIES AND RULES FOR SPECTATORS

Fans can significantly influence a game's atmosphere and possibly even a game's result. Think about the home crowd advantage, through which your fans can motivate your team and intimidate opponents. Have you ever played an away game when the crowd was so hostile that your athletes were intimidated? Partisan crowds at matches played on "neutral" grounds can also make a difference—think of professional tennis or golf events at which fans favor one player over others. At the extremes are examples of crowds becoming unruly, even violent, before, during, or after a game. Crowds may even turn against their own team when dissatisfied with their performance.

If you create a set of rules or a code of conduct for spectators, you might consider how you would publicize this information. If your spectators all come from a defined group, say a school or club, you might consider including the information in posters, flyers, and newsletters and also posting it on a Web site. If your spectators come from a more diverse group, a spectator's code of conduct could be publicized in the media, printed on the back of tickets, or announced at the start of games.

Respectfulness

When hosting a competition, how would you like your fans to behave? You'd probably like to encourage and harness your fans' enthusiasm and use this to motivate your team. At the same time, you might not want their behavior to become a spectacle that distracts from the action on the field. You might not have a great deal of control over spectator behavior unless your spectators come from a common group. For example, if your fans are the friends and families of your players, you have the opportunity to communicate with them about their expected behavior. On the other hand, if your team attracts fans from a wider base, rules about fan behavior will likely have a more limited impact.

Spectators' Respect for the Team and Its Opponents

Fans love a winner, but the true test of their respect and loyalty is how they treat their team when it is losing in a game, going through a slump, losing key players because of injury, or going through a rebuilding phase. If your spectators come from a small community (i.e., mainly family and friends of your athletes), they are more likely to understand and sympathize with the ups and downs of sport. In contrast, fans with few personal connections with a team may not be as understanding.

Option 1 is very general and simply asks spectators to treat competitors on both sides with respect. This option might work when the sport has a tradition of decorum among spectators, such as in tennis, golf, and swimming. Option 2 is more restrictive and clearly spells out what is unacceptable. This option might be appropriate for sports that draw large audiences or when there is a history of unruly crowds. Some might consider this option "overkill" and unnecessary when there is no hint that anyone might act disrespectfully.

☐ *Coach A's rule*: Spectators should act respectfully toward all team members and opponents.

☐ *Coach B's rule*: Spectators should be good sports and accept victory and defeat with honor. Spectators should treat all participants with respect and refrain from disrespectful language, gestures, and actions directed at any participant including all athletes, coaches, officials, and other spectators. Disrespectful behavior includes violence, offensive language and gestures, profanity, taunts, trash talk, comments of a sexual nature, and demeaning cheers.

Interacting With Other Spectators

Research has shown that spectators can become as emotionally charged as players during a sporting event. Although players can actively release their emotion through exertion during the game, spectators are usually confined in crowded seats. Although most sporting events take place without problems, there are enough examples of spectator violence from school, club, and professional sport for you to consider whether you should have a rule about spectators interacting with others. Consider the level of competition, the number of fans who attend your games, their usual demeanor, the size and layout of the venue (e.g., do fans from opposing sides sit together or on opposite sides), and whether the venue has security to intervene if needed.

Option 1 is fairly low key and might suit sport in which spectators from opposing sides do not generally interact. Option 2 is more prescriptive in giving specific examples of unacceptable behavior. Some parents might be surprised to see such a rule if there's little risk or no history of inappropriate behavior by spectators.

☐ *Coach A's rule*: Spectators should display respect for other spectators.

☐ *Coach B's rule*: Spectators should display respect for other spectators. They should not insult, taunt, or fight or display verbal or physical aggression or act violently toward other spectators.

Spectators' Behavior Toward Officials

Have you been involved in a game or match in which fans expressed their frustration and dissatisfaction by abusing the officials? Previous chapters have discussed rules to ensure that coaches and athletes treat officials respectfully and

COACHING TIP

"Fun is the idea behind sport programs for most young people. They want to have fun. You can have fun, work hard toward a team goal, improve each individual's performance, and still be successful."

—Mark Logan, track and field and cross country coach, RHAM High School, Hebron, Connecticut

accept their decisions without dissent. It makes sense, then, that you might try to convey such ideals to your spectators as well. Of course, you have far less control over their behavior and attitudes than over those of your coaches and athletes.

Option 1 is more open to interpretation and asks spectators to exercise restraint and discretion. This option might work when the audience is small, sits far away from the officials, or usually acts appropriately. Option 2 is more prescriptive and clearly defines what is acceptable and not acceptable. This option might be difficult to enforce in large crowds (how would your team or organization deal with offenders)? You might consider ways for your coaches and athletes to let your spectators know that they enjoy their support when expressed positively.

☐ *Coach A's rule*: Spectators should exercise self-control when reacting to officials' decisions.

☐ *Coach B's rule*: Spectators should accept officials' decisions without dissent and should not "boo," throw items, taunt officials, or make offensive or obscene comments or gestures to officials.

Observing Pregame and Other Rituals

The pregame ritual is an established part of showing respect for everyone involved in sport, and, if it involves the national anthem or another cultural display, places sport in a wider context of regional or national identity. You might consider whether your team should have a specific rule about its expectation of spectator behavior during pregame rituals.

Option 1 is minimal; one would hope most people involved in sport would act this way without a reminder. The second option has a higher level of expectation that spectators should actively participate and watch rituals associated with the game. You might choose this option for larger programs, when your games attract large crowds, or if your games involve more than a simple pregame ritual such as singing the national anthem.

☐ *Coach A's rule*: Spectators should act respectfully during pregame rituals and half-time shows.

☐ *Coach B's rule*: Spectators should act respectfully during pregame rituals and should stand and join in singing the national anthem or other songs. Spectators should act respectfully during half-time shows or demonstrations.

Responsibility

Spectators come to games to be entertained and are expected to act responsibly. Spectator behavior, whether positive or negative, reflects back on your team. A community that expects its coaches and other adults to act as positive role models for athletes and other young people probably expects its spectators to do the same.

Acting Responsibly During Games

Spectators often sit near enough to the field of play to disrupt play. In some sports, spectators can interfere with and affect the outcome (e.g., the spectator who tackled the lead marathon runner at the 2004 Olympic Games in Athens just short of the finish). Some spectators' actions, such as throwing bottles, can injure athletes or officials; other actions, such as blowing a whistle or calling a ball "out," might confuse a participating player. Coaching is hard enough without having to worry about disruptive spectators.

Option 1 might suit venues where fans sit some distance from the field of play or when it's unlikely that fans might disrupt play. Option 2 might work better in sports that attract large crowds or in situations in which spectators are close or unruly enough to interrupt play. You might also consider this rule in combination with the rule on what to do about disruptive spectators, discussed later.

☐ *Coach A's rule*: Spectator.5s should not disrupt competition.

☐ *Coach B's rule*: Spectators should display self-control and act as positive role models for athletes and young spectators. Spectators should understand and follow the venue rules when attending competitions. Spectators should sit or stand only in designated areas and should not act in any way that disrupts play or that could injure a player, coach, official, or other spectator.

Spectators Attending Practice

You might decide that you want to have a rule about visitors at practice. Consider who might come to watch and why. A newcomer to your school might wish to watch to decide whether to join your team; your athletes' friends might attend out of curiosity or to support their friends; younger athletes might attend to learn from more experienced athletes or to watch their idols. You might also consider other factors, such as your own personal style, whether spectators distract your athletes, the space available to accommodate spectators, and whether other teams in your organization permit visitors at practice.

These options are similar to those proposed for parents, as discussed earlier in the chapter. Option 1 opens practice to anyone and might work if you have a lot of space so that spectators do not distract your athletes, or if you think others (e.g., younger athletes) might benefit by watching your team practice. Option 2 might be appropriate when you have limited space, when you want your athletes to focus without any distractions, or when there is a history of spectators disrupting your practice.

☐ *Coach A's rule*: Spectators may attend any practice.

☐ *Coach B's rule*: Spectators may not attend practice.

Dealing With Disruptive Spectators

How much authority do you have over spectators? Some sports or sport associations have rules about unruly behavior by spectators that can lead to ejection from a game and even barring further attendance for repeat offenders. The police might pursue some types of offenses, such as assault. However, it can be difficult to identify and document such behavior when you are dealing with a large crowd.

In deciding whether you want to have a rule dealing with unruly spectators, you might consider the size of crowds your sport attracts, where your team draws its fans from, whether there is a history of unruly behavior, and the resources available to monitor and enforce your rule.

Both rule options below make it clear that spectators are not to disrupt games or practice. The first option expects spectators to voluntarily monitor their own behavior. Option 2 is stricter and gives an expansive definition of disruptive behavior. This rule also lays the basis for barring repeat offenders from attending matches or practice. This option might work with larger programs or those that attract big crowds, especially partisan crowds, or when there is a history of spectators causing disruption. If you adopt this option, however, you need to consider how to enforce a ban against a disruptive spectator.

☐ *Coach A's rule*: A spectator who disrupts practice or games will be given a warning and asked to avoid such behavior in the future.

☐ *Coach B's rule*: A spectator who disrupts practice will be asked to leave and not to attend any more practices. A spectator who disrupts a competition will be ejected from the grounds. A second incident of disruptive behavior will result in that spectator being barred from competition for the remainder of the season. Disruptive behavior includes verbal or physical abuse, drunkenness, and offensive or obscene language or gestures.

Caring

As discussed earlier, rules about caring focus on cooperation, compassion, praise, and concern for health and safety. From the spectator's viewpoint, it might not always be apparent why a star player is on the bench at a critical time, why the coach has decided to call a certain play, or why athletes can't seem to score. In an ideal world, your fans trust the coach and athletes to always give their best; in reality, there are probably too many "armchair coaches" in the stands. As an adult and professional coach, you have the maturity to deal with spectators who don't always support your team. In contrast, your athletes might not have the experience or self-confidence to deal with negative attitudes expressed by spectators. You might consider having a simple rule to communicate your team's expectation of spectators' attitudes toward the team.

The first option asks spectators to show their support for the players regardless of whether they are winning or losing. From the athlete's viewpoint, this is minimum one might expect of loyal fans. Option 2 is more educational because it gives examples of the way you'd like your spectators to behave.

☐ *Coach A's rule*: Spectators should cheer for their players regardless of the likely outcome.

☐ *Coach B's rule*: Spectators should support and encourage their players and applaud their effort regardless of performance and the likely outcome of the match. Spectators should not encourage dangerous play that might cause injury to any player.

Honesty

Honesty involves integrity, loyalty, and playing according to the spirit of the rules. As mentioned before, loyalty is a vital part of sport and is needed to create a positive team culture. Honesty runs two ways: If we expect young athletes to demonstrate their loyalty by representing their school or club with pride and integrity, then the team can expect some degree of honesty and loyalty in return from its devoted fans. You might consider having a simple rule to help define your expectation of spectator loyalty.

Option 1 is minimal. You might choose this option for a team that does not draw big crowds. The second option gives a more expansive definition of loyalty and an expectation about respecting both written and unwritten rules. This rule educates spectators that their responses have the potential to influence athlete behavior on the field.

☐ *Coach A's rule*: Spectators should encourage athletes to play by the written rules.

☐ *Coach B's rule*: Spectators should be loyal to the team in either victory or defeat. Spectators should encourage athletes to play by the rules and honor the spirit of the rules of the sport. Spectators should not encourage or applaud players who bend the rules or who display dishonest or unsporting behavior.

Fairness

Fairness includes issues such as playing to the best of one's ability regardless of outcome; competing honestly and playing to win within the rules; and avoiding gamesmanship. Everyone involved in sport, including spectators, can influence how the concept of fairness is put into practice. For example, a young athlete might be tempted to act inappropriately by a crowd that cheers unfair play and gamesmanship. A young athlete would be much less likely to act inappropriately if he or she knew the behavior would attract no attention, or a negative response, from team supporters.

The first option is simple. You might choose this option when you are confident of your athletes' self-discipline despite the crowd response or if your team usually attracts very supportive spectators who understand the sport. Option 2 gives more direction to your spectators about the type of behavior you'd like to see and educates spectators about the value of sport beyond simply winning (e.g., acknowledging effort). Some might find this option too prescriptive, but you might choose it when you think your spectators need to consider the wider issues about the value of sport for young people.

☐ *Coach A's rule*: Spectators should encourage athletes and their team to play fairly.

☐ *Coach B's rule*: Spectators should acknowledge effort and outstanding performance by any athlete, including those on opposing team(s). Spectators should applaud when athletes play fairly and should not encourage or applaud unfair play.

Coach's Exercise

A local reporter has asked you for some information for an article about spectator behavior at games. Describe the importance of spectators to your team and the concept of home court advantage. Give some tips for ways that spectators can help your players perform their best.

Good Citizenship

Spectators expect athletes and coaches to strive for excellence; many in the community expect athletes to be good citizens and role models. If we expect athletes and coaches to demonstrate good character and to contribute to the community, then it's reasonable to expect the same from spectators. Consistent pressure to win at all costs and unruly behavior when fans are dissatisfied can put young athletes on the defensive, which is a distraction.

Depending on the venue where you compete and the size of the crowds your team attracts, you might feel you need another rule about spectator behavior during games to complement your rules about respect and responsibility. Here are two simple rule options about following venue rules and cooperating with security personnel. The first option is minimal and might suit teams that do not attract large crowds. Option 2 expects a lot more of spectator behavior and best suits teams that attract large or diverse crowds. If you choose this option, you will need to consider how you would regulate such problems as spectator use of tobacco, alcohol, and controlled substances; whether your school has the resources to hire security personnel; and how you would handle spectators who violate the rules.

☐ *Coach A's rule*: Spectators should follow the venue rules and cooperate with security personnel at games.

☐ *Coach B's rule*: Spectators should follow all venue rules and observe all local community laws when attending competition. Spectators should not attend competition when drunk or under the influence of other controlled substances. Spectators should cooperate with security personnel.

Sample Codes of Conduct for Spectators

Coach A's Choices

Spectators are important to us; our team wants and appreciates their support. We encourage spectators to attend our games and to actively support our team. We expect spectators to be polite, civil, and considerate of everyone involved in the game or match.

As a spectator, I understand that I am expected to act with honor and dignity at all sporting events and to show self-respect and respect for athletes, coaches, officials, and others involved in sport. I will behave in ways that are consistent with the following values:

Respectfulness

- Show respect for athletes, coaches, officials, and other spectators.
- Exercise self-control when reacting to officials' decisions.
- Act respectfully during pregame rituals and half-time events.

Responsibility

- Not disrupt competitions or practices.

Caring

- Cheer for the team regardless of the likely outcome of the competition.

Honesty

- Encourage athletes to play by the written rules.

Fairness

- Encourage the team to play fairly.

Good citizenship

- Follow the venue rules and cooperate with security personnel at games.

Coach B's Choices

Spectators are an important part of sport, and our team appreciates their support. Our team values the principles espoused in the six moral values: respectfulness, responsibility, caring, honesty, fairness, and good citizenship. We encourage spectators to attend our games and to actively support our team.

As a spectator, I will act with respect and dignity, will demonstrate self-respect, and will act respectfully at all times towards everyone involved in sport, including athletes, coaches, other parents, support staff, officials, opponents, volunteers, and spectators. I will behave in ways that are consistent with the following values:

Respectfulness

- Treat all participants with respect and accept victory and defeat with honor. I will refrain from disrespectful language, gestures, and actions directed at any participant, including all athletes, coaches, officials, and other spectators. I understand that disrespectful behavior includes violence, offensive language and gestures, profanity, taunts, trash talk, comments of a sexual nature, and demeaning cheers.
- Accept officials' decisions without dissent. I will not "boo," throw items, taunt officials, or make offensive or obscene comments or gestures to officials.
- Act respectfully during pregame rituals and half-time shows. I will stand and join in singing the national anthem or other songs.

(continued)

(continued)

Responsibility

- Act as a positive role model for athletes and for young spectators. I will follow the venue rules when attending competitions, sit or stand only in designated areas, and not act in any way that disrupts play or that could injure a player, coach, official, or other spectator.
- Accept that I may not attend practice.
- Accept that I will be ejected from competition if I disrupt the game and that a second incident of disruptive behavior will result in my being barred from matches for the remainder of the season. I understand that disruptive behavior includes verbal or physical abuse, drunkenness, and offensive or obscene language or gestures.

Caring

- Support and encourage my team and applaud their effort regardless of performance and the likely outcome of the match. I will not encourage dangerous play that might cause injury to any player.

Honesty

- Be loyal to the team both in victory and defeat and encourage athletes to play by the rules and honor the spirit of the rules of the sport. I will not encourage or applaud players who bend the rules or who display dishonest or unsporting behavior.

Fairness

- Acknowledge effort and outstanding performance by any athlete, even those on opposing team(s), and applaud when athletes play fairly. I will not encourage or applaud unfair play.

Good citizenship

- Follow all venue rules and observe all local community laws when attending games. I will cooperate with security personnel and will not attend matches when drunk or under the influence of other controlled substances.

SELECTING POLICIES AND RULES FOR SUPPORT STAFF AND VOLUNTEERS

Depending on your team's and organization's size and level, you might have support staff or volunteers, such as trainers, physical therapists, sport scientists, fitness consultants, medical practitioners, dietitians, or marketing and business consultants. Some of these people might be paid, whereas others might volunteer their time and expertise. Other volunteers might help organize travel, administration, equipment, scoring, uniforms, or refreshments. Volunteers might be parents of your athletes, students from your school or local colleges, or members of your community.

You might consider whether you want or need to have team policies and rules covering the activities of support staff and volunteers. The previous chapter on rules for coaching staff should include assistant coaches. You could probably apply or modify those rules to cover your support staff and volunteers. To make it easier, the next section discusses some of the issues you might consider in your policies and rules for support staff and volunteers. The main issues focus on confidentiality, lines of communication and authority, competency, and the behavior of support staff or volunteers.

Respectfulness

In chapter 4, you were asked to consider the ways in which you convey your respect for people, especially your athletes, and how you strive to act with class and teach your athletes to do the same. In chapter 4 we also discussed how young people respond best to positive role models and constructive criticism. Support staff such as doctors, trainers, or physical therapists often spend a lot of time with athletes. You would hope that these people would share your philosophy about such issues as showing respect and care toward your athletes. Consider the possible effect of drastically different philosophies. For example, your philosophy is to show respect for athletes by keeping them informed and involving them in important decisions, but your therapists and trainers take a more autocratic approach and refuse to answer an injured athlete's questions about treatment or when he or she will be able to return to play. Consider the possibility of the athlete being confused, frustrated, and demoralized about his or her recovery from injury.

COACHING TIP

"I tell my support staff: Praise in public, disagree in private. We need to present a united front to players and spectators. It's okay to disagree, but have the courtesy to come directly to me, and we'll work it out together."

—Jim Caputo, boys' soccer coach, Blue Ridge High School, Farmer City, Illinois

Language and Gestures

Any adult can be a role model, be it positive or negative, for young athletes. If your support staff spends a lot of time with athletes or represents your school in the wider community, you might consider whether you want to have rules about their language and gestures. These rules might be similar to those you have adopted for athletes, coaches, parents, and spectators.

Option 1 is more general and reminds support staff that they are role models for young athletes. This option might work best with professional or experienced support staff who have worked with young athletes a long time. Option 2 is more prescriptive, distinguishing which behaviors should be avoided and which should be encouraged.

☐ *Coach A's rule*: Support staff and volunteers should remember that they are role models and consider how their language and behavior might set an example for young athletes.

☐ *Coach B's rule*: Support staff and volunteers should avoid using offensive language or gestures in the presence of athletes or when representing the team. Support staff and volunteers should use positive words when talking with or about athletes.

Respect for Athletes, Coaches, and Others Involved in Sport

In some situations support staff or volunteers might need to speak with officials or opponents. For example, a trainer might need to tell an official about an injured player, or a volunteer might need to explain to an official about errors in scoring or timing. In a small program, you might not need rules about support staff talking with officials and members of the opposition. In larger programs, or those with various roles filled by support staff, you might consider rules outlining support staff behavior during competition.

Option 1 permits support staff and volunteers to speak to officials and the opposition when necessary. This option makes it clear that you are discouraging direct contact unless absolutely necessary. Option 2 is more restrictive and might be most appropriate in larger programs or when volunteers do not receive extensive training.

☐ *Coach A's rule*: During games, support staff and volunteers should speak to officials or opposing players, coaches, parents, and fans only if needed and should do so respectfully.

☐ *Coach B's rule*: Support staff should not talk directly with officials or opposing players, coaches, parents, and fans at any time before, during, or after competition.

Maintaining Professional Relationships

You expect your coaching staff to maintain objective, professional relationships with everyone involved in sport, and you expect your support staff to do the same. In the following section we look at rules about physical contact and touching, harassment, and socializing with athletes.

Close Physical Contact and Touching   Some support staff, such as trainers, physical therapists, masseurs, fitness consultants, and sport scientists, might be involved in activities that provide an opportunity for close physical contact with the athlete. As mentioned in chapter 4, close physical contact with an athlete is sometimes unavoidable (e.g., when examining an injury) and sometimes happens spontaneously (e.g., when embracing after a victory). Depending on the size of your program and the number and roles of support staff, you might consider whether you want to have rules about when and how support staff may touch or have other physical contact with athletes.

Option 1 permits close physical contact when necessary and lists situations in which contact is appropriate. Requiring others to be present might help avoid misinterpretation of physical contact or the appearance of impropriety. Option 2 is quite strict and might be appropriate for support staff whose roles do not involve close physical contact (e.g., administrators or those not working directly with athletes).

☐ *Coach A's rule*: Support staff may have close physical contact with athletes only when necessary to instruct or test an athlete, to ensure athlete safety, or to examine or treat an injured athlete. Support staff should touch an athlete only when others are present.

☐ *Coach B's rule*: Support staff may not have close physical contact with or touch any athlete.

Harassment   Chapter 3 defined harassment, and rules for coaches were described in chapter 4. You might wish to also include rules on harassment for support staff, depending on the number of staff and their roles. If your school has a broad harassment policy, it might be easiest to extend this rule to support staff. In deciding if you want to have a policy on harassment for support staff, consider the professional level of your support staff, how much contact they have with athletes and with each other, and how likely harassment is to become an issue. If you decide to have rules on harassment, you might also consider how to inform and educate your staff about your policy.

Option 1 is general and could be open to interpretation. Experienced, professional staff will usually understand its intended meaning and subtleties. Option 2 is more prescriptive in clarifying what is unacceptable and stating which staff are expected to be proactive in discouraging and reporting unacceptable behavior.

☐ *Coach A's rule*: Support staff should maintain an appropriate relationship with all athletes and with other staff members.

☐ *Coach B's rule*: Support staff should maintain a professional relationship with all athletes and with other staff members. Staff should not engage in conduct, gestures, actions, or comments of a sexual nature with any athlete. Support staff should discourage athletes from acting or talking in a way that could be perceived as sexual harassment. Support staff should report any incident of alleged harassment, including sexual harassment, to the coach.

Socializing With Athletes   Support staff might become an integral part of the team and become quite close to the athletes. Chapter 4 discussed the need for coaches to define and maintain boundaries between themselves and their athletes. You might consider if the concept of boundaries also applies to support staff who might spend a lot of time with athletes.

Option 1 gives some flexibility. Depending on the size of your program and community, who your support staff are and their roles, you might need this flexibility. For example, if fellow students and parents fill all of the support staff roles, it would be ridiculous to try to limit social interaction. Option 2 is most appropriate when your team has professional support staff or is part of a larger, more complex program.

☐ *Coach A's rule*: Support staff should use discretion in deciding whether to socialize with athletes outside of official team activities.

☐ *Coach B's rule*: Support staff should not socialize with athletes except for at official events (e.g., awards banquets) or other community events (e.g., fund-raisers).

Coach's Exercise

Plan a meeting for your volunteers and support staff in which you define and discuss your rules for confidentiality and touching athletes. Prepare a handout that includes examples to illustrate these rules and concepts.

Responsibility

Some support staff might have few or light responsibilities, such as selling tickets, helping raise funds, or working the concession stand during games. In contrast, professional support staff, whether paid or volunteer, might have far greater or more serious responsibilities relating to their expertise and amount of contact with athletes. For professional staff, responsibility includes the concepts of "duty of care," competency, confidentiality, and conflict of interest; each of these is discussed separately in the following section.

Duty of Care

The term "duty of care" refers to the legal responsibility of those in authority. Professional support staff such as trainers, physical therapists, exercise scientists, sports medicine physicians, and dietitians have a duty of care to use sound professional practice to train and treat athletes. The expectation of a duty of care might be defined in their professional code of ethics, by law, or by their professional indemnity insurance.

Option 1 is minimal and simply calls for support staff to use accepted methods when working with athletes. You might choose this option for volunteer staff with little professional training. The second option has a much higher level of expectation about the level of care, requiring support staff to continually update their knowledge to ensure they use "best practice" methods when treating or working with athletes. This option might be better for professional support staff or those with extensive professional training (e.g., doctors, therapists, trainers).

☐ *Coach A's rule*: Professional support staff should use accepted professional practice when advising, working with, or treating athletes.

☐ *Coach B's rule*: Professional support staff have a duty of care to athletes they treat, supervise, or train. Support staff should use sound professional practice when advising, working with, or treating athletes and should regularly update their accreditation to ensure they are using the most recent practices.

Confidentiality

As discussed in chapter 4, coaches and support staff often learn of personal information about the athlete and his or her family. Regardless of how relevant that knowledge is to the athlete's participation, support staff has a responsibility to treat that information confidentially. An offhand comment to someone else could be embarrassing or even damaging to the athlete and his or her family and would certainly violate the rules about trust and respect.

Option 1 is more general, indicating that support staff are expected to treat all personal information confidentially. Option 2 is more prescriptive, requiring support staff to seek the athlete's permission to discuss personal information (i.e., discussing an athlete's injury with the coach or team doctor or telling the coach about personal issues that might influence the athlete's attendance or performance). This option also suggests that support staff should be proactive in recognizing signs of personal problems and encouraging the athlete to resolve them. Your choice of option might depend on the number and type of support staff, the size of your sport program, the level of athlete, the level of your support staff (e.g., professional paid staff versus volunteers), and how closely support staff work with athletes.

☐ *Coach A's rule*: Support staff will treat all personal information about an athlete confidentially.

☐ *Coach B's rule*: Support staff will treat all personal information about an athlete confidentially and will not discuss personal information about an athlete with anyone else without permission from the athlete. Support staff should be alert for signs of personal problems in an athlete that might affect his or her school or sport performance and should encourage the athlete to seek assistance for significant personal problems.

Communication With the Coach and Athletes

The more complex and large your team and its support network, the higher the probability that miscommunication might occur. How important is it that your support staff keep you up to date about your athletes' progress in practice or recovery from an illness or injury or about important management issues such as travel arrangements? Your ability to prepare and manage your team could be hampered by not knowing all the relevant information.

The first option expects that support staff will recognize the importance of communicating with the coach. This option might work with volunteer support staff who have few responsibilities or do not spend much time with athletes. Option 2 expects much more of support staff and places an obligation on them to immediately report relevant information to the coach. You might choose this option with larger programs at which professional support staff spend a lot of time with athletes.

 COACHING TIP

"I tell volunteers, 'When in doubt, ask.' Volunteers sometimes make mistakes in trying to help because they don't know or understand something about the sport. The error is never in the trying. Volunteers want to do the right thing. I let volunteers know that they can ask any question at any time. If you don't show patience with volunteers, you'll be in for more work."

—Mark Logan, track and field and cross country coach, RHAM High School, Hebron, Connecticut

☐ *Coach A's rule*: Support staff should communicate effectively with the coach.

☐ *Coach B's rule*: Support staff should maintain open communication with the coach. Unless bound by confidentiality, support staff must inform the coach immediately of any relevant information about an athlete that affects his or her ability to train or compete.

Representing the Team

Support staff often work very closely with athletes and coaches. In sports or on teams that attract great public interest, competitors, media, or members of the public might approach support staff for information about the team or individual athletes. Rules about confidentiality should prevent support staff from divulging personal information about team members. However, you might consider if you need a more general rule that goes beyond confidentiality to cover how support staff represent themselves and the team. For example, the media or the public might not always recognize that the opinion of a member of the support staff does not always reflect official team policy or the coach's viewpoint.

The first option allows the staff member some flexibility in deciding whether and how to talk about the team and individual athletes. You might select this option for highly professional and experienced support staff who understand the subtleties involved in representing the team. The second option is much more restrictive and requires support staff to seek approval before talking or writing about the team. You might choose this option if you want to have more control over who speaks for your team or to protect the privacy of your team or individual athletes.

☐ *Coach A's rule*: Support staff may use their discretion in talking with others about individual athletes, the team, or their role on the team.

☐ *Coach B's rule*: Support staff should seek the coach's permission before talking or writing about individual athletes, the team, or their relationship with the team.

Competency

Depending on the roles and functions of support staff, you might have rules about their expected level of competency. Obviously, such rules are unnecessary for support staff who perform simple administrative functions. However, if your support staff have direct contact with athletes or their roles require specialized knowledge, you might consider setting some minimum criteria for their involvement. For some professions, such as the team doctor, physical therapist, or dietitian, this is relatively easy because of accreditation by professional organizations. For other roles, such as trainer, first-aid attendant, or fitness consultant, you might consider including rules about minimum level of competence. When choosing your rules, consult your organization's insurance policy, which might indicate the level of competence required in some roles.

Option 1 calls for support staff to restrict their actions according to their training or expertise. Option 2 sets the minimal level of competence and encourages support staff to seek further professional development to update their knowledge and skills.

☐ *Coach A's rule*: Each member of support staff working with athletes should stay within the boundaries of his or her expertise.

☐ *Coach B's rule*: Members of support staff working with athletes should have the minimal level of accreditation required to work in their area and should stay within the boundaries of their expertise. Staff members are expected to become members of their relevant association and to continually update their knowledge.

Conflict of Interest

Chapter 4 defined conflict of interest as a situation or relationship in which a conflict might arise between a team's interests and an individual's interests. Conflict of interest might apply to support staff, such as a trainer, physical therapist, or marketing consultant who works with more than one team. We hope that these people are able to act objectively and professionally. However, we are concerned with the potential for and the appearance of conflict. When choosing support staff and rules for support staff, consider factors such as the role they play on your team, whether it is important that they work only for your team, and situations in which it might be inappropriate for them to also work with other teams.

Option 1 is very general and asks support staff simply to consider the issue. Option 2 is more restrictive, and some support staff, such as therapists or trainers, might be less comfortable with it. When deciding whether to have such a rule, consider the support staff you work with and whether you foresee any possible problems.

☐ *Coach A's rule*: Support staff are expected to consider if there is any conflict of interest when working with a team.

☐ *Coach B's rule*: Support staff should act in the best interests of the athletes and the team and should avoid any real or apparent conflict of interest by avoiding commitments, contracts, or relationships with others that might prevent the staff member from effectively performing his or her role. Members of the support staff must declare any possible conflict of interest in advance and should exclude themselves from involvement in decisions in which a potential for conflict of interest exists.

Caring

Caring involves giving priority to a team's needs and the well-being (both physical and psychological) of the athletes and others involved on the team. As mentioned earlier, it is possible to strive for excellence while also caring about health and safety. Professional support staff who work directly with athletes, especially those attending to athletes' health needs, are critical in contributing to a caring environment for athletes. For example, consider the contradiction of a coach who gives the highest priority to athletes' health and safety and a trainer who values winning above the health of athletes and is willing to allow an injured athlete to play.

Athlete Health and Well-Being

The first option simply asks support staff to be concerned about individual athletes. This option might suit teams with volunteer support staff who have limited direct contact with athletes. Option 2 has much higher expectations, requiring support staff to value both athlete health and safety and to help create a caring team environment. You might choose this option for professional support staff who spend more time with athletes or who deal with health issues.

☐ *Coach A's rule*: Support staff should demonstrate concern for the health and well-being of individual athletes.

☐ *Coach B's rule*: Support staff should consider the athletes' health, safety, and well-being as the top priority. They should actively encourage athletes to look out for each other and should put the team's success and needs ahead of personal recognition and glory.

Cooperation Among Athletes

If your team values cooperation among athletes and feels teamwork is an important part of team culture, you might consider creating a rule that encourages support staff to contribute to a cooperative environment. Option 1 is a simple reminder of support staff's role in supporting a caring team environment. The second option expects support staff to actively participate in creating a caring team environment. This option might work better with professional support staff or those who spend a lot of time with athletes.

☐ *Coach A's rule*: Support staff should encourage all athletes to work together as a team and to contribute to a team effort.

☐ *Coach B's rule*: Support staff should encourage athletes to cooperate with and to care about teammates. They should support the coach's efforts to encourage athletes to play selflessly and for the good of the team. All members of the support staff should cooperate with each other.

Honesty

Support staff play varied roles, some of which require a high level of honesty and trust. For example, volunteers might handle financial aspects such as fundraising or ticket selling, and you need to be able to trust that they are performing these roles honestly. Professional support staff might work directly with athletes without supervision (e.g., trainers or physical therapists) or be involved in making decisions about athletes. You need to rely on their professional integrity.

Staff Honesty

Option 1 asks support staff to be honest when working with the organization and team members. As mentioned before, the word "honesty" can be interpreted differently in different contexts. The second option has a higher level of expectation and more explicitly defines honesty in terms of checking facts, being forthcoming with relevant information, and correcting false information. This option requires support staff to actively demonstrate the highest level of integrity. You might select this option if support staff have a range of duties, if they spend a lot of time with athletes, or if they are involved in important decisions.

☐ *Coach A's rule*: Support staff should be honest in all verbal and written communication with the school, athletes, parents, and the coach.

☐ *Coach B's rule*: Support staff should check all facts discussed or included in written communication with the school, athletes, parents, and others involved in sport (e.g., volunteers, the media, or the local community). Support staff should present information honestly; should not withhold any relevant information from the organization, an athlete, or parent; and should make a reasonable effort to correct any false statements.

Loyalty to the Team

The term "support" implies that support staff assist your team in achieving its goals. One might assume that loyalty to the team is also implicit in the concept of support or assistance. Volunteers usually contribute from a sense of commitment and generosity, especially if they have a vested interest in the team (e.g., parents or students), and you can probably safely assume their loyalty. You might wish to consider the issue of loyalty for other support staff, especially professional support staff who work with other teams or have different motives for working with yours.

The first option supplies a simple reminder for support staff regarding loyalty to the team. Option 2 defines loyalty in terms of the balance between personal interests and the team's needs. You might find this option works better with teams that rely heavily on professional support staff.

 COACHING TIP

"High school sports should teach lessons in life. The kids need to learn to be good people first and good athletes second. Our kids learn to look past individual differences and focus on common goals together. To have a happy and successful team—and life— you have to do this daily."

—Arnie Miehe, cross country coach, Darlington High School, Darlington, Wisconsin

☐ *Coach A's rule*: Support staff should be loyal to the team.

☐ *Coach B's rule*: Support staff should be loyal to the team and school and should put the team's interests ahead of personal interests and glory.

Fairness

Fairness is an integral part of sport. There is more to fairness than simply following the rules; fairness also reflects one's attitude and approach to life in general. As a coach and educator, you want to help your athletes realize their potential and achieve your team's goals. If fairness is an important part of your team's philosophy, it would be consistent to expect support staff to act in accordance with your rules about fairness in regards to athletes, coaches, and parents. If your support staff spend time with athletes, you might consider creating a rule regarding how they can demonstrate fairness toward athletes.

The first option requests that support staff simply be aware of the issue of fairness and to treat each athlete fairly. You might select this option if your support staff do not spend much time with or have much opportunity to influence athletes. Option 2 asks support staff to treat athletes fairly and to become actively involved in teaching athletes about fairness.

☐ *Coach A's rule*: Support staff should treat each athlete fairly.

☐ *Coach B's rule*: Support staff should treat each athlete fairly and encourage athletes to play by both the written and unwritten rules. Support staff should discourage athletes from gamesmanship and from bending or knowingly breaking rules to gain an advantage.

Good Citizenship

Good citizenship involves encouraging excellence, acting lawfully, and avoiding and discouraging abuse of illicit or harmful substances such as tobacco, alcohol, and performance-enhancing and illicit drugs. If your support staff have some influence over your athletes, you might consider rules encouraging support staff to act as positive role models for good citizenship.

Striving for Excellence

Although young people like to win, most are motivated to participate by other factors, such as enjoying themselves and taking on new challenges. Striving for excellence is part of the challenge of learning new skills and testing oneself. Encouraging young people to strive for excellence involves getting them to take some level of risk, even if they might fail (e.g., might lose a game or might not achieve their personal goals). Support staff who work directly with athletes, including trainers, physical therapists, sport scientists, and dietitians, can become an integral part of your plan to help your athletes strive for excellence.

The first option is fairly basic and might be assumed for most support staff. This option might work for a sport that promotes participation and learning new skills. Option 2 underscores the expectation of the support staff to actively contribute to the team's efforts to encourage excellence and improvement, regardless of outcome.

☐ *Coach A's rule*: Support staff should encourage each athlete to strive for excellence.

☐ *Coach B's rule*: Support staff should encourage athletes to improve and strive for excellence. Support staff should focus on and acknowledge each athlete's efforts and good performance and should not overemphasize outcome.

Substance Use and Abuse

Rules about cigarette smoking, alcohol consumption, and substance abuse have been discussed earlier in the context of athletes, coaches, and parents. If you have established rules about smoking and alcohol for these groups, it would be consistent to have similar rules for support staff.

One option might be to have a general rule that covers everyone involved in sport (athletes, coaches, parents, spectators, support staff, and volunteers). For example, if your school prohibits smoking and alcohol for all activities, it's easy to establish a rule that covers everyone. If this is not feasible and you decide to include a rule about substance use for support staff, consider doing so within the context of your rules for others, such as coaches and parents.

Use of Tobacco and Controlled Substances Support staff might spend significant time with your athletes, and your school and community expect them to act as positive role models for young athletes. If you do not have a general rule that covers everyone's use of tobacco and other controlled substances, you might wish to create a rule that addresses the issue of whether your support staff are permitted to smoke or use controlled substances when involved in your team's activities.

Option 1 is most liberal in allowing support staff and volunteers to smoke or consume alcohol, if permitted, in designated areas. Option 2 is more restrictive, forbidding the use of tobacco, alcohol, and other controlled substances. You might consider whether your rule for support staff should be consistent with your rules on coaches, athletes, and parents in regard to smoking and consuming alcohol, as discussed earlier. Issues such as negligence and liability, which could arise if a member of the health or medical support staff treats athletes while under the influence of alcohol or other controlled substances, should also be considered.

☐ *Coach A's rule*: Support staff and volunteers may smoke cigarettes and consume alcohol as permitted in designated areas during team activities.

☐ *Coach B's rule*: Support staff and volunteers should not smoke cigarettes or consume or be under the influence of alcohol or any controlled substance during any team activity, including games.

Supplying Tobacco or Controlled Substances   Along with a rule about support staff's use of controlled substances, you might also consider a rule that expressly prohibits support staff from supplying such substances to athletes and whether support staff should play a role in discouraging or monitoring substance abuse by athletes.

The first option forbids support staff from supplying illicit substances to athletes. The second option goes much further, specifying a range of forbidden substances and stating a clear expectation that support staff will play an active role in discouraging athletes and in reporting substance abuse.

☐ *Coach A's rule*: Support staff should not supply alcohol, tobacco, or any controlled substance to any athlete.

☐ *Coach B's rule*: Support staff should not supply, distribute, or sell tobacco, alcohol, controlled substances, performance-enhancing substances, or drug-related paraphernalia to any athlete at any time. Support staff should actively discourage athletes from using illicit or performance-enhancing controlled substances. Support staff should report infractions to the coach.

Sample Codes of Conduct for Staff and Volunteers

Coach A's Choices

Support staff and volunteers are important contributors to our team, and we encourage their active involvement.

As a volunteer or a member of support staff, I will behave in ways that are consistent with the following values:

Respectfulness

- Remember that I am a role model and consider how my language and behavior might set an example for young athletes.

(continued)

(continued)

- Speak to officials or opposing players, coaches, parents, and fans only if needed, and I will always do so respectfully.
- Have close physical contact with athletes only when necessary to instruct or test an athlete, to ensure athlete safety, or to examine or treat an injured athlete. I will touch an athlete only when others are present.
- Maintain a professional relationship with all athletes and other staff members.
- Use discretion in deciding whether to socialize with athletes outside of official team activities.

Responsibility

- Use accepted professional practice when advising, working with, or treating athletes.
- Treat all personal information about an athlete confidentially.
- Communicate effectively with the coach.
- Use discretion in talking with others about individual athletes, the team, or my role in the team.
- Stay within the boundaries of my expertise.
- Consider if there is any potential for a conflict of interest when working with the team.

Caring

- Demonstrate concern for the health and well-being of individual athletes.
- Encourage all athletes to work together as a team and to contribute to team effort.

Honesty

- Be honest in all verbal and written communication with the school, athletes, parents, and the coach.
- Be loyal to the team.

Fairness

- Treat each athlete fairly.

Good citizenship

- Encourage each athlete to strive for excellence.
- Refrain from supplying alcohol, tobacco, or any controlled substance to any athlete.

Coach B's Choices

Support staff and volunteers are important contributors to our team, and we encourage their active involvement.

As a member of the team's support staff or volunteers, I will support the principles espoused in the six moral values: respectfulness, responsibility, caring, honesty, fairness, and good citizenship.

I will act with respect and dignity toward everyone involved in sport. I will display the highest ethical and professional standards and put the needs of the athletes and the team ahead of my own. I will behave in ways that are consistent with the following values:

Respectfulness

- Avoid using offensive language or gestures in the presence of athletes or when representing the team. I will use positive words when talking with or about athletes.

- Not talk directly with officials or opposing players, coaches, parents, and fans at any time before, during, or after competition.

- Not have close physical contact with or touch any athlete.

- Maintain a professional relationship with all athletes and with other staff members and not engage in conduct, gestures, actions, comments, or a relationship of a sexual nature with any athlete. I will discourage athletes from acting or talking in a way that could be construed as sexual harassment, and I will report any incident of alleged harassment, including sexual harassment, to the coach.

- Not socialize with athletes except for official events (e.g., awards banquets) or other community events (e.g., fund-raisers).

Responsibility

- Have a duty of care to athletes I treat, supervise, or train, and use sound professional practice when advising, working with, or treating athletes. I will regularly update my accreditation to ensure that I use the most recent practices.

- Treat confidentially all personal information about athletes and will not discuss personal information about athletes with anyone else without permission from the athletes. I will be alert for signs of personal problems in athletes that might affect their school or sport performance. I will encourage athletes to seek assistance for significant personal problems.

- Maintain open communication with the coach. Unless bound by confidentiality, I will inform the coach immediately of any relevant information about an athlete that affects his or her ability to train or compete.

- Seek the coach's permission before talking or writing about individual athletes, the team, or my relationship with the team.

- Have the minimal level of accreditation required to work in my area and will stay within the boundaries of my expertise. I will become a member of an association relevant to my area and will continually update my knowledge.

- Act in the best interests of the athletes and the team and avoid any real or apparent conflict of interest by avoiding commitments, contracts, or relationships with others that might prevent me from effectively performing my role. I will declare any possible conflict of interest in advance and will exclude myself from involvement in decisions in which potential for conflict of interest exists.

(continued)

(continued)

Caring

- Consider the athletes' health, safety, and well-being as the top priority. I will actively encourage athletes to look out for each other and will put the team's success and needs ahead of personal recognition and glory.

- Encourage athletes to cooperate with and to care about teammates. I will support the coach's efforts to encourage athletes to play selflessly and for the good of the team and will cooperate with other support staff.

Honesty

- Check all facts discussed or included in written communication with the school, athletes, parents, and others involved in sport (e.g., volunteers, the media, local community). I will present information honestly and will not withhold any relevant information from the school, an athlete, or parent and will make a reasonable effort to correct any false statements.

- Be loyal to the team and school and put the team's interests ahead of personal interests and glory.

Fairness

- Treat each athlete fairly and encourage athletes to play by both the written and unwritten rules. I will discourage athletes from gamesmanship and bending or knowingly breaking rules to gain an advantage.

Good citizenship

- Encourage athletes to improve and strive for excellence. I will focus on and acknowledge each athlete's efforts and good performance and not emphasize outcome.

- Not smoke cigarettes or consume or be under the influence of alcohol or any controlled substance during any team activity, including games.

- Not supply, distribute, or sell tobacco, alcohol, controlled substances, performance-enhancing substances, or drug-related paraphernalia to any athlete at any time. I will actively discourage athletes from using illicit or performance-enhancing controlled substances and will report infractions to the coach.

SELECTING POLICIES AND RULES FOR THE MEDIA

Consider how you would like your team and staff to be portrayed in the media. If you have experience with the media, how would you describe that experience? Were you happy with the way you or your team was portrayed? Can you recall times when a team was depicted in a way that was, while not entirely inaccurate, perhaps unflattering or one-sided? If the media have portrayed your athletes or team in a positive way, did this have a positive effect on your athletes' morale? Have there been occasions when the media built up expectations about an athlete or team beyond their capabilities? Has there been a time when the media harshly criticized a team or athlete for poor performance?

The media have their own rules and codes of ethics about issues such as honesty, integrity, confidentiality of sources, accountability, independence, and fairness. Many of these are the same principles underpinning good sportsmanship and respect for the game that we hope to instill in young athletes.

What can you expect from the media? According to codes of ethics of organizations representing the media (e.g., see the Radio–Television News Directors Association & Foundation Web site at www.rtnda.org/ethics/coe.shtml or the Society of Professional Journalists Web site at www.spj.org/ethics_code.asp), you can expect members of the media to do the following:

- Act in the interest of public trust

- Seek the truth

- Present information fairly

- Be accountable for their actions and publications to the public and to their profession

- Gather and report information independently without external influence and self-interest

- Respect the dignity and privacy of private individuals (as opposed to public officials)

- Act with integrity and honesty

Except for pursuing legal action for reporting untruths, you might not be able to control what the media say and write about you or your team. However, you might consider having rules about the media's access to your team and coaching staff. When deciding whether you want to include such rules, consider the age and experience of your athletes, the level of competition, whether your team or sport is likely to be reported by the media, and how comfortable you, your staff, and your athletes feel in dealing with the media.

Respectfulness

In accordance with the media codes of ethics mentioned previously, the media can be expected to treat all athletes, especially young athletes, respectfully when seeking information and in interviews.

Respecting Athletes and Their Families

Young athletes have likely had limited experience in talking with or being the focus of the media. Think about your previous experience with the media: Is it sometimes difficult to clearly say what you think on the spur of the moment? How good are young athletes at thinking on their feet, especially after a close match or if they are disappointed with their performance? What would be the implications for your team if an athlete said something that he or she should not say? The community might sometimes idolize high-profile athletes and forget that they are normal young people.

Option 1 asks the media to consider the age and experience of your athletes when covering their activities. This option implies that a young person should not be held to the same level of scrutiny in reporting as an adult. You might choose this option if you have an open and trusting relationship with the local media, or if you feel little need to protect your athletes from the media. Option 2 starts with the same approach but expects more from the media, specifically mentioning the privacy of your athletes and their families and the possible long-term consequences of reporting negatively about an athlete. You might choose this option if you coach a high-profile team that is often mentioned by the media or if you think you need to protect your athletes from overzealous media scrutiny.

☐ *Coach A's rule*: The media should recognize that our athletes are young people and should act accordingly when interviewing them or publishing information about them or the team.

☐ *Coach B's rule*: The media should recognize that our athletes are young people and should act accordingly when interviewing them or publishing information about them or the team. The media should respect athletes' dignity and privacy and that of their families, and they should avoid publishing information about athletes that might damage their future educational or career opportunities.

Interviews

Reporters might want to formally or informally interview coaches, athletes, or support staff. Such interviews might be done in face-to-face meetings, over the telephone, or during a team activity such as training or before or after a game. Consider whether you want to have rules limiting access to athletes or other team personnel.

Option 1 is quite liberal, allowing media free access to team members. Option 2 implies permission by the head coach; this rule requires interviews to be conducted in the presence of the coach or another team representative. You might consider this option if you coach young athletes with limited experience with the media, if your sport is high profile and covered regularly in the media, if past experience has shown that athletes need guidance, or if your team or sport is somehow connected to a controversial situation.

☐ *Coach A's rule*: Reporters and other representatives of the media may seek to interview any athlete, coach, or other team representative.

☐ *Coach B's rule*: Reporters and other representatives of the media may interview a member of the team or coaching or support staff only in the presence of the head coach or the coach's representative.

Responsibility

As mentioned previously, the media codes of ethics expects journalists to seek the truth, to present information fairly, and to be accountable for what is reported. Thus, you can expect the media to act responsibly when reporting on your athletes, team, or school. This might include checking the facts and details to ensure that only true information is published and that coverage is fair and balanced. This doesn't mean that you are preventing the media from taking a critical look at your team but that you expect them to present information objectively and fairly and to consider the "angle" of the story in the context of sport and the long-term effects on your athletes and community.

Confirming Details

The media obtain information from various sources. A central tenet of the journalist's practice and code of ethics is to publish the truth and to confirm all information before publication. Defamation laws are designed to prevent publication of untrue information that might damage someone's reputation or livelihood. In reality, there is a diversity of opinion and practice about the extent to which journalists should substantiate information before publishing or broadcasting it. Consider if you want the media to confirm information about your team before issuing the information to the public. In deciding on this issue, you might think about how much time you want to spend confirming details, your relationship with the media most likely to report on your team, how accessible you want to be, how likely it is that your team will be reported on, and how likely it is that the media will abide by the rules you set.

Option 1 gives the media the option of confirming information, presenting doing so as a courtesy rather than a requirement. Option 2 clarifies that you expect the media to confirm stories before they are published. In reality, you might have little control over whether or how a story is published or broadcast, but you do have the option of refusing future access to reporters if you are unhappy with their reporting about you or your team. Voluntarily providing information, say in a press release, is one way to increase the chance that correct information is published.

☐ *Coach A's rule*: We ask the media to extend the courtesy of confirming all information or stories about the team with the head coach.

☐ *Coach B's rule*: The media should ask the head coach to confirm all information or stories about athletes or the team and should provide the opportunity to respond before publication or broadcast.

Reporting Negative Information About Athletes

Occasionally, the media might become aware of negative information about an athlete, which may or may not be relevant to his or her participation in sport.

For example, discovering that an athlete was recruited from another team in violation of the conference rules might have implications for your team and might be in the public interest. Contrast this with a media report that an athlete's parent was arrested for tax evasion, which has no real bearing on the athlete's participation on the team but could cause significant problems for the athlete if the media chose to link the athlete with his or her parent's legal problems.

Option 1 requests the media to consider in advance the implications of publishing information about an athlete or team member. This option gives the media more discretion in balancing their function of reporting newsworthy information against the interests of the individual. Option 2 restricts what the media may report on but may not be enforceable in some situations. However, this option makes it clear that you believe the media should stick to reporting only information relating to the athlete and team's performance.

☐ *Coach A's rule*: The media should consider the potential impact of reporting negative information about our athletes or other team members.

☐ *Coach B's rule*: The media should report negative information about our athletes or other team members only if it is directly relevant to the team's performance.

Reporting on Abusive or Violent Behavior

The media often sensationalizes information. We all know that sex, disagreement, and conflict attract attention, even when only tangentially related to sport. Despite the emphasis on playing with honor, violence can and does occur in association with sport; examples of violent behavior by spectators, athletes, and coaches are plentiful. One might question whether the media have the power to influence such behavior and if the media could play a more active role in discouraging aggression and violence. How many times have you seen television coverage of a game that spent more time focusing on a few minutes of brawling between opposing players or crowd violence than on outstanding play during the game?

Option 1 asks the media to avoid focusing on violence, implying that the media should focus on the sport itself. You might consider this option if there is little history of violence in your sport or if your team does not attract much media attention. The second option expects more of the media. Again, you might not have much choice about what aspects of sport the media choose to report, but you can, through rules such as this one, articulate the approach you think appropriate for the media to take when reporting on your team and, by implication, sport in general. The last sentence of this rule makes it clear that you believe the media can play an active role in discouraging violence and abusive behavior in sport.

☐ *Coach A's rule*: The media should not emphasize or focus on examples of abusive or violent behavior during games or matches.

☐ *Coach B's rule*: The media should not report on sport in a way that appears to condone, excuse, or incite abusive or violent language or behavior by athletes, coaches, or spectators. The media should support the coach, team administrators, and officials in trying to discourage or control such language or behavior.

Let's now consider the media's role relating to the third moral value of caring. This is perhaps a more subtle aspect of sport policies than is normally considered.

Caring

Can you think of a decision that you made in the best interest of your team that was reported negatively in the media? Perhaps you rested one of your stars because he or she was ill or injured and instead played a less-talented player to give him or her more experience and confidence. If you have a good relationship with the media, perhaps they understand that such decisions are part of a caring team environment. On the other hand, the media might not know or care about your personal or team philosophy and choose to focus more on results. Consider whether you should have a rule that explains your team philosophy about the moral value of caring to the media.

Option 1 asks the media simply to recognize the importance the team places on a providing a caring environment, implying that the media should respect this. Option 2 clarifies team values and the expectation that the media will respect these values. In our previous example, the media might negatively report your decision to rest your star player at a crucial time in the game because they don't understand your team policies about caring.

☐ *Coach A's rule*: The media should recognize our efforts to provide a caring team environment.

☐ *Coach B's rule*: The media should support our team's emphasis on cooperation and playing for the good of the team. The media should acknowledge that the health and well-being of our athletes is our highest priority.

The fourth moral value, honesty, and its components, integrity and accountability, are integral facets of journalism ethics. Let's look at a few rules regarding how you might expect the media to act in the context of this moral value.

Honesty

You can expect members of the media to gather and report information honestly, to be accountable for that information, and to act with integrity and honesty. Although you might assume these ideas because they form part of the media's own codes of ethics, you might also consider having a rule to articulate your team's expectations as well.

Option 1 mirrors the media code of ethics discussed at the start of this section and is the minimum of what you can expect of the media. Option 2 spells out your expectation that the media will report only true and relevant information. You might choose this option if you coach a team that is frequently portrayed by the media or if your team has had previous negative experiences with the media. Although this rule cannot prevent the media from reporting negatively about your team, it does tell them that you have a high expectation and that your cooperation is closely related to their ethical behavior.

☐ *Coach A's rule*: The media should act with integrity and honesty when reporting on members of our team.

☐ *Coach B's rule*: The media should act with integrity and honesty when reporting on members of our team. The media should use honest means to gather information and report only information that they know to be factual and directly relevant to the team's performance in sport.

The fifth moral value, fairness, is also a key component of journalism ethics. Consider whether you want to establish a rule stating that you expect your team to be covered fairly and objectively by the media.

Fairness

Ideally, you should be able to expect the media to gather and present information fairly and objectively, without bias or conflict of interest.

Balanced Reporting

The first option is liberal, simply stating that you expect media coverage of your team to be fair. The words "balanced and fair reporting" could be interpreted differently by different individuals. This option might work best if you have a good rapport with the media and have been satisfied with how the media have reported on your team in the past. The second option expects more regarding how the media gather and report information about your team, particularly requiring media members to maintain objectivity and independence. You might consider this option if you coach a high-profile team, if you do not have a well-established relationship with the media, or if you have been dissatisfied with previous reports about your team.

☐ *Coach A's rule*: The media should use balanced and fair reporting to present information about our athletes or members of our staff.

☐ *Coach B's rule*: The media should present only a balanced and fair representation of our team. The media should gather information independently and objectively and without external influence or self-interest. The media should avoid presenting only one side or a biased view of athletes, the team, or any situation involving the team.

Supporting Sportsmanship

In *Coaching for Character*, Clifford and Feezell state that everyone involved in youth sports is a "moral educator, whether they want to be or not." One could argue that this statement also applies to the media, which can be a powerful force—positive or negative—in forming public opinion about the issues of fair play and sportsmanship. You might consider a rule that lets the media know that you would welcome their active involvement in encouraging these ideals.

The first option is rather general and easily enforced because even the crustiest of journalists would probably agree that sportsmanship is a central tenet of sport. You might select this option if your team is not a frequent center of attention or if you have confidence in the way the media portrays the ideals of sportsmanship. The second option clarifies that you expect the media's active support of the ideals of pursuing victory with honor and good sportsmanship. You might select this option if your past experience tells you that such a rule is needed or if you wish to effect a change in attitude among the media and public.

☐ *Coach A's rule*: The media should support the ideal of good sportsmanship.

☐ *Coach B's rule*: The media should actively encourage athletes and spectators to demonstrate good sportsmanship by positively acknowledging sportsmanlike behavior in their reporting. The media should support the coach's efforts to encourage the ideals of sportsmanship, fair play, and pursuing victory with honor.

Coach's Exercise

How would you deal with a sports writer from your community who seems to always report negatively about your team? List and explain the different options you could take to change how this reporter writes about your team.

We come to the final moral value of good citizenship. The media can do much to promote the ideals of good citizenship and to convey the community's expectation about it.

Good Citizenship

Besides expecting the media to obtain and report information fairly and objectively, you can also expect them to use legal and transparent methods to gather information. All athletes have a right to a certain level of privacy and to protection from illegal information gathering.

The first option is minimal and would fit within the general code of ethics for the media. Option 2 goes further, expecting that the media will not use information obtained illegally or through deceptive means. This option might suit a team that is covered frequently by the media or if you have had previous bad experiences with the media; this rule articulates the expectation that you expect the media to use legitimate and transparent means to obtain their information.

☐ *Coach A's rule*: The media should use legal means to obtain information about our athletes or members of our team.

☐ *Coach B's rule*: The media should use legal and ethical means to obtain information about our athletes or members of our team. The media will not publish or broadcast information obtained illegally or unethically or through deceptive methods.

Sample Codes of Conduct for the Media

Coach A's Choices

We recognize that media representatives are experts in reporting information of public interest and that they have their own professional ethical standards. When reporting on our team, we request that the media adhere to the highest professional ethical standards and to our code of conduct for the media. We ask representatives of the media to behave in ways that are consistent with the following values:

Respectfulness

- Recognize that our athletes are young people and act accordingly when interviewing them or publishing information about them or the team.

Responsibility

- Extend the courtesy of confirming all information or stories about the team with the head coach.
- Consider the potential impact of reporting negative information about our athletes or other team members.
- Do not emphasize or focus on examples of abusive or violent behavior during games or matches.

Caring

- Recognize our efforts to provide a caring team environment.

Honesty

- Act with integrity and honesty when reporting on members of our team.

Fairness

- Use balanced and fair reporting to present information about our athletes or members of our staff.
- Support the ideal of good sportsmanship.

Good citizenship

- Use only legal means to obtain information about the members of our team.

Coach B's Choices

We recognize that media representatives are experts in reporting information of public interest. We also recognize that the media have their own rules and codes of ethics about issues such as honesty, integrity, confidentiality of sources, accountability, independence, and fairness—many of the same principles underpinning good sportsmanship and respect for the game that we hope to instill in young athletes.

When reporting on our team, we ask the media to adhere to the highest professional ethical standards and to our code of conduct for the media. We ask media representatives to behave in ways that are consistent with the following values:

Respectfulness

- Recognize that our athletes are young people. The media should respect our athletes' dignity and privacy and that of their families and avoid publishing information about athletes that might damage their future educational or career opportunities.

- Interview a member of the team or coaching or support staff only in the presence of the head coach or the coach's representative.

Responsibility

- Ask the head coach to confirm all information or stories about athletes or the team and provide the opportunity for the coach to respond before publication or broadcast.

- Report negative information about our athletes or other team members only if the information is directly relevant to team performance.

- Avoid reporting on sport in a way that appears to condone, excuse, or incite abusive or violent language or behavior by athletes, coaches, or spectators. The media should support the coach, team administrators, and officials in trying to discourage or control such language or behavior.

Caring

- Support our team's emphasis on cooperation and playing for the good of the team; acknowledge that the health and well-being of our athletes is our highest priority.

Honesty

- Act with integrity and honesty when reporting on members of our team. The media should use honest means to gather information and report only information that is factual and directly relevant to the team's performance in sport.

Fairness

- Present a balanced and fair representation of our team. The media should gather information independently and objectively and without external influence or self-interest. The media should avoid presenting only one side or a biased view of athletes, the team, or any situation involving the team.

- Actively encourage athletes to demonstrate good sportsmanship and spectators to support the ideal of good sportsmanship by positively acknowledging sportsmanlike behavior in their reporting. The media should support the coach's efforts to encourage the ideals of sportsmanship, fair play, and pursuing victory with honor.

Good citizenship

- Use legal and ethical means to obtain information about our athletes or members of our team. The media will not publish or broadcast information obtained illegally or unethically or through deceptive methods.

Now that you've read the codes of conduct written by Coach A and Coach B, it's time to write your own! Visit www.humankinetics.com/CoachesGuideToTeam Policies to create your code of conduct. You will also find other helpful documents to use for your team.

SUMMARY

Continuing to build on the framework of the six moral values (respectfulness, responsibility, caring, honesty, fairness, good citizenship), this chapter has discussed ideas and options for your team policies and rules for other people involved with your team such as parents, spectators, support staff, and the media.

These people will play varying roles, depending on the skill level of your athletes and size of your school. No doubt parents are vital to achieving your team goals and getting the most out of your athletes. Most parents have the best interests of their children at heart and will support and cooperate with your efforts. For them, it may be sufficient to clearly communicate your team goals, philosophy, and expectations, and how these are translated into team rules. We hope that only a minority of parents will require further efforts to be convinced that your team rules form the basis of a successful program. Involving parents directly in the process of developing or revising your team policies is more likely to gain their understanding and active support.

Choosing policies and rules for spectators can be more complex, depending on who your regular spectators are. If your spectators are mainly parents and other members of your organization (e.g., students), a single policy that combines rules for parents and spectators may suffice. In contrast, spectators who come from outside your school require a different and more creative approach in communicating your team's expectations. Your first step might be to find out about policies or rules developed by your conference or venue(s) where you compete. You can use these as a starting point for your own policies.

Your policies and rules for support staff and volunteers might need to be customized to suit your situation. For example, if all your support staff are professionals (e.g., doctor, physical therapist, trainer), your policies can borrow from their professional codes of ethics and accreditation guidelines. You might need explicit policies and rules for volunteer or nonprofessional support staff, or if your support staff come from a mixture of backgrounds (e.g., paid and unpaid, professional and nonprofessional, wide range of tasks undertaken).

The media has its own code of ethics, which you can use as a basis for your policies and rules. Although you cannot control what the media reports about your team, you can develop policies to clarify your team philosophy and goals and your expectation that the media will act within its own established ethical code. If your team is frequently in the news, it is in everyone's best interest to cultivate and maintain an open, cordial, and constructive relationship with the media.

When developing your policies and rules for parents, spectators, support staff, and the media, always consider how closely they fit with your policies and rules for athletes, as discussed in chapter 3, and coaches, as discussed in chapter 4. As mentioned earlier, good policies have a sense of consistency or logic that allows people to see the reasons behind them. People will then be much more likely to accept and support the policies.

GLOSSARY

abuse—Any form of physical, emotional, or sexual behavior or mistreatment or neglect that results in physical or emotional harm. Abuse takes many forms, including sexual, emotional, physical, verbal, and neglect. Abuse and harassment are similar, but the term *abuse* is generally used to describe behavior toward a child, whereas harassment describes behavior among peers or adults.

code of conduct (or ethics or behavior)—A statement about expected behavior and the consequences for violating those expectations.

conflict of interest—A situation or relationship in which a conflict might arise between the team or club's interests and the individual's interests.

due process—The legal process to ensure that an individual's rights are protected in any decision making or proceedings.

duty of care—Legal responsibility of those in authority (e.g., the coach has a duty of care to ensure the safety of the athletes he or she is coaching).

ethics (or code of ethics)—Moral values or principles that guide behavior; expected behavior from an individual (athlete on your team) or group (e.g., coaching staff, media) based on those moral values.

fair play—A general concept that encompasses the ideals of sport, such as playing by the rules and within the spirit of the game; self-respect and respect for others; good sportsmanship; and avoiding violence, harassment, abuse of drugs or illegal supplements, and corruption.

gamesmanship—Winning a game through use of questionable practices while not technically breaking the rules.

harassment—Conduct or behavior that intimidates, humiliates, harms, or is offensive to a person or group. Harassment includes hostile talk; unwelcome jokes or innuendo, especially relating to sex, religion, race, or ethnic background; hazing or initiation rites; practical jokes intending to embarrass the victim; and bullying or intimidation.

objectives—Goals or measurable plans to help achieve your stated mission. Objectives can be short term (e.g., teaching your team specific ball skills) or long term (e.g., improving your win–loss record, qualifying for the championships, recruiting more athletes to your team).

philosophy—A basic theory or group of beliefs, ideas, and principles held by an individual or group that represent what is valued by that individual or group.

policy—A course of action or set of organizational guidelines that guide decision making. Team policies comprise a set of principles, guidelines, and procedures to direct behavior, rules, and decision making.

principles—Predetermined set of beliefs used to make decisions and formulate policies and rules.

rules—Guidelines dictating specific behavior or actions; specific procedures based on a more general policy.

REFERENCES

Alternative Dispute Resolution for Sport, Canadian Centre for Ethics in Sport, Montreal, QU. www.adrsportred.ca (first accessed April 7, 2003).

American Academy of Pediatrics Policy Statement. Testing for drug abuse in children and adolescents. *Pediatrics* 98(2): 305–307, 1996. http://aappolicy.aappublications.org (first accessed December 3, 2003).

Bailey, W.J. Current issues in drug abuse prevention: Suspicionless drug testing in schools. Indiana Prevention Resource Center at Indiana University. www.drugs.indiana.edu/publs/archive/pdfs/drugtesting_athlete.pdf

Bukowski, B.J. A comparison of academic athletic eligibility in interscholastic sports in American high schools. *The Sport Journal* 4(2), Spring, 2001. www.thesportjournal.org/2001Journal/Vol4-No2/athletic-eligibility.asp (first accessed December 2, 2003).

Centre for Sport and Law, Inc., Brock University, St Catherines, ON, Canada. www.sportlaw.ca

All Centre for Sport and Law sites were first accessed April 12, 2003.

> Code of Conduct Policy, sample document: www.sportlaw.ca/cocpol.htm
>
> Discipline Policy, sample document: www.sportlaw.ca/discippol.htm
>
> Harassment Policy, sample document: www.sportlaw.ca/haras.htm
>
> Appeals Policy, sample document: www.sportlaw.ca/appealpol.htm
>
> Alternative Dispute Resolution (ADR) Policy, sample document: www.sportlaw.ca/adrpol.htm
>
> Fair Treatment: www.sportlaw.ca/articles/coach/coach6.htm
>
> Conflict of Interest Policy, sample document: www.sportlaw.ca/coipol.htm
>
> About Policy Writing: www.sportlaw.ca/policyW.htm
>
> Policies: www.sportlaw.ca/policies.htm
>
> Violence in sport—it's your responsibility too: www.sportlaw.ca/articles/coach/coach36.html

Clifford, C., and R.M. Feezell. *Coaching for Character.* Champaign, Human Kinetics, 1997.

Drug Policy Alliance. Drug testing fails our youth. www.drugtestingfails.org (first accessed December 4, 2003).

Flannery, T., and M. Swank. *Personnel Management for Sport Directors.* Champaign, Human Kinetics, 1999.

Martens, R. *Successful Coaching.* Human Kinetics, 2004.

Mom's Team. www.momsteam.com (first accessed December 23, 2003).

Positive Coaching Alliance. www.positivecoach.org (first accessed December 23, 2003).

INDEX

Note: The italicized *f* and *t* following page numbers refer to figures and tables, respectively.

ABOUT ASEP

ASEP has been developing and delivering coaching education courses since 1981. As the nation's leading coaching education program, ASEP works with national, state, and local sport organizations to develop educational programs for coaches, officials, administrators, and parents. These programs incorporate ASEP's philosophy of "Athletes first, winning second."

Content provider Dr. Laurel T. Mackinnon is a former associate professor, now an adjunct professor, of exercise physiology at the University of Queensland, Brisbane, Australia. Dr. Mackinnon is a fellow of the American College of Sports Medicine and was internationally recognized for her research on immune function and overtraining in elite athletes. She has been involved in youth sport for 15 years by coaching and managing her sons' participation in soccer, track and field, and basketball.

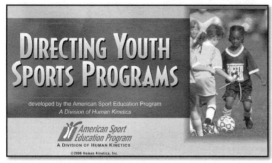
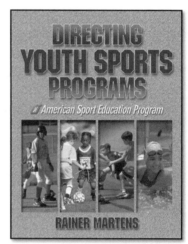

 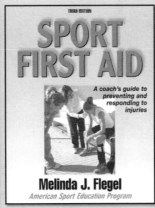 

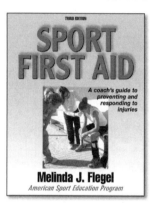

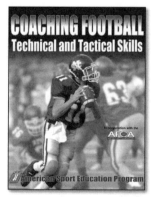